Mexican American Literature

Mexican American Literature is one of the first book length studies to focus on what is arguably the most important period in the development of Mexican American writing, the Chicano Movement of the 1960s. It offers an extended analysis of Chicano and Chicana identity politics over several decades through readings of some of the major works of contemporary Mexican American literature while exploring the Movement's historical, political and conceptual effects.

Mexican American Literature examines the identity politics in Chicano and Chicana literary and political texts dating from the 1960s to the present day. Offering original readings of the works of several major figures of the Chicano Movement and the canon of contemporary Chicana writing, it brings together a broad range of legal, political, geographic and cultural concerns. In its approach it also covers a large part of the historical map of the Mexican American experience in the United States from colonisation and annexation, to civil rights and contemporary developments in Chicano and Chicana political identity.

This book is an important contribution to the study of Mexican American literature. The careful consideration given to the politics of identity in a number of key literary works illuminates the way in which literature reflects and incorporates political ideology in a way no other critical work on this subject does. Crossing several disciplinary boundaries, this book will be of use to those studying literature, history, feminism and politics.

Elizabeth Jacobs is Research Fellow at the Rothermere American Institute, Oxford University, UK.

Routledge transnational perspectives on American literature

Edited by Susan Castillo
University of Glasgow

In an age of globalisation, it has become increasingly difficult to characterise the United States as culturally and linguistically homogenous and impermeable to influences from beyond its territorial borders.

This series seeks to provide more cosmopolitan and transnational perspectives on American literature, by offering:

- in-depth analyses of American writers and writing literature by internationally based scholars
- critical studies that foster awareness of the ways in which American writing engages with writers and cultures north and south of its territorial boundaries, as well as with the writers and cultures across the Atlantic and Pacific.

1. New Woman Hybridities
Femininity, feminism, and international consumer culture, 1880–1930
Edited by Ann Heilmann and Margaret Beetham

2. Don DeLillo
The possibility of fiction
Peter Boxall

3. Toni Morrison's *Beloved*
Possible worlds
Justine Tally

4. Fictions of the Black Atlantic in American Foundational Literature
Gesa Mackenthun

5. Mexican American Literature
The politics of identity
Elizabeth Jacobs

Mexican American Literature

The politics of identity

Elizabeth Jacobs

Routledge
Taylor & Francis Group

LONDON AND NEW YORK

First published 2006
by Routledge
2 Park Square, Milton Park, Abingdon, Oxon OX14 4RN

Simultaneously published in the USA and Canada
by Routledge
270 Madison Avenue, New York, NY 10016

Routledge is an imprint of the Taylor & Francis Group

Transferred to Digital Printing 2009

© 2006 Elizabeth Jacobs

Typeset in Garamond by
RefineCatch Limited, Bungay, Suffolk

British Library Cataloguing in Publication Data
A catalogue record for this book is available from the British Library

Library of Congress Cataloging in Publication Data
Jacobs, Elizabeth, 1956-
Mexican American literature/Elizabeth Jacobs.
p. cm.
Includes bibliographical references.
1. American literature–Mexican American authors–History and
criticism. 2. American literature–20th century–History and criticism.
3. Mexican Americans–Intellectual life. 4. Mexican Americans in
literature. I. Title.
PS153.M4J33 2006
810.9′86872′09046–dc22
2005023540

ISBN10: 0–415–36490–6 (hbk)
ISBN10: 0–415–54406–8 (pbk)

ISBN13: 978–0–415–36490–4 (hbk)
ISBN13: 978–0–415–54406–1 (pbk)

Contents

Acknowledgements   vi

Introduction   1

1   The Chicano movement   6

2   Chicana feminism   26

3   Critical approaches to Chicana/o literature   39

4   The relationship between Chicano and Chicana literature   64

5   Mexican American theatre and the politics of Chicana/o identity   81

6   Women, confinement and *familia* ideology   98

7   The search for Aztlán: the Chicano nation   118

8   Mestiza Aztlán: a nation without borders   134

Conclusion   152

Notes   157
Bibliography   159
Index   176

Acknowledgements

In addition to using a large number of secondary works to form this study, I have also utilised a wide selection of primary source material from the archives of the Chicano Research Collection at Arizona State University. I would like to thank the staff of the Department of Archives and Manuscripts at the Hayden Library for their help and direction in using the collection. I would also like to thank the staff of the Hispanic Research Center and the Department of Chicano and Chicana Studies for their assistance with my research. My thanks go to the British Association for American Studies and the Department of English and Board of American Studies University of Wales, Aberystwyth, for enabling this research visit to take place. The study also benefited from my time spent as a Postdoctoral Research Fellow at the Rothermere American Institute, University of Oxford (2003–5) where the holdings in the Vere Harmsworth Library proved to be of great use and the staff generously provided support and excellent office and research facilities.

Finally, I would like to express my eternal gratitude to all my family for their constant support throughout.

Introduction

This study of Mexican American writing was first of all motivated by a more general interest in minority literatures of the USA. Like other minority groups, Mexican Americans have a rich and lengthy cultural and literary heritage from which to draw on in order to express their sense of self in the midst of what often appears to be an alienating American society. In order to explore the fullest range of Mexican American literary and political expression possible within the framework of a single study, I have chosen to focus on certain historical moments when issues of identity became central facets of Mexican American writing. During the decades of the 1980s and 1990s, writing by Mexican American women displayed such a concern with self-identity, a concern that was deeply rooted equally in their self-awareness as marginalised women of colour in the USA and in their awareness as women within their own profoundly masculinist Mexican American community. Additionally, writing from this period seemed to be inevitably related to that other period in contemporary history when the Mexican American community strongly articulated their sense of self and identity largely for political ends. The 1960s and early 1970s were the decades of Mexican American civil-rights protests, and a period in Mexican American history that saw a resurgence in cultural and political activity.[1]

As such it was part of the wider radical climate of national political protests that took place in the USA during the 1960s and 1970s and should be viewed alongside the political activity of other ethnic groups such as the Native American movement and the Black Civil Rights and Black Power Movements. In a similar way to these groups Chicanos attempted to forge a unique collective identity and a socio-political programme based around that identity. Like their movements, *el movimiento* served a dual purpose, balancing support for the expansion of the democratic process through direct political action on the one hand, with a more separatist cultural nationalism on the other. In many respects it was a like-minded attempt to counter discrimination through a celebration of indigenous roots and organised political protests. Grouping themselves into organisations such as the UFW (United Farm Workers) in California and Texas, the Alianza Federal de Mercedes (Alliance of Free City States) in New Mexico, the Mexican

American Youth Organisation (MAYO), the United Mexican American Students (UMAS), the Mexican American Legal Defence and Education Fund (MALDEF), the Movimiento Estudiantil Chicano de Aztlán (MEChA), Chicanos por la Causa (CPLC) in Arizona, and La Raza Unida Party (LRUP) in Texas, the Chicano movement also presented unique and comprehensive forms of political activism.

A primary theoretical concern of this study centres on the ideology that connected these groups as research has indicated that their collective politics formed a master narrative that was problematic. More specifically for the thematics of this study, a certain tendency within the movement sought to construct a selective and homogenous identity that was both paternalistic and exclusionary. While this internalised practice repressed Chicanas in subordinate roles, it simultaneously celebrated machismo and male heroic activity, especially that formed in the face of American domination. Many male Chicano writers privileged these ideas, thereby reinforcing hegemonic discourses that were part of the movement's own dominant political rhetoric. More specifically Chicano literature became a vehicle for concentrated expressions of ethnic and cultural pride. Mirroring external modes of repression, Chicano literary practice perpetrated its own ideology of containing differences, only in this case within selected Chicano rather than American identities. Chicano publications such as *El Malcriado, El Grito, Aztlán, Con Safos*, and *El Grito del Norte* and publishing houses such as Quinto Sol further entrenched this ideology by implicitly prioritising the publication of male texts over those written by women.

This book explores the Chicana activism and literary production that emerged in response to this entrenched ideology. It is my contention that Chicana writers endeavoured to displace the masculinised identity politics of the movement by proposing new constructions of Chicana subjectivity that were both oppositional to the male bias of movement rhetoric as well as American racist discourses. As a framework for the study the chapters focus on certain 'locations' of identity which played a formative role in the development of movement politics and which have subsequently been reworked by women writers. These are myths of descent, the family and home and national identity. The study also brings together a wide range of narrative forms including historiographic material, political manifestos as well as more conventional literary texts such as poetry, the novel and drama. The first three chapters analyse cultural, political and critical material. The remaining chapters deal with literary analysis, and in each case are organised around the work of at least two authors with some reference to other works where appropriate. Thus a reading of writers associated with movement rhetoric such as Tomás Rivera, Rudolfo Anaya, Alurista, Luis Valdez and Rodolfo 'Corky' Gonzales are analysed alongside texts from Chicana writers such as Sandra Cisneros, Alma Villanueva, Ana Castillo, Lorna Dee Cervantes, Gloria Anzaldúa and Cherríe Moraga.

In order to focus my argument more specifically I have selected the work of writers living in the borderland states of California, Texas and New Mexico, although in assessing the movement's trajectory Arizona and Colorado also feature in the study. The cultural and historical frameworks of these states provides a viable and particularly pertinent structure, first, as they have historically had the most concentrated populations of Mexican Americans in the USA. For instance, the Spanish-speaking population of these states grew by nearly 50 per cent between 1950 and 1960, or from 2.9 million in 1950 to 3.46 million in 1960 (Vargas 2001: 385). According to the 2000 census, this figure has continued to grow at a similar rate, as people of Mexican origin now comprise approximately 66 per cent of the total Hispanic population of 32.8 million, many of who still reside in these states.

In addition to this, the south-western states provide a pertinent focus because historically the Spanish colonisation of the south-west has led to the development of distinct subcultures and identities in these regions (Gutiérrez 1986, Griswold del Castillo and de León 1996, Gonzales 2000, Hine and Faragher 2000). Most historians also agree that it was the loss of these states following annexation in 1848 that underlay the militant resistance of the movement including the boycotts and farm workers' strikes in California, the land seizures and land-grant struggles in New Mexico, the revolt of the electorate in Texas and the high-school walkouts in Los Angeles. It is also of particular significance, as Chávez (1984) argues, that dating from the late nineteenth century nearly every major Chicano civil-rights, labour and political organisation originates from one of these states (Chávez 1984: 131). Collectively then, the south-western states provide important insights into the diversity of cultural positions within the grouping of Chicana/os, as individually each has a complexly stratified Mexican American community that in varying degrees participated in the protest decades. They thus suggest on the one hand a material context for studying the production of identity and culture in historically and geographically specific spaces. On the other hand they are also important 'contested' sites through which Chicana/o literary and political forms of expression have been differently signified and mediated over time.

As the Chicano movement influenced and created a catalyst for the development and dissemination of Chicano/a writing, the purpose of the first two chapters is to provide a broad-based introduction to and analysis of the movement's dynamics and progression. For the sake of clarity Chapter 1 focuses on the related issues between Mexican American social activism and issues of Chicano identity, in particular land, political rights and education. Subheadings are organised around key figures and organisations that played a significant role in relation to these issues such as Reies López Tijerina and the Alianza Federal de Mercedes in New Mexico, César Chávez and the UFW in California, the student organisations and Rodolfo 'Corky' Gonzales and The Crusade for Justice. The chapter concludes with a summary of the movement's achievements and offers some reasons for its decline. In conjunction with this analysis, the chapter introduces some of the major works of

Chicana/o literary production that emerged during the protest decades and situates them in relation to movement ideology.

Following on from the observations of the Chicano movement made in the first chapter, Chapter 2 provides an assessment of the parallel development of Chicana feminist discourse and the emergence of women's writing. Tracing the development of a self-consciously feminist agenda, subheadings in this chapter include 'Chicana and American Feminism' and 'Women and the Movement'. An introduction to Chicana writers' post-movement politics forms a subsection to this analysis, as by the decade of the 1980s, through both collective and individual effort, women writers began to supersede their male counterparts and to establish their own platform for their oppositional identity politics. Rather than supporting the earlier male-oriented stance, Chicana writers and critics began to invoke a collective identity that deconstructed the ethnic, political and gendered separatism of movement discourse. The publication of the anthology *This Bridge Called My Back: Writings by Radical Women of Color*, edited by the Chicana writers Cherríe Moraga and Gloria Anzaldúa, marks the beginning of this trajectory (Moraga and Anzaldúa 1983). As I go on to explore, it was their formulation of a more pluralistic and multiple sense of self that most radically influenced subsequent representations of Chicana subjectivity. Succeeding chapters build on this analysis and examine the most significant 'locations' of Chicano and Chicana identity in a range of literary genres.

The methodological model when approaching the literary works is based on a framework that is interdisciplinary and cross-cultural, and that places an emphasis on the historical and sociological context of the writing. In seeking to establish a firm historical base for the analyses, I draw largely on the work of Chicano and Chicana historians such as David Gutiérrez (1995), Carlos Muñoz (1989), John Chávez (1984), Vicki Ruiz (1998), Alma Garcia (1997) and Emma Pérez (1999a). Similarly, cultural and critical perspectives are based on the works of among others Juan Bruce-Novoa (1990a), Wilson Neate (1998), Rafael Pérez-Torres (1995) and Sonia Saldívar-Hull (2000). The works of these critics are discussed in more detail in Chapter 3, which provides an assessment of the differing tendencies within critical approaches to Chicana/o literature. In order to more broadly establish the dialectical involvement between writing by Mexican American women and the politics of the Chicano movement, the chapter moves on to consider the most recent developments and debates within Chicana feminist and cultural criticism.

The concluding chapters explore the issues associated with nationhood and national identity that surfaced at the height of the movement. During this time Chicanos claimed that they were an unassimilated nation that had been oppressed by the political, economic and cultural dominance of the US Government. Nationalist conceptions of a homeland began to coalesce around the idea of a separate Chicano nation, Aztlán, and were consolidated with *El Plan Espiritual de Aztlán* (1969), the manifesto that presented the social philosophy of the Chicano movement. Despite the plan's objective to galvanise the Chicano community into collective action, Aztlán was significantly stratified along lines of gender and was figured almost exclusively as a male nation. Chapter 8 explores how this rhetoric found its corollary both politically at the grass-roots level and culturally at the level of literary production, both of which were based ideologically on the exclusion of women. The closing chapter explores the response by Mexican American women to the contours of the male nation widely imagined by movement politics. While myths of descent and the reacquisition of land form the basis for their rebuilding of this idealised state, the community imagined by Chicanas is formed through coalitions that move across borders and beyond the confines of the separatism promoted by movement rhetoric. The study concludes with the suggestion that the rewriting of Aztlán by Chicana writers effectively displaces the agenda of the protest decades and supersedes previous manifestations of Chicana/o identity politics.

1   The Chicano movement

As the Chicano movement influenced and created a catalyst for the development of Chicano/a writing, this chapter's purpose is to provide an historical and ideological base for the later analysis of Chicano/a literary texts. Before considering these issues further, my main objective should be stated at the outset, as I don't intend to provide an exhaustive interpretation of the activities associated with the Chicano movement. Its highly complex trajectory and character preclude the possibility of giving such an account here. Instead, for the sake of clarity, this analysis aims to provide a synopsis of what were the seemingly diverse civil-rights and nationalistic activities of Chicano groups during the protest decades, and as such focuses on selected phases and leaders in the development of movement activism.

For this reason I have based my initial analysis on a 'four-phase framework' similar to that suggested by Ignacio M. García (1997) in his study of the Chicano movement. This kind of framework, he states, enables an understanding of the movement 'as a process by which Mexican Americans came to debate their place in American history' (I. M. García 1997: 16). Following this interpretation, I characterise the first phase of the movement by the role played by Reies Lopez Tijerina and the Alianza de los Pueblos Libres (Alliance of Free City States), which advocated the reclamation of Chicano lands in New Mexico. The second stage follows the activism of César Chávez and the UFW in California. The third phase follows the organisation of the Crusade for Justice and student groups and the political programme put forward at the Denver Youth Conference in 1969. The fourth and final stage marks the decline of movement activism.

The development of Mexican American political activism

The Chicano movement grew out of an alliance of diverse groups including farm workers in California and Texas, land-grant owners in New Mexico, the urban working classes of the south-west and mid-west, and the growing radicalisation of student groups across the country. The politics of these diverse groups initially coalesced around a consensus of socio-political and cultural concerns. These included arguing for such basic rights as just representation in government and the courts, fair treatment from the police and the military, a decent standard of living, and bilingual and bicultural education (Chávez 1984, Chávez 2002). Organisations such as the UFW, the Alianza Federal de Mercedes, MAYO, UMAS, MALDEF, MEChA, CPLC and LRUP were established in order to press the existing authorities and achieve these aims.[1] To this end, several plans were also drawn up including the ground-breaking *El Plan de Delano* (1965) a stated proclamation of rights by the UFW; *El Plan de Santa Bárbara* (1969) MEChA's educational programme and *El Plan Espiritual de Aztlán* (1969), arguably the movement's most radical statement concerning issues of Chicano identity and land rights.

Most interpretations of these organisations and manifestos indicate that they were an extension of previous acts of Mexican American political activism. In this sense the events of the 1960s did not necessarily mark a new direction for Chicano political activity since it was only 'quantitatively rather than qualitatively' different from their previous acts of struggle (Sanchez 1994: 24). Many Chicana/o critics and historians in fact trace the political impetus behind the movement as far back as the Mexican revolution (1910–20). For instance, according to Alfred Arteaga (1997) the concept of the 'plan', which dominated the movement's rhetoric, owed much to the Mexican revolutionary tradition (Arteaga 1997: 12). The Chicana historian Emma Pérez (1999a) concurs with this view and writes that leaders actively sought to establish this kind of connection in order to reassert both an organisational structure and a specific discourse based on prior revolutionary rhetoric. She states that during the movement, 'Posters of Emiliano Zapata . . . decorated the homes of college Mechistas and "Tierra y Libertad" [land and liberty] . . . also the slogan of Zapata . . . was now imaged for contemporary leaders' (Pérez 1999a: 72). Zapatista-Indianist philosophy, historical confrontation and land-rights claims were the three dominant philosophies of revolutionary Mexico. According to Pérez, the 'doubling' of its rhetoric in movement discourse was a deliberate strategy designed to connect to earlier forms of political activism and to instil a revolutionary consciousness (Pérez 1999a: 72). Historian Rodolfo Acuña (1988) also shares this view and concurs with Pérez by noting that the organisation and *caudillismo* (leadership by personality) of the movement, 'closely resembled the pattern of the Mexican Revolution, where revolutionary juntas and local leaders emerged' (Acuña 1988: 360).

Others see the events of the 1960s as taking root more recently. George Sanchez (1993) argues that many of the political issues associated with the movement were shaped in the decade before the Second World War. Sanchez (1993) states that it was during this time that a distinct cultural identity and sense of self began to emerge among second-generation Mexican Americans in the barrios of Los Angeles. It was also at this point he argues that the first Chicano organisation formed, the Mexican American Movement (MAM), which, like many other groups, promoted advancement through education (Sanchez 1993, Chávez 2002). Other interpretations of the developments in the 1960s set the context for successful protest more firmly in the class-structural changes accompanying the Second World War or the GI Bill of 1947 that enabled a first-generation of working-class Chicanos to enter higher education (Montejano 1999b: 235). Others see the grass-roots activism for voter registration as well as desegregation of schools, housing, public facilities and working conditions in the post-war era as being instrumental in the later formation of Mexican American civil-rights activities (Vargas 2001: 397). Vargas (2001) argues that:

> after World War II, hundreds of experienced Mexican American union members worked tirelessly to mobilize their communities for social change. These men and women were a major force in the early Mexican American civil rights movement and also worked in electoral politics.
>
> (Vargas 2001: 399)

Though, arguably, the key factor in the development of Chicana/o political activity lay in the establishment of new political groups in the 1950s and early 1960s. The most important of these groups were the Mexican American Political Association (MAPA) founded in California in 1959 and the Political Association of Spanish Speaking Organisations (PASO or PASSO), which was originally founded in Arizona in 1960, but also proved highly influential in Texas where it evolved from the Viva Kennedy Clubs. These organisations spearheaded a significant shift in political strategy by Mexican American groups in that they targeted the electoral process by supporting Mexican American candidature. This kind of tactic also featured significantly throughout the movement when it proved instrumental in laying the foundation for the later unprecedented politicisation of thousands across the country. But as organisations they did not embrace or even articulate the separatist and nationalist position that would later be adopted during the movement decades. Their politics were characterised by an assimilationist perspective to civil-rights protest, such as the League of United Latin American Citizens (LULAC) in Texas (Gutiérrez 1995, de León 2001). This meant that they advocated a pro-assimilationist stance unlike aspects of the Chicano movement, which largely advocated a militant separatism.

Reies López Tijerina and the Alianza Federal de Mercedes

The first stages of the accelerating social and political activism associated with Chicano civil-rights struggles began as a series of localised protests erupting in New Mexico, Colorado, Texas and California in the early part of the 1960s. It was characterised most strongly by the pioneering efforts of Reies López Tijerina and the Alianza Federal de Mercedes in New Mexico and by César Chávez and the UFW in California. Initially scattered in their activism, by the latter half of the decade their collective protests provided a focus for the later organisation and cohesive structure of the Chicano social movement.

Reies López Tijerina, a former Pentecostal preacher and one of the movement's more enigmatic leaders, founded and directed New Mexico's Alianza de los Pueblos Libres (Alliance of Free City States) and the Alianza Federal de Mercedes (later renamed La Confederacion de Pueblos Libres) in the early years of the movement (Tijerina 2000). These organisations were primarily concerned with reinstating Spanish and Mexican land grants and property entitlements dating from the colonial period. Tracing a direct lineage back to these times, many New Mexican residents legitimated their claims to land through their Spanish forebears, thus predating American annexation of Mexican land after the US–Mexican war of 1846–8. In 1966 Tijerina led Alianza members in an attempt to reclaim part of the Kit Carson National Forest in New Mexico. Calling for a stricter adherence to the civil and property rights promised by the treaty of Guadalupe Hidalgo (1848) and by the constitution of New Mexico, he aimed to reappropriate the Echo Amphitheatre Campground, which was on the site of the 500,000-acre San Joaquin del Cañon de Chama grant dating from the Spanish conquest.

This kind of tactic galvanised Chicano political opinion by focusing attention on the treaty and the various miscarriages of justice associated with its implementation. Originally, the treaty of Guadalupe Hidalgo formed the international border separating Mexico from America after the US–Mexican war of 1846–8. While annexing most of Mexico's northern territory onto the USA, it also clearly stated that it was a 'Treaty of Peace, Friendship, Limits and Settlement between the United States of America and the Mexican Republic' and, according to the articles of the treaty, the Hispanic residents of the region were also to be granted certain rights. According to Article 8:

> Mexicans now established in territories previously belonging to Mexico and which remain for the future within the limits of the United States, as defined by the present treaty, shall be free to continue where they now reside, or to remove at any time to the Mexican Republic . . . Those who shall prefer to remain in the said territories may either retain the title and rights of Mexican citizens, or acquire those of citizens of the United States. But they shall be under the obligation to make their election within one year from the date of exchange of ratifications of this treaty.
>
> (Meier and Gutiérrez 2000: 277–8)

Article 9 of the treaty also detailed Hispanic rights and issues of citizenship:

> The Mexicans who, in the territories aforesaid, shall not preserve the character of citizens of the Mexican Republic, conformably with what is stipulated in the preceding article, shall be incorporated into the Union of the United States, and admitted as soon as possible, according to the principles of the Federal Constitution to the enjoyment of all the rights of citizens of the United States. In the meantime, they shall be

maintained and protected in the enjoyment of their liberty, their property, and the civil rights now vested in them according to the Mexican laws. With respect to political rights, their condition shall be on an equality with that of the inhabitants of the other territories of the United States; and at least equally good as that of the inhabitants of Louisiana and the Floridas, when these provinces by transfer from the French republic and the Crown of Spain, became territories of the United States.

(Meier and Gutiérrez 2000: 277–8)

The failure to uphold the treaty and the subsequent implementation of Mexican American civil and property rights became the basis of Tijerina's argument and formed much of his political rhetoric, though he also based his arguments on the *Recopilación de Leyes de las Indias*, a seventeenth-century document that had been the legal framework for the Spanish land grants (Griswold del Castillo and de León 1996: 129–30, Tijerina 2000: 62). By using these foundational documents, ultimately he sought to bring these issues to national attention, and for the most part he was successful. He also worked with different groups and befriended African American militants such as H. Rap Brown and Stokely Carmichael of the Black Panthers in order to strengthen the Alianza's protests. He also attempted on one occasion to make a citizen's arrest of the District Attorney in Arriba County, and on another occasion he and his supporters stormed a courtroom in Tierra Amarilla, New Mexico, in order to free Alianza members held in custody there. These activities certainly attracted large-scale interest, although not necessarily of the kind he hoped. Tijerina's style of militant armed action meant that his politics became the subject of heated debate and his credentials as a bona-fide movement leader were questioned as some of the Alianza's activities clearly went beyond the movement's praxis of 'nonviolent revolution' (I. M. García 1997: 4, Tijerina 2000: viii). Many Chicanos also resented the close ties between Tijerina and African American civil-rights leaders and tactics, preferring a more separatist stance for their protest activity. Likewise, most of the Mexican American middle classes strongly objected to what they saw as Tijerina's 'bandit-like' activities. He also never advocated Chicano nationalism or the quest for Chicano identity and power as other members of the movement did. Tijerina and his followers in fact consistently referred to themselves as Indo-Hispanos and not as Chicanos.

These differences and Tijerina's own confrontational style ultimately undermined the cohesion of his own organisation. As a result of the raid on Tierra Amarilla he was jailed for two years in 1969 and the Alianza never subsequently regained the degree of cohesion and political bite that characterised its early years (Griswold del Castillo and de León 1996, Gonzales 2000). Despite these major setbacks, Tijerina was nonetheless successful in several ways, first, by bringing Hispanic land-grant issues to national attention and, second, by mobilising thousands of Mexican Americans in the name of the Alianza's cause. Beginning with about 6,000 members in the early 1960s, by the latter part of the decade this number of followers had grown to approximately 20,000 in all.

César Chávez and the United Farm Workers

Another key organisation of these early years was undoubtedly the UFW, a union that was particularly powerful in the south-west and especially in the states of California and Texas. Initially termed the Farm Workers Association (FWA), it was organised under the leadership of César Chávez and Dolores Huerta and was primarily concerned with solving farm workers' labour conditions. The popularity of the union was greatly enhanced through its support for the abolition of the Bracero programme, which eventually ceased operation in 1964. This labour programme, first established in the 1940s, took the form of an agreement between America and Mexico for the temporary migration of Mexican agricultural workers into the USA. Despite written protocols, which stated that these workers should not suffer discriminatory acts, the Bracero programme exploited the Mexican workers economically while at the same time discriminating against them through racist practices and bars to citizenship (Gutiérrez 1995: 153–60). This socio-economic disparity has continued to exacerbate over time and has become particularly divisive as the economic relationship between Mexican immigrant labour and American capital has evolved. David Gutiérrez (1995) argues this point, by stating that 'American employers and their allies in government have worked in close partnership . . . to ensure that the flow of immigrant workers from Mexico is regulated for the maximum benefit of American businesses and consumers' (Gutiérrez 1995: 211). Significantly, as Gutiérrez argues, the economic workings of this alliance between business and government 'also helped to erode the clear cut distinctions between juridically bona-fide American citizens and members of American society who in every respect except their formal citizenship status were as American as anyone else' (Gutiérrez 1995: 211).

The UFW's campaign to bring about the cessation of the Bracero programme indicated a new level of convergence between civil-rights efforts and the issue of the rights of Mexican agricultural labour in the USA. On 16 September 1965, these issues further cohered when the newly formed National Farm Workers Association (NFWA) voted to join a grape strike initiated in Delano, California by the Filipino Agricultural Workers Organising Committee. Striking to gain higher pay and rights guaranteed to industrial workers by the National Labour Relations Act of 1935, the Filipino and Mexican American agricultural workers collectively presented a cohesive but greatly disaffected workforce. Because of their greater numbers, Mexican Americans soon dominated the action, as did Chávez who was rapidly acknowledged as the leader of the campaign.

It was Chávez and the UFW who later called for a nationwide consumer boycott of table grapes, a strategy that was so successful that it sowed the seeds of further unionised disruption across the mid- and south-western states of America. The Grape Strike lasted from 1965 to 1970, during which time the union also turned its attention to the workers in the lettuce fields of the Salinas valley, as well as towards the farm workers of Texas and the mid-west (Chávez 1984: 134). Shortly after voting to strike in Delano, Chávez appealed to religious and civil-rights groups and radical student associations for support for the farm workers' cause. An indication of the degree of its unity and power of consensus across differing social groups can be found in *El Plan de Delano*, which was published in the union's newspaper, *El Malcriado* in March 1966. Written by Luis Valdez, it followed in the rhetorical style of the US Declaration of Independence and the African American gospel style of Dr Martin Luther King Jr. In this manner it unequivocally stated the discontent and oppression of Mexican and Mexican American agricultural workers, while at the same time endorsing a more widespread unification of political interests:

> The Mexican race has sacrificed itself for the last 100 years. Our sweat and our blood have fallen on this land to make other men rich . . . [W]e know that our cause is just, that history is a story of social revolution, and that the poor shall inherit the land . . . We know that the poverty of the Mexican or Filipino worker in California is the same as that of all farm workers across the country, the Negroes and poor whites, the Puerto Ricans, Japanese, and Arabians; in short, all of the races that comprise the oppressed minorities of the United States.
>
> (Jensen and Hammerback 2002: 17–18)

The plan, which has a clear religious resonance, proclaimed the farm workers' struggle a non-violent movement 'for social justice' led by 'the sons of the Mexican revolution', and called for social unity across working-class communities including farm workers, people of differing races and oppressed minorities throughout the USA. Arguably it was this broadening of the UFW's scope across different social groups that effectively converted what began as a labour dispute into a recognisable social movement (Gutiérrez 1995: 196).

The achievements of the UFW were numerous and included much-needed reforms in medical, pension and unemployment benefits. A skilled organiser and leader, Chávez used the strategy of civil disobedience, the power of the media and carefully chosen political rhetoric on behalf of his campaign:

> It is now clear to me that the war in Vietnam is gutting the soul of our nation. Of course we know the war to be wrong and unjustifiable, but today we see it has destroyed the moral fiber of the people.
>
> Our resistance to this, and all wars, stems from a deep faith in nonviolence. We have to acknowledge that violent warfare between opposing groups – be it over issues of labor or race – is not justifiable. Violence is like acid – it corrodes the movement's dedication to justice.
>
> (Jensen and Hammerback 2002: 48)

As well as speeches such as these, organising boycotts and implementing the tactic of the *huelga* (strike), Chávez and the UFW also relied on demonstrations, marches and hunger strikes in order to attract attention to the farm workers' cause (Chávez 1984, Gutiérrez 1995). Catholicism also became an integral part of UFW rhetoric and protest and played a significant role in attracting more moderate Mexican Americans (I. M. García 1997: 87, Jensen and Hammerback 2002: 6). Alongside banners bearing the image of the Virgin of Guadalupe, a parish priest often led UFW demonstrations (as was the case in Mexico in 1810 when the village priest Hidalgo began the resistance against Spain), and several of Chávez's marches, as well as his famous twenty-five-day fast in 1968, also ended with a mass.

The farm workers' heroic struggle also became an integral part of movement discourse and consistently surfaced in Chicano literature and cultural production. In an interview published in 1980, Tomás Rivera clearly situated his work firmly within the parameters of the Mexican American farm workers' struggle for social and political justice. He stated that, 'in . . . *Tierra* . . . I wrote about . . . the migrant farm worker . . . I began to see that my role . . . would be to document that period of time, but giving it some kind of spiritual strength or spiritual history' (Bruce-Novoa 1980a: 148). A discussion of Rivera's award-winning novel, *Y no se lo trago la tierra/And the Earth Did Not Devour Him* (1987) in Chapter 6 further highlights this connection. Set explicitly within the political and social contexts of the post-Second World War agricultural workers' life in south Texas, Rivera's text recalls and parallels many of the issues associated with the UFW's cause.

Oscar Zeta Acosta's novel *The Revolt of the Cockroach People* (1989b) presents a slightly different perspective on the UFW's activities that nonetheless indicates the profound impact that the union and its leader made on the lives of many Chicanos. During the course of the novel the lawyer Buffalo Zeta Brown experiences an epiphany upon meeting César Chávez during a hunger strike. This forces him to reconsider his life and its meaning, and motivates him to write 'about the whole struggle':

> I know that for twenty-five days now, César has not tasted a morsel of solid food. He has starved himself like Gandhi. He believes that physical resistance to oppression only produces lesser men. By way of example to his followers, he gives up his flesh and strength to their cause. The height of manhood, César believes, is to give of one's self.
>
> (Acosta 1989b: 44)

The iconic status accorded to Chávez by Acosta is an accurate representation of Mexican American public opinion concerning the heroic activities of the UFW's charismatic leader. Even today Chávez remains a 'folk saint' and one of the greatest leaders of the Mexican American and Chicano people. But in terms of literary and cultural production, arguably his most significant influence was found in the performances of the Teatro Campesino or the

Farmworkers Theatre, established in 1965 by Luis Valdez. The Teatro Campesino was intimately linked to the UFW in the sense that the actors were often striking farm workers and the *actos* performed were brief sketches that satirised the capitalist system of agribusiness and the American land-owner bosses. Generally there was no written script; instead actors impro-vised and often performed the rapid dialogue characteristic of the *acto* on the back of trucks, in the fields or on picket lines. A statement made by Valdez at the time of the UFW's dominance indicates the level of cohesion between the Teatro Campesino, the UFW and movement discourse:

> Our campesinos, the farm-working raza find it difficult to participate in this alien North American country. The acculturated Mexican Americans in the cities, ex-raza, find it easier. They have solved their Mexican con-tradictions with a pungent dose of Americanism, and are more concerned with status, money and bad breath . . . We are repelled by the human disintegration of peoples and cultures as they fall apart in this Great Gringo Melting Pot.
>
> (Muñoz 1989: 6)

The connection between the *campesinos* (farm workers), *raza* (the Chicano people), and an oppositional stance towards those who 'sell out' to white American society is typical of movement rhetoric. The reciprocal relationship between the UFW, movement politics and Valdez's *teatro* was, however, prob-lematic. According to Acuña (1988), it was 'César Chávez [who] gave the Chicano Movement a national leader', but the UFW, like Tijerina's Alianza, was never part of the movement as such (Muñoz 1989: 7). Chávez made it clear, especially during the movement's formative years, that the UFW did not support Chicano nationalism or neo-separatism, which Valdez initially did, and stated firmly that he did not consider himself to be a Chicano leader but the organiser of a union of rank-and-file farm workers (Muñoz 1989: 7).

In 1967, because of these profound ideological differences, Luis Valdez and the Teatro Campesino parted company with César Chávez and the UFW to pursue their own political objectives within the broad sphere of the move-ment's activities. Before this, however, the collaboration between the UFW and the Teatro Campesino popularised many of the movement's most fun-damental aims. It was mainly because of their collaboration that the farm workers' heroic struggle became a focal point for more widespread social analysis and action, and by 1966 their combined efforts opened the way for a second phase of Mexican American political activity.

The student organisations and protest

Chávez's fight for social justice proved to be a catalyst for Mexican American students, who, without ever abandoning the focal concern of the agri-cultural worker, soon embraced other political and cultural concerns. In

Muñoz's (1989) estimation it was 'Mexican American youth and particularly students [who] were central to the building of the Chicano movement, and especially to the shaping of its ideology . . . which evolved in the context of a quest for Chicano identity and power' (Muñoz 1989: 7). Certainly Chicano students were dissatisfied with the existing educational system, which was perceived as perpetuating ideological and cultural hegemony and racial discrimination. In response, Chicano student groups readily embraced militant forms of political protest. Initially their political activity was directed towards establishing Chicano student organisations, such as UMAS, MAYO, MASC (Mexican American Student Confederation), MEChA as well as promoting the institutionalisation of Chicano Studies programmes and community organisations.

In his autobiography *Always Running: Gang Days in L.A.* (1995), Luis J. Rodriguez recalls his experiences of the Chicano movement in East Los Angeles, and details how several of his neighbourhood schools formed student organisations similar to those mentioned above, including ToHMAS (To Help Mexican American Students), MASO (Mexican American Student Organisation) and HUNTOS (Together) (Rodriguez 1995: 174–5). These groups 'targeted the physical deterioration' of Rodriguez's school and enabled one of the first stagings of Chicano culture to take place at the annual show there. With the backing of these groups, the Latino students were prepared to experience the painful lessons of racism and discrimination in order to assert their pride in their culture and race:

> How are we going to win when the Anglos do all the judging? We plan to do an authentic Aztec dance, in authentic Aztec dress [but] if they deny us, then everyone will know how racist this school is.
>
> (Rodriguez 1995: 175)

Replicating the emphasis placed on the iconography of indigenous culture by movement politics, the show becomes a positive assertion of Chicano identity and is a massive success. Though, arguably, the sense of pride in winning over the American judges and displacing prior prejudices occurs most overtly when Rodriguez appears as a descendent of the Aztecs, dressed in 'leather top, arm bands and loin cloth, with a jaguar imaged headgear' and finally wins the contest (Rodriguez 1995: 175). For the students this meant that 'another barrier had been torn down and an important aspect of our culture recognised' (Rodriguez 1995: 175).

Despite the facticity of localised successes such as these, it was when the student organisations came into contact with community politics and other movement groups including the Brown Berets, Black Berets, and La Junta, that they became a much more cohesive group of militant activists.[2] The Brown Berets, the Chicano Moratorium Committee, LRUP and the Center for Autonomous Social Action-General Brotherhood of Workers (CASA) were among the more militant of the Los Angeles urban-based groups that were committed to Chicano liberation during the movement's most radical years. At first, cultural nationalism and a shared political perspective meant that all of these organisations believed in direct confrontation over problems of housing, education, employment and political empowerment, though their individual organisational structures, aims and methods varied in the implementation of these concerns. CASA's philosophy of *un pueblo sin fronteras* (a people without borders) and emphasis on organising domestic and foreign labourers greatly differed from the Chicano Moratorium Committee's focus on America's military intervention in Vietnam. Tactically, the paramilitary activities of David Sánchez and the Brown Berets again contrasted greatly with LRUP's challenges to the state's political system through electoral politics. Despite these somewhat glaring differences, all of the organisations were, in varying degrees, successful in forming a concerted political programme. The Brown Berets, organised and led by Sanchez, were initially extremely popular and influential. Originally they aimed to mediate between the Chicano community and the Los Angeles Police Department (LAPD), but instead they proceeded to expose the corruption of both the LAPD and other bureaucratic institutions on a number of different levels. The group also played an important role in the student 'blowouts' (boycotts) and mass demonstrations held in the spring of 1968 in East Los Angeles when more than 10,000 high-school students walked out of their classes and staged a sit-in at the Board of Education.

In 1969, the Chicano Co-ordination Council on Higher Education in Santa Barbara, California formed MEChA, one of the most important Chicano student organisations of the movement decades, as the move to bring all existing student groups together under the umbrella of MEChA facilitated the organisation of a national-level student movement. According to MEChA's programme, set forth in *El Plan de Santa Barbara* (1969), education, access to higher education, and the institutionalisation of Chicano Studies programmes 'held the key to Chicanos destiny' (Muñoz 1989: 192). It proposed direct political action to achieve these goals and set out a programme based on the development of 'political consciousness, mobilisation and tactics' (Muñoz 1989: 192).

In addition to this, and due to the diversity of racial groups in the area, students in the state of California emphasised *chicanismo* (cultural nationalism) as a source of political unity and strength, a strategy that would eventually characterise dominant sectors of the movement. Yet in other states interpretations of what constituted *chicanismo* varied greatly. In New Mexico the ethnic categories employed by Hispanos of Spanish/Mexican origin have always been problematic. As stated earlier, many New Mexican residents traced a direct lineage back to their Spanish forebears, and Tijerina and his followers consistently referred to themselves as Indo-Hispanos and not as Chicanos. This was mainly because compared to other states such as Texas and California, New Mexico had experienced a much longer period as part of New Spain. From colonisation and the founding of Santa Fe in 1610 to New Mexican statehood in 1912 comprises some 320 years. The relatively brief period when New Mexico was part of the Mexican nation, from independence from Spain in 1821 to conquest by the USA in 1846 was only twenty-five years. The logical outcome of these longer periods of time spent under Spanish rule encouraged Hispanicisation and the rejection of miscegenate identities. At the time of independence from Spain in 1821, the population of New Mexico was approximately half *mestizo* yet most denied their *Indio* heritage and considered themselves to be *Hispano* or Spanish American. This impulse was reinforced throughout the nineteenth century when 'the ethnic confrontations created by the Texas Revolution, the US–Mexican war, the Gold Rush and large scale immigration' meant that the Hispanos of New Mexico began to emphasise their Hispanicity in an attempt to thwart anti-Mexican sentiment as well as Anglo assimilation (Gutiérrez 1986: 97).

In Texas, the ethnic categories employed by Tejanos, or Texans of Spanish/ Mexican origin, have been similarly problematic. When the Tejanos joined forces with the American settlers of Texas to form their own independent republic in 1836, certain sectors of the community clearly rejected their Mexican identity. Later, faced with the same prejudice that the Mexican immigrants suffered in the 1920s, Tejanos insisted on being called Latin Americans. Not surprisingly then the first major civil-rights group in Texas reflected this identity and was consequently titled the League of United Latin American Citizens (LULAC) an organisation that was assimilationist and openly pro-English speaking (Gutiérrez 1995, de León 2001). Years later, during the movement, LULAC was still active, particularly concerning issues of immigration, but was more moderate in its approach to social activism than the ideology and the goals of the Chicano movement had been (de León 2001: 163–84). Their middle-class philosophy was based on the duality in ethnic life expressed as 'Mexican in culture and social activity, but American in philosophy and politics', instead of the more separatist and nationalistic approach favoured by movement discourse (Gutiérrez 1995: 193).

Conversely, other groups in Texas during the protest years advocated cultural nationalism and rejected this type of assimilation. José Angel Gutiérrez founded one such group, MAYO, in 1967, together with four associates, who collectively named themselves Los Cinco (The Five). Like other student organisations, MAYO was concerned with the educational status of Chicanos and what it saw as the threat posed to Chicano culture by the American educational system. In his account of MAYO, Navarro (1995) observes that Gutiérrez stated that 'We wanted to be a group of active crusaders for social justice Chicano style', and in this regard MAYO were responsible for thirty-nine student walkouts between 1968 and 1970 (Vargas 1999: 393). While this indicates a degree of cohesion with other radical student groups of the 1960s, at the same time MAYO's focus on the material terms of oppression differentiated them from other styles of Chicano militants. Initially concerned to support the Texas Farmworker Movement, MAYO's focus soon moved towards dissatisfaction with other Chicano organisations and the perceived lack of political action towards changing conditions in the urban barrios. This impetus was matched by the funding of the Ford Foundation who fully supported their campaign to 'maximise Mexican political power in a ten county area along the Rio Grande' (Gonzales 2000: 206).

One of the most significant of MAYO's urban projects took place in Crystal City in Texas. In 1963, a Mexican American 'political revolt' enabled Chicanos to elect their own councillors there, thus ending decades of American control. However, progress was undermined by American authority, which eventually seized power again two years later. In 1969 a second wave of militant activism, in which MAYO played a part, addressed the issue of high-school discrimination in the city. During this time Chicanos in Crystal City gained control of the school system and city government and introduced many innovative programmes. Needless to say, these events provoked a variety of responses from other Texan groups. For instance, Americans dubbed Crystal City 'Little Cuba', thereby precipitating an exodus of businesses and finance (Meier and Gutiérrez 2000: 63). In the spring of 1969, several US representatives including Henry B. Gonzalez (D-Texas) attacked MAYO and Angel Gutiérrez in a series of speeches that ultimately resulted in the termination of Chicano control in the city. Despite these major setbacks, MAYO activism did nonetheless bring about broad educational changes and the organisation in 1970 of LRUP, arguably the most significant organisation in Chicana/o politics on a national level.

The Crusade for Justice

One of the most important thrusts of this second stage of increasing political activism, and arguably the development that ultimately had the most impact in transforming Mexican American political opinion, was the adaptation and promotion of a new Chicano identity. A decisive moment in the shaping of the emerging identity politics came about with the National Chicano Youth Liberation Conference held in Denver, Colorado in 1969. The conference took place at the headquarters of La Cruzada para la Justicia (Crusade for Justice), the first Mexican American civil-rights organisation in the USA that was founded by Rodolfo 'Corky' Gonzales in 1965 (Vigil 1999). Ostensibly a community self-help group, through their own fund-raising efforts members of the Crusade for Justice established a barrio service centre, providing such assistance as health care, legal aid, housing and employment counselling (Chávez 1984: 142). Besides co-organising the Poor People's March in Washington DC in 1968, along with Martin Luther King Jr., the Crusade for Justice also supported the cause of the Native American movement, as well as the controversial African American scholar and activist, Angela Y. Davis. They also founded and published *El Gallo: La Voz de la Justicia*, a newspaper that promoted their political programme between 1967 and 1980 (Esquibel 2001: xvii–xxxvi).

As one of the strongest proponents of nationalism, the Crusade was also outspoken concerning Chicano cultural rights and issues of identity. It was in this vein that over 100,000 copies of 'Yo soy Joaquín' ('I Am Joaquín', 1967), a poem by Rodolfo 'Corky' Gonzales, were distributed by members of the Crusade during the movement's most radical years. The poem is an epic assertion of Chicano identity, during which Gonzales draws from Mexican history in order to make Chicanos aware of their identity and their centuries-old heritage of struggle for justice and property ownership. This can be seen in the following short extract:

> I am Cuauhtémoc
> Proud and Noble
>   Leader of men,
> King of an empire,
> Civilised beyond the dreams
>   of the Gachupín Cortez,
> Who also is the blood,
>   The image of myself.
> I am the Maya Prince.
> I am Nezahualcoyotl
> Great leader of the Chichimecas
> (Hernández-Gutiérrez and Foster 1997: 207–22)

A full discussion of the construction of Chicano identity in 'Yo soy Joaquín' appears in Chapter 5 of this study. As I state there, in essence it is progressively defined by a genealogy constructed from the past.[3] Through the course of the epic, Joaquín allies himself with several key figures from Chicano history including the village priest Hidalgo who began the war of independence against Spain in 1810 with a loud *grito* (shout), and others that fought for Mexican independence from Spain in 1810 such as 'Morelos! Matamoros! [and] Guerrero!' Also included are Juan Diego, who first saw the Virgin of Guadalupe in a series of apparitions in 1531, and Don Benito Juarez, a Zapotec Indian who supported republican rule in the nineteenth century and fought against French colonisation. Joaquin Murietta, the famous Mexican rebel of the mid-nineteenth century, and the leaders from the Mexican revolution, Emiliano Zapata and Francisco 'Pancho' Villa who fought against the ruler of Mexico Porfirio Diaz (1830–1915) in the early years of the twentieth century similarly play a vital role in the construction of Chicano identity (Hernández-Gutiérrez and Foster 1997: 210).

Despite the emphasis placed on the importance of the past, the poem captured the imaginations of Chicanos involved in present-day struggles. According to Gonzales, it was not only due to the fact that it was 'the first work of poetry to be published by Chicanos for Chicanos' but also because of 'the sounds of movement, the literary and anthropological quest for our roots, the renewal of a fierce pride and tribal unity' that made the poem appeal to such a wide audience (Arteaga 1997: 147). Commenting later on the poem's significance from a slightly different perspective, the Chicano critic Alfred Arteaga (1997) states that 'while it does outline a genealogy, its focus is decidedly contemporary and with a vision toward the future' (Arteaga 1997: 148).

This vision of a past and future marked out by strong symbolic ethnic boundaries undeniably appealed to those sectors of the movement who stridently advocated separatism and the rejection of inherent American superiority. Many Chicano groups also rejected the Mexican American identity itself, as they saw it as assimilationist, and instead favoured a more separatist identity such as that of the poem, which was based on *chicanismo*. According to MEChA's programme set forth in *El Plan de Santa Barbara*, around the same time as the Denver Youth Conference, *chicanismo* involved a crucial distinction in political consciousness 'between a Mexican American and a Chicano mentality' (Muñoz 1989: 194). Whereas a Chicano embraced and nurtured his cultural roots, 'the Mexican American is a person who lacks respect for his cultural and ethnic heritage' and subsequently 'seeks assimilation as a way out of his "degraded" social status' (Muñoz 1989: 194).

Advocating the separatist ideology of *chicanismo*, those attending the Denver Youth Conference also emphasised the importance of Aztlán, the Chicano homeland, both as a separate state and as an important part in the construction of Chicano identity. Aztlán was the territory that Mexico ceded to the USA in 1848 with the signing of the treaty of Guadalupe Hidalgo. This territory included the future states of California, Arizona and New Mexico as well as parts of Colorado, Nevada and Utah. Significantly, these states also symbolised Aztlán, the ancestral homeland of the Aztecs and, by extension, the Chicano people. According to Chávez (1984), to reclaim this land simultaneously meant to enact a process of decolonisation, because with the ancient myth of Aztlán 'Chicanos re-discovered a tie between their homeland and Mexican culture that antedated the republic of Mexico, the Spanish exploration of the borderlands, and even the establishment of Tenochtitlan [Mexico City] itself' (Chávez 1984: 131).

The spiritual manifesto *El Plan Espiritual de Aztlán* re-emphasised these sentiments when first presented during the youth conference. Written largely by the San Diego poet Alurista and 'Corky' Gonzales, it considered Aztlán as an idyll that was lost, and its reclamation by Chicano groups a reality that could and should be regained. Structurally, the plan had four basic points, that were laid out in steps to achieve these aims (I. M. García 1997: 96). First, it declared the use of nationalism as the bond that would unify various factions of the movement; second, it set out a specific set of organisational goals including greater community and barrio control; third, it called for action; and last but not least, it called for Chicano liberation from oppression through the attainment of social, cultural, political and economic independence from the USA (I. M. García 1997: 96). Aztlán, it states, should be a nation 'autonomous and free':

In the spirit of a new people that is conscious not only of its proud historical heritage but also of the brutal 'gringo' invasion of our territories, we, the Chicano inhabitants and civilizers of the northern land of *Aztlán* from whence came our forefathers, reclaiming the land of their birth and consecrating the determination of our people of the sun, declare that the call of our blood is our power, our responsibility, and our inevitable destiny . . . *Aztlán* belongs to those who plant the seeds, water the fields, and gather the crops and not to the foreign Europeans. We do not recognise capricious frontiers on the bronze continents.

(Anaya and Lomelí 1989: 1)

Ignoring the boundaries of the American nation established through the treaty of Guadalupe Hidalgo, the plan reclaims the land once deemed to belong to the Chicano people. It also delineates a separate Chicano culture and nation and as such marks an important turning point in refining a collective idea of Chicano identity. Presenting a nationalist vision of the Chicano people that extolled a pre-Columbian, native ancestry while simultaneously diminishing or rejecting their connection with American culture, the plan stated that Aztlán, 'belongs to those who plant the seeds, water the fields, and gather the crops and not to the foreign Europeans' (Anaya and Lomelí 1989: 1). This perspective, while promoting an ethnic and political separatism, simultaneously established a context for a variety of demands including restitution from the USA for past economic, cultural and political oppression associated with the loss of the land. Chapters 8 and 9 of this study provide a discussion of these issues in more detail as well as highlighting the differing ideological implications the politics of Aztlán held for Chicana/o women and men.

Achievements of the Chicano movement

In enabling a large number of important coalitions and reforms to be passed, few could deny that the Chicano movement, like the larger civil-rights movement, was instrumental in raising awareness of the problems facing the Mexican American population in the USA. Organisations associated with the movement made considerable advances in education and legal matters. MALDEF was and still is an important organisation dedicated to using the legal system to protect the civil rights of Chicanos. Initially concerned with attacking the courts on charges of racism, MALDEF soon filed suits in a range of cases including police brutality and harassment, segregation in schools and citizen rights under social security and welfare legislation (Meier and Gutiérrez 2000: 146).

This trend accelerated after 1971 when a US district court ruled that Mexican Americans constituted an identifiable minority group entitled to special federal assistance (Gutiérrez 1995: 187). Some Mexican American moderates who had previously opposed cultural nationalism also began to acknowledge and act upon the militants' demands. As one prominent scholar noted:

> The success, of the movement . . . In focusing government attention on Mexican problems softened the initial resistance and pejorative attitudes of the established Mexican American community leadership which realised its own interests could be served best by working in the movement framework.
>
> (Gutiérrez 1995: 187)

For many Chicanos, participation in these activities also earned them valuable experiences that they would later put to use in their membership in the major political parties and in their election or appointment to public office (Montejano 1999a). Again, MALDEF reduced barriers to participation in the US political system and led to considerable gains in local governance. By the mid-1970s, many former activists had become involved in mainstream politics. Both the Democratic Party and Republican Party were acknowledging the importance of the Chicano vote and Mexican American congressional representation eventually increased. At the state legislative level, Mexican American elected officials began to represent important areas of the south-west, a previously unthinkable proposition as traditionally the Mexican American electorate was routinely considered to be a 'sleeping giant' (Montejano 1999: 234–57). Though, arguably, the widest and most successful degree of political cohesion during the movement years occurred through the Chicano Moratorium against the Vietnam War in 1970. This was when more than 30,000 Chicanos and Chicano representatives came from all over the south-west and gathered on 29 August in Los Angeles in order to protest the disproportionate number of Mexican American casualties during America's military intervention in Vietnam.

In terms of literary and cultural production, the movement years also achieved unprecedented successes. Anthologies and festivals of Chicano literature appeared, as did theatre groups, journals and several important publishing houses. This study goes on to explore the ways in which the movement, with its strong emphasis on cultural regeneration, encouraged the rise of a whole generation of artists and writers including Tomás Rivera, Rudolfo Anaya, Rolando Hinojosa, Alurista, and Rodolfo 'Corky' Gonzales and many others whose literary concerns centred on forging issues of identity from out of the Chicano past.

The decline of the Chicano movement

Before beginning this assessment of the decline of the Chicano movement, its trajectory needs to be seen in a wider context, in the sense that all the militancy associated with the broader civil-rights movements of the 1960s waned, and not just that of *el movimiento*. This is not meant to suggest that a continuation of civil-rights protests does not exist to the present day. On the contrary, it is quite commonly accepted that multicultural politics of the ensuing decades represent goals and tactics that are similar in aim to that of the earlier activism. But the change in the political and intellectual climate of the USA that came with Richard Nixon's presidency and the end of the Vietnam war in 1975 meant that Mexican Americans, like other minority groups, were forced to adopt different tactics in order to retain the gains made during the movement years.

Much earlier than this, in fact by the end of the 1960s, state and federal authorities had mobilised to meet the challenge from Chicano civil-rights protests. In New Mexico, Tijerina was incarcerated for two years, and what began as an organised and peaceful demonstration with the Moratorium in Los Angeles quickly escalated into a police riot. Over 400 people were injured and several million dollars in property damage inflicted. Three people were killed, including the *Los Angeles Times* reporter Ruben Salazar, whose 'mysterious' death at the hands of the LAPD spawned further rioting and protest (Gutiérrez 1995, Ruiz 1998, Vigil 1999, Chávez 2002). The Crusade for Justice also lost support when organisers were continually discredited by local, state and federal law-enforcement agencies including the FBI (Vigil 1999: 93). The Crusade even attracted the attention of the US Congress. The US Representative Larry McDonald provided an extensive report on the Crusade for Justice under the title of 'Colorado Terrorism' that suggested there was 'evidence of national and international revolutionary support for the Crusade' (Esquibel 2001: xxxv).

In a similar vein, the police and military repeatedly infiltrated the Brown Berets. While arguing that ideological conflicts within movement organisations themselves undoubtedly contributed to its demise, studies such as that by Muñoz (1989), Vigil (1999) and Chávez (2002) also consider this climate of government harassment and political surveillance as being instrumental in bringing about the decline of the Chicano movement. Muñoz states that divisions within the movement were attributable to 'agents of the FBI and other intelligence agencies, their paid informants and provocateurs' (Muñoz 1989: 172–3). Political surveillance, infiltration of movement organisations and arrests of movement leaders were certainly forms of ideological repression that played a major role in the decline of Chicano activism. However, other factors also come into play when considering its demise.

Initially, *chicanismo* or cultural nationalism served as a dynamically effective tool capable of mobilising divergent struggles within the Chicano movement. It provided an ideological link between such diverse groups as LRUP, the UFW, the Crusade for Justice and the various student movements. But despite MEChA's claim put forward in *El Plan de Santa Barbara* that 'Chicanismo was flexible enough to relate to the varying levels of consciousness within la raza', internal divisions and ideological differences within the movement itself meant that a cohesive political programme was difficult (Muñoz 1989, Vigil 1999, Chávez 2002). A case in point is LULAC, which, as previously stated, neither promoted or supported the ideology or the original goals of the Chicano movement. LRUP also faced internal problems and differing perspectives to other movement groups. José Angel Gutiérrez, the co-founder of the organisation, in contrast to LULAC's assimilationist philosophy, accused other activists of holding 'gringo tendencies' and maintained that Mexican Americans who subscribed to the ideology of assimilation were *vendidos* or sell-outs (Gutiérrez 1995: 186). Arguably, the most significant split in the movement as a whole occurred as a result of the national-level political infighting at LRUP when ideological differences formed a rift between Chicano pragmatists led by Gutiérrez and Chicano cultural nationalists led by 'Corky' Gonzales (Gutiérrez 1995, Vigil 1999). These events resulted in fragmentation and pockets of localised militant strength, but ultimately left the movement without a national leadership or a coherent nationally based political strategy.

By the early 1970s, a pattern of political realignments within and outside of the Chicano movement was also beginning to evolve. The UFW formed new liberal alliances in order to succeed in their campaigns and were forced to seek the intervention of the AFL–CIO (American Federation of Labor–Congress of Industrial Organisations) and the Democratic Party. According to Xavier (1999), by 1972 the UFW had become the main link between Chicanos and the Democratic Party liberals (Montejano 1999a: 182). These alliances were unacceptable to the more militant wing of the movement and, as the previously assumed emphasis on nationalism was being scrutinised in light of their organisation, they effectively sharpened differences between opposing factions.

Apart from these sometimes-glaring conflicts, Gutiérrez (1995) argues that it was nationalist ideology specifically in conjunction with the immigration issue that helped to expose some of the more obvious contradictions between members of the movement. In his view, leaders who advocated Chicano nationalism did not 'fully and critically examine the sources of their ethnicity, their relationship to Mexicans who had arrived from across the border, or their relationship with America itself' (Gutiérrez 1995: 204). This, he states, presented 'an ideological dilemma that was never resolved' (Gutiérrez 1995: 204).

In sum, then, the movement was extremely varied, and by the late 1970s internal debate over the most basic questions of ethnic and cultural identity and historical disagreements over the best political strategy effectively combined to foil concerted Chicano activism. Moreover, in time, the dominance of *chicanismo* gave rise to a parallel movement formed in ideological opposition to its masculinist politics. This parallel movement not only began to gain momentum, but also further highlighted the differences within *el movimiento* itself (A. Garcia 1997: 3). Chicano nationalism encouraged resistance to American domination and the continuity of ethnic traditions by embracing and delineating a common Chicano identity. Yet this effectively excluded anyone who was not a man. In the following chapter, I detail the steadily increasing presence of Chicanas and their own brand of militancy which evolved as a response to the paternalistic ideology that dominated certain sectors of the movement. As I go on to argue, their emerging political programme ultimately survived the years ahead much better than the fractured and divisive politics, which characterised the activism of their male counterparts during the movement years.

2   Chicana feminism

Following on from the observations of the Chicano movement made previously, this chapter provides a study of the parallel development of Chicana feminism and Chicana feminist discourse. Most early studies of the movement failed to adequately discuss or include the role of Chicanas in the political activities of the protest decades, and so this is an area that is now being more thoroughly explored. Alma Garcia (1997) cites Ignacio García's study of LRUP, *United We Win*, and Muñoz's *Youth, Identity, Power* (1989) as examples of the lack of attention accorded to Chicanas by male scholars of the movement. She also cites Navarro's (1995) study of MAYO, which does include issues of gender, but she argues that this is not central to the analysis (A. Garcia 1997: 11). Many of the sources cited in the previous discussion of the Chicano movement likewise either give little attention to gender issues or consistently trivialise the complexity of women's political position during these years. More recent studies such as García's *Chicanismo: The Forging of a Militant Ethos among Mexican Americans* (I. M. Garcia 1997) do include sections on Chicanas and so more adequately reflect more recent trends in Chicano/a scholarship. Up until the relatively recent publication of studies such as these, Chicano research in to the movement decades tended to exclude gender as a category of analysis and those factors that were unacceptable to a masculinised agenda. By the late 1980s David Gutiérrez (1989) noted that there still existed an almost total absence of gender as a category of analysis in recent historiographic research (D. Gutiérrez 1989: 281–96). While in the early 1990s according to the Chicana historian Vicki Ruiz, 'among Chicano historians there appears [to be] a fascination with second-generation men . . . so much so that the life-styles and attitudes of their female counterparts have gone unnoticed' (de la Torre and Pesquera 1993: 110).

Despite this long-term invisibility, Chicanas not only participated in the movement, they also inherited a strong tradition of political activism dating back to the turn of the century and to social movements on both sides of the US–Mexico border (A. Garcia 1997, Ruiz 1998, Pérez 1999a). Chicana feminism can be traced as far back as the middle to late nineteenth century, and in particular to women's role in the Partido Liberal Mexicano (PLM) from 1905 to 1917 in Mexico itself (Cotera 1977, Pérez 1999a). The Liga Feminil

Mexicanista (Mexican Feminist League), a Mexican American organisation established in 1911 by Jovita Idar in Laredo, and the civil-rights activities of María L. Hernandez, also in Texas, are perhaps the earliest forms of organised political protest by Mexican American women in the USA. By the 1930s, however, women began to play increasingly important roles in the emerging union movement and labour activism in the south-west. Several prominent Mexican American women activists emerged in the decade of the 1930s including Luisa Moreno, Emma Tenayuca, and Josefina Fierro de Bright (Ruiz 1998: 79–80). According to Ruiz (1998), subsequent expressions of women's politics leading up to the movement decades 'whether it was through commadrazgo, mutualistas, labor unions, or political organising', was marked by a similar 'tenacity of intention' (Ruiz 1998: 102).[1] Of these strategies the most traditional were *mutualistas* or mutual aid organisations that were used to help maintain Mexican culture, identity and political life, and *commadrazgo* or *compadrazgo* which creates connections and family ties (Segura and Pierce 1993, Gutiérrez 1995).

During the movement, in order to force male activists to change their perspective and to accept women's issues, Chicanas adopted two main approaches, one of which was to work outside of the movement by creating alliances with the mainstream women's rights movement (Sánchez 1985: 5). The other approach favoured a close role within *el movimiento* itself forcing Chicano men to recognise women's issues, including educational, political, social and economic advancement programmes for Chicanas (A. Garcia 1997: 137). By the early 1970s a broader platform for women's politics had emerged and Chicana feminists were writing as well as actively protesting their exclusion from movement activities. Mirta Vidal (1971) was one of the most radical and outspoken among this new generation of women activists. Her essay titled 'New Voice of La Raza: Chicanas Speak Out' was among the first to document and record the developing Chicana feminist movement. *The Woman of La Raza* by Enriqueta Longeaux Vasquez (1972), *La Chicana* by Elizabeth Martinez (1972), and *Our Feminist Heritage* by Marta Cotera (1973) likewise contribute important insights to the debates concerning Chicana feminism that intensified throughout this period of social protest.

According to Garcia (1997) the development of Chicana feminism 'proved to be a contentious political struggle and transformed Chicanas into an oppositional group in relation to Chicano men' (A. Garcia 1997: 5). Chicanas who adopted feminist ideologies and who fought against gender oppression within the movement as well as class and race oppression against the dominant culture were considered to be *malinches* (betrayers), untrustworthy *vendidas agabachadas* (sell-outs) who were destroying the most basic bonds of *la familia* (family) and *carnalismo* (brotherhood). This chapter goes on to trace the development of a Chicana feminist discourse that emerged in response to this paternalistic ideology. Whereas group consciousness within the movement proved to be untenable in the long run, Chicanas, both activists and writers, were responsible for ushering in a cohesive post-movement politics that displaced and superseded the static political agenda of the earlier years. In subsequent chapters I explore this response in more detail by focusing on the recodification of Chicana/o identity politics and key issues associated with movement discourse. This chapter first of all explores the trajectory of Chicana feminism, its socio-political as well as cultural activities, before moving on to consider how following the protest decades it found its most concentrated expression in the literature produced by Chicana writers.

Chicana and American feminism

Sánchez (1985) among others argues that during the 1960s Chicanas found themselves at the juncture of two parallel, and apparently opposing move- ments in the USA (Sánchez 1985, Segura and Pesquera 1988–90). These were the mainstream women's movement and the Chicano movement itself (Sánchez 1985: 5). On the one hand Chicano men dominated the movement, whereas on the other hand the women's movement was primarily white and middle class. Sharing similar ideologies with both, Chicanas wanted to affirm their commitment to the struggle against racism as well as supporting the political goals of feminism. Despite their efforts to organise their political activity, their own Chicano groups were characterised by a restrictive hier- archy that precluded their participation. Likewise, the women's movement with its emphasis on individualism and Eurocentric perspectives was often seen as effectively denying Chicanas their rights. The realisation of these biases motivated some to challenge the prerogatives accorded to men by Chicano culture and to white middle-class women by feminism. Con- sequently, Chicanas were active in supporting some of the causes Chicanos espoused, but their focus was also on women's issues and its exclusion from movement discourse. According to Nieto Gomez this meant that in the main male concerns of access to political power and community autonomy gave way to issues of birth control, welfare rights, child care, sexual discrimination in employment, access to institutions of higher education and women's position within the Chicano movement itself (A. Garcia 1997: 52–7).

Because of their particular relevance to Chicanas, these issues also naturally problematised the categories of feminism as defined by the more mainstream feminist movement at the time. The editors of the first edition of the Chicana Studies publication *Encuentro Femenil* stated this more explicitly: 'As a Chicana feminist journal [we] recognise the fact that the Chicana feminists' struggle is necessarily distinct from that of the Anglo women's popular feminist movement, although we may indeed have many similarities' (A. Garcia 1997: 115). It is interesting to note that this journal together with *Regeneración*, named after a Mexican women's underground newspaper published during the 1910 Mexican revolution, according to Segura and Pesquera (1988–90) 'provided Chicanas with a means to frame their local agendas within a larger critique of race, class, and gender domination' (Noriega et al. 2001: 393). But before the publication of journals such as these, Alarcón (1989) and Segura and Pesquera (1988–90) argue that initially much Chicana feminism resembled American feminism and was similarly organised oppositionally to men from a perspective of gender differences (McClintock et al. 1997, Noriega et al. 2001). Influenced by the politics of the movement, however, this position soon shifted towards a parallel awareness of their race and class situation. Virdal (1971) stated at the First National Conference of La Raza Women in Houston that 84 per cent of the women there felt that 'there [was] a distinction between the problems of the Chicana and those of other women' (A. Garcia 1997: 23). She concluded that '*Raza* women suffer a triple form of oppression: as members of an oppressed nationality, as workers, and as women' (A. Garcia 1997: 23).

When taking these factors into consideration, the developments in Chicana feminism bore only a faint resemblance to the feminist movements in the USA and northern Europe at that time. It became increasingly clear that the 'normative subject' of American feminist theorising was radically different from Chicana womanhood. As Alarcón (1990b) points out, mainstream feminism effectively excluded the 'native female' or 'woman of colour' from its discourse (Anzaldúa 1990: 357). The mainstream American women's movement initially revealed its indifference to Chicanas and other women of colour in the USA, by minimising or neglecting to focus on issues of race or poverty as categories of analysis. Chicana feminists on the other hand were keen to attend to the dynamics of each social location that frame a woman's experiences. Pesquera and Segura (1993) argue that the multiple axes of class, race, ethnicity as well as gender and sexuality inform a Chicana's social position (A. Garcia 1997: 295). Gloria Anzaldúa (1987), one of the more outspoken Chicana feminists among the generation of Chicana writers of the 1980s, states this more explicitly. In *Borderlands/La Frontera* (1987) she uses a phrase normally associated with mainstream feminism when she claims that, 'I am every woman's sister' (Anzaldúa 1987: 80–1). Yet she goes on to qualify this notion by highlighting the internal differences within the category of 'woman' itself. The subversive image of female identity that recurs throughout the text is developed with reference to Anzaldúa's own lesbian sexuality and a genealogy of indigenous female figures beginning with Coatlicue the Aztec goddess of life and death. In relation to this, Alarcón (1990a) states that 'the strategic invocation and recodification of the native woman' in Chicana feminist discourse 'has the effect of conjoining the historical repression of the "noncivilised" dark woman with the present moment' (Trujillo 1998a: 376). This 'strategic invocation', together with Anzaldúa's non-European and non-Western perspective clearly calls into question mainstream feminism's myth of 'sisterhood'. Yet the growing strength of the mainstream women's movement was an important catalyst in the development of Chicana political discourse. Likewise, as Garcia (1989) and Segura and Pesquera (1988–90) point out, Chicana feminism as it came to be known emerged as a result of the gendered dynamics within the Chicano movement itself (Dubois and Ruiz 1990, Noriega et al. 2001).

Women and the movement

In his description of the debate between Chicanos and Chicanas during the movement years, Rendon (1972) polarises men and women into the mutually exclusive categories of male and female or *machismo* and *malinchismo* (de la Torre and Pesquera 1993: 40). Rendon (1972) asserts that whereas the former is synonymous with revolutionary struggle, commitment and progress, the latter is synonymous with retrocession, betrayal and conquest (de la Torre and Pesquera 1993: 40–1). The degree of participation allowed to women in movement-based activities and politics upheld this perspective and brought home to Chicana activists the fact that they were being denied positions of authority within their own culture. CPLC, a Chicano civil-rights organisa- tion mainly based in Arizona, reflected these divisions. Despite women's considerable interest and willingness to participate, men held the most primary positions in the organisation, whereas women were confined to clerical and secretarial roles. Joe Eddie Lopez who was Chairman of the organ- isation together with his male colleagues appointed all other personnel, including secretaries and treasurers, posts nominally given to women in the organisation.[1]

MAYO is another case in point. In his study, *The Mexican American Youth Organisation: Avant Garde of the Chicano Movement in Texas* (1995), Navarro outlines the ways in which the leadership pattern was essentially male and 'machismo was a factor' in constructing this hierarchy (Vargas 1999: 403). While women participated in its activities and membership ranks, no women were allowed to serve in a state leadership capacity and were essentially considered second-class participants by and large. According to Navarro (1995), statements made by Carlos Guerra, a participant and one of the leaders of the organisation substantiate this point:

> Actually, we are going through a very serious rewriting of history in dealing with the role of women in the movement. We would like to think that in the old days we were progressive about it, but we were not. We were pretty sexist. They were essentially second-class participants by and large.
>
> (Vargas 1999: 402)

Chicanas who did play a role were made aware of the iniquities within the organisation. Their roles were clearly vital and supportive, but were relegated to picketing or distributing the organisation's literature. Commenting on the wider participation of Chicanas in the movement, García (1997) states that through women's 'clerical skills, their willingness to do tedious jobs well, and their ability to follow through on assignments', they 'became the organ- isational backbone of the movement' (I. M. García 1997: 64). Yet this kind of activism has consistently meant that the most visible participants in movement-based organisations were clearly Chicano men.

This masculinist tendency of the movement and its related activities can be seen in Lucha Corpi's autobiographical novel, *Delia's Song* (1989). The narrator is a student at Berkeley during the most turbulent period of the movement and is a witness to the volatile events of the times. The book is dedicated to 'all the Chicano students who participated in the Third World Strike, at the University of California at Berkeley' (Corpi 1989: 3). Yet Delia, as a woman, is relegated to the role of recorder and of chronicling events, rather than participating in the protest activities themselves. This duty not only effectively prevents her physical participation in the events, but also bars her from writing in her own journal; in fact it essentially silences her:

> Rallies, riots, the arrival of the National Guard for the first time on campus, the chancellor's refusal to meet with any of them, the support for the strike vote . . . the Regents' vote for immediate suspension of all students who violated rules, the 150 people arrested, 38 students placed on interim suspension, 18 of them falling under the Regents' ruling.
>
> (Corpi 1989: 50)

The recording of these 'facts' supersede any other forms of activism including her own writing, as she 'entered all events and dates in the chronology during the weeks to follow, but she stopped writing in her journal' (Corpi 1989: 50). Literary representations of the machismo politics of the movement such as these foreground its marginalising and masculinist tendencies from a personal perspective. These exclusions, however, also carried over into the public sphere and, as I continue to explore, the position of Chicanas in many of the other organisations and events was similarly limited.

Women's place within the UFW during the struggle for union recognition and collective bargaining rights was also circumscribed by this ideology. Although César Chávez selected Dolores Huerta, one of the best-known activists for social justice as one of his chief organisers, originally few Mexican or Mexican American women were active in the UFW. Rose (1990b), for instance, demonstrates how Huerta's position within the union was 'non-traditional' in comparison to the more 'traditional' roles assigned to both women and men (Rose 1990b: 26–32). In her other analysis of women in the UFW, Rose (1990a) argues how the recruitment of farm-worker families began to strengthen the boycott and suggests that women did eventually find some form of political inclusion in the sense that they were encouraged to accompany their husbands on picket and boycott duties (Vargas 1999: 404). Over time, and as the UFW's tactics developed, Huerta similarly pointed out that 'no married man went out on boycott unless he took his wife . . . excluding women, protecting them, keeping women at home, that's the middle class way. Poor people's movements have always had whole families on the line . . . it's a class not an ethnic thing' (Acuña 1988: 352). Yet from one perspective, Huerta here appears to be upholding the Chicano mandate of privileging one social location over others by emphasising class rather than race and more importantly gender in her evaluation of women's activism within the union. In so doing she ignores the ways in which the family, and by implication the UFW, reinforced established gender relations by confining women to traditionally female-defined work and social activism. Rose (1990a) argues that in much the same way as other movement groups, a patriarchal order characterised the organisational structure and personal relations of the UFW from the leadership down to the rank-and-file levels (Vargas 1999: 405). Additionally, most women who were active in the boycott received much less attention than men and were refrained from public speaking. Moreover, women who engaged in supportive roles in the offices did not participate in the formal decision-making process, which again was reserved for men. Rose (1990a) states that this resulted in the situation that women's activism in the UFW, like that of most other Chicanas in other groups, was relegated to secondary roles and seemed to be largely invisible (Vargas 1999: 407). By June 1969 this situation remained largely unchanged for 'out of the forty-three boycott coordinators in major cities, thirty-nine were men and five were women' (Rose 1990b: 30).

Thus it was through their attempts to be included in political organisations and activities such as these that Chicanas became exposed to the dynamics of gender subjugation and the male hegemony of movement thought. To a large extent it was because of their exclusion from any decision-making process in these years that Chicana activists began to problematise the consensually held view that Chicano groups cohered through a politics based on a 'communal consciousness of allegiance' (Saldívar 1997: 113). Muñoz (1989) states that a collective ethnic consciousness based on *chicanismo* crystallised the essence of nationalist ideology (A. Garcia 1997: 3). Yet these ideas of 'group consciousness' were based on a deeply entrenched patriarchal and heterosexist hierarchy that placed women in the movement far below their male activist colleagues.

In Ana Castillo's novel *So Far from God* (1994a), the episodes which detail Esperanza's troubled relationship with her boyfriend Rubén, satirically reflect on the Chicano movement, its machismo politics and general disregard for Chicanas. Rubén, who renames himself Cuauhtémoc after the Aztec emperor during 'the height of Chicano cosmic consciousness', appears as an unflattering caricature of a Chicano activist (Castillo 1994a: 25). His actions designate him as a *vendido* or a sell-out, ironically a term usually ascribed to Chicanas, as he marries a white woman from outside of the community and effectively 'dumped [Esperanza] for a middle-class *gabacha* with a Corvette' (Castillo 1994a: 26).

This accurately mirrors movement ideology in the sense that on the one hand the Chicano movement called for justice and demanded equity for Mexican American people in the USA, but on the other hand little was said about the rights of women. Within its main organisational tool, the Chicano family, sexism and internal oppression were widespread and deeply entrenched. Consequently its ubiquitous ideology affected the female participants of the movement in a number of profound ways. As one Chicana activist stated, 'When a family is involved in a human rights movement, as is the Mexican American family, there is little room for a women's liberation movement. There is little room for having a definition of women's role as such' (A. Garcia 1997: 31).

Chicanas, both activists and writers, were responsible for ushering in a cohesive post-movement politics that displaced and superseded this entrenched ideology. Their critique of the Chicano family contributed significantly to their reformulation, and more generally to the new wave of Chicana feminist politics. According to Baca Zinn (1975), within movement discourse the Chicano family represented a source of cultural and political resistance to various types of discrimination experienced in American society. At the cultural level the Chicano movement emphasised the family as a safeguard for their tradition and cultural values. At the political level the Chicano movement used the family as a strategic organisational tool for protest activities (Noriega et al. 2001: 455–72).

Traditionally Chicano families were depicted as warm and nurturing, and any evidence of conflict within them was kept to a minimum. But as a unit it solidified male dominance, and the oppression of women was considered necessary in order to maintain the myth of its stability. Rose (1990a) states that in the UFW the family approach to organisation preserved gender-designated forms of labour activism and gave the male of the household more prominence, authority and responsibility (Vargas 1999: 408). These views were also expressed at meetings of LRUP where a separate stand on the rights of women was considered unnecessary. Instead, LRUP, like the UFW, preferred a political familism, and strongly believed that 'the strength of unity begins with family' (A. Garcia 1997: 165–7).

According to Orozco (1986) the lack of recognition given to women in community action because of this family-based ideology was also mirrored in university-based Chicano Studies programmes where Chicana feminism was also undermined (A. Garcia 1997: 266). She goes on to state that Chicano academics, who were also by and large activists in the movement, argued that race and class were the determining factors in understanding the subordinate position of Mexican Americans in the USA and that gender was irrelevant (A. Garcia 1997: 266). Chicanas were in a minority in academia both in professional posts and as students; likewise there were no Chicana Studies courses or recognition of women's writing as such. Orozco (1986) points out that in the Chicano Studies document *El Plan de Santa Bárbara* (1969), which provided the rationale for Chicano Studies at that time, a lack of analysis concerning sexuality and gender can be inferred as neither women nor female liberation are mentioned (A. Garcia 1997: 267). Likewise, *El Plan Espiritual Aztlán* (1969), first presented at the Denver Youth Conference, also seemed to raise the question of gender mainly through its absence:

Brotherhood unites us, and love for our brothers makes us a people whose time has come and who struggles against the foreigner *'gabacho'* who exploits our riches and destroys our culture. With our heart in our hands and our hands in the soil, we declare the independence of our *mestizo* nation. We are a bronze people with a bronze culture. Before the world, before all of North America, before all our brothers in the bronze continent, we are a nation, we are a union of free pueblos, we are *Aztlán*.

(Anaya and Lomelí 1989: 1)

Women's reaction to the overt masculinist bias of this document first appeared in print in 1971 when 600 Chicanas produced a manifesto titled *Chicanas Speak Out*. It took up concerns not addressed by the plan producing resolutions on sex, marriage and religion. The gendered dimensions of the mythical homeland of Aztlán were also questioned. In terms of identity construction, the ethnic identity associated with Aztlán was linked to the Aztec heritage and much like its earlier patriarchal model, it was constructed largely as a male identity. This crucial aspect of Aztec society was not only idealised by Chicano men but also implicitly encoded the domination of women. Moreover, the debate put forward in the plan over national entitlements implicitly suggested that civil liberties were to be granted only to subjects of the Chicano nation, in other words, only to Chicano men. Chicanas as such were denied similar rights. According to López (1977) statements made at the conference by Chicano men reinforced this position by reminding the women attending that the role of the Chicana in the movement was to 'stand behind her man'. Those that failed to do so delegates resolved 'must be opposed to their own liberation' (A. Garcia 1997: 103).

Chicana activism

Beginning in the late 1960s and early 1970s Chicana feminist writings began to document the ideological debates that intensified throughout this period of social protest. Although a few Chicano publications published Chicana feminist writings, Chicanas believed that existing publishing outlets did not provide them with an appropriate platform to voice their concerns. The development of their own small but influential feminist publications such as *Regeneración* and *Hijas de Cuauhtémoc* (1971), and the first feminist Chicana journal, *Encuentro Femenil* (1973) were successful attempts to counter this kind of literary and political exclusion. In the first issue of *Hijas de Cuauhtémoc* (1971), Nieto Gomez stated that a major issue facing Chicanas was the need to organise to improve their status as women within the larger Chicano movement. Their disagreements revolved around the following key points: the control of the leadership of the movement by men and the exclusion of women from key leadership positions, the negative role of machismo within the movement, the contradictions inherent to the oppression of Chicanas by Chicanos, and the prioritising of issues of race and class over others

(A. Garcia 1997: 71). In attempting to rectify these points numerous political groups and several dynamic leaders emerged, most notably Bernice Rincon and Francisca Flores. It was Flores who stated that:

> [Chicanas] can no longer remain in a subservient role or as auxiliary forces in the [Chicano] movement. They must be included in the front line of communication, leadership and organisational ability . . . Anyone opposing the rights of women to organise has no place in the leadership of the movement.
>
> (A. Garcia 1997: 5)

Together with Ramona Morin, Flores also helped to co-found the California League of Mexican American Women, a political association, in the mid-1960s. She was also the Chief Editor of *Regeneración* in the 1970s and co-founded the Los Angeles-based Comisión Feminil Mexicana Nacional (CFMN, National Commission of Mexican Women) the first major Chicana feminist organisation of the 1960s (A. Garcia 1997, Ruiz 1998). She also co-founded the Chicana Service Action Center (CSAC), one of the largest employment programmes in Los Angeles, whose newsletter was used as a means to disseminate knowledge of Chicanas and employment opportunities (Ruiz 1998: 114). During these years Chicanas also held workshops at several of the major Chicano conferences held throughout the south-west, including all three Youth Liberation Conferences held in Denver in 1969, 1970 and 1971. During the first National Conference of La Raza Women that met in Houston in 1971, workshops were held on identity and movement issues. Several resolutions were passed including calls for the legalisation of abortion, equal educational opportunities and the abolition of traditional marriage. Finally religion, specifically the Catholic Church, was condemned as 'an oppressive institution' – a move that according to López (1977) further exploded the stereotype of the passive Chicana (A. Garcia 1997: 104). Arguably the most significant idea or resolution to emerge from the conference though was the promotion of *hermanadad* (sisterhood) among Chicanas.

Post-movement politics

During the 1970s and 1980s Chicana feminism continued to develop. Academic groups were the most successful in this regard as they combined with larger Chicano organisations such as the National Association of Chicano Studies (NACS, now known as the National Association of Chicana and Chicano Studies or NACCS) to launch several successful campaigns in order to make their selves heard. Moreover, Mujeres Activas en Letras y Cambio Social (MALCS, Women Active in Letters and Social Change), another academic organisation, became a national association in 1982 (Gonzales 2000: 247). Perhaps the most significant nationwide initiatives that arose outside of academia were the Mexican American Women's National Association (MANA), which by the mid-1980s was 'the most prominent Mexican American women's organisation nationally' and the National Association of Hispanic Women (NAHW), which was also at its peak during these years (Gonzales 2000: 247). Among academics Martha Cotera played a leading role as a major participant in LRUP, she also founded the Texas Women's Political Caucus in 1973 as well as publishing two pioneering texts, *Diosa y Hembra: The History and Heritage of Chicanas in the US* (1976) and *The Chicana Feminist* (1977), both of which refute the entrenched cultural stereotypes of Chicanas as passive and apolitical (Ruiz 1998: 115–19).

In terms of literary production most presses in the main continued to ignore books written by women. The establishment of several women's presses, including Scorpion Press by Eliano Rivero and the poet Margarita Cota-Cardenas, provided some of the major outlets for women's writing at this time. Like Cota-Cardenas many women writers produced self-published texts including Estela-Portillo Trambley's *Rain of Scorpions* (1975), Bernice Zamora's *Restless Serpents* (1976), Angela de Hoyos's *Chicano: Poems from the Barrio* (1975) and *Arise Chicanos and Other Poems* (1976), and Isabella Rios's *Victuum* (1976). These works caused much controversy among Chicano literary critics, who were in the main male dominated, and were subsequently condemned for their oppositional stance towards Chicano ideology. The politics of the movement demanded a reassertion of traditional Mexican American family values and issues of identity associated with selected aspects of the indigenous historical past. In contrast Chicana writers began to reassert an entirely different set of values.

The publication of *This Bridge Called My Back: Writings by Radical Women of Color* (1983), edited by Cherríe Moraga and Gloria Anzaldúa, marks the beginning of this trajectory, the overarching aim being the redefinition of feminism in order to invoke a more collective identification for women of colour. Taking their critique a step further than prior formulations the editors aimed to bridge differences not only between races but also between genders, thus contributing to the ongoing process of deconstructing dominant formulations of the theoretical subject of feminism. Anzaldúa presents this vision of a multiracial and gendered coalition in her foreword to the second edition of *This Bridge Called My Back* when she states that, 'We have come to realise that we are not alone in our struggles nor separate nor autonomous but that we – white black straight queer male female – are connected and interdependent' (Moraga and Anzaldúa 1983).

This ground-breaking volume contributed to a major development in the history of Chicana feminism and feminist consciousness. The explicit engagement with the intersecting oppressions of race, gender and sexuality were issues that American feminism and the movement had previously ignored. The profound shift this text made was marked by an emphasis on inclusion, heterogeneity and difference. Writing by Chicanas that reflected these issues became more fully developed with the publication of *Cuentos:*

Stories by Latinas in 1983, this text representing the first step in the creation of a written literary tradition that grew out of the specific realities of Latina women in the USA. It also broke new ground in the sense that it was the first anthology by both Latinas and feminists that openly engaged with issues of sexuality. The 1989 edition of *Third Woman: On the Sexuality of Latinas* is perhaps the culmination of this trend (Rebolledo 1995: 27).

Up until then, the patriarchal posturing of leading Chicano activists silenced gay Chicanos as well as lesbian women as the vast majority of Chicano heterosexuals perceived Chicana lesbians as a threat to the family and the community. Bruce-Novoa observes that homosexuality was absent from the Chicano movement, and attempts to gain recognition had little success. He goes on to state that, 'homophobia may not be more prevalent among Chicanos ... but as products of Mexico and the US, neither of which tolerates gays, Chicanos reflect norms of their wider socio-cultural context' (Pérez-Torres 1995: 27). Despite the number of literary works published by gay and lesbian Chicana/o writers during the 1980s they continued to suffer the effects of homophobia within Chicano communities as well as the mainstream women's movement. In *Loving in the War Years/Lo nunca pasó por sus labios* (1983) Cherríe Moraga states her politics unequivocally in this regard:

> A political commitment to women must involve, by definition, a political commitment to lesbians as well ... [T]o refuse to allow the Chicana lesbian the right to free expression of her own sexuality, and her politicisation of it, is in the deepest sense to deny one's self the right to the same ... Any movement built on the fear and loathing of anyone is a failed movement. The Chicano movement is no different.
>
> (Moraga 1983: 140)

Moraga's concern with issues of sexuality forges a politics that aims to deconstruct the basic dualisms that underpin the belief in two fixed and opposing genders. As such she simultaneously condemns the dominant, binary and hierarchical systems of conceptualising the self and other that underwrote the politics of the movement. In a similar way Anzaldúa's text *Borderlands/La Frontera* (1987) challenges the dualisms that underpin a variety of patriarchal power structures as she attempts to create new representations of Chicana subjectivity that will break down borders as they exist in geo-political, cultural and gendered terms. Her conception of the new mestiza is based on a fluctuating subjectivity that moves through a number of races, cultures and genders, so that identity becomes multiple, contradictory and fluid. It is among this generation of 'self-identified Chicanas', as Deena González (1997) points out, that 'more fluid identities can be located' (Noriega et al. 2001: 421). The shifts in the notion of self and the evocation of crossings by these writers represent the ability to transgress the power lines of patriarchy, as well as establish a 'linkage between identity and homeland' (Noriega et al. 2001: 421). In order to more fully explore these and other recent developments in Chicana feminism, the next chapter provides an overview of critical approaches to Chicana/o literature, its trajectory during and since the movement and the implications its ideology holds for recent trends in Chicana feminist criticism.

3 Critical approaches to Chicana/o literature

This chapter provides an overview of certain interrelated literary and theoretical issues concerning male and female cultural production that are central to this study. I consider that an examination of such issues is necessary in order to more broadly establish the ways in which writing by Chicanas is formed in opposition to the patriarchal politics of the Chicano movement. Leading up to the mid-1970s most Chicano criticism was based on how the literature conformed to the political agenda of the movement. By and large this meant that the most acceptable literary works were those that were seen to offer resistance to the oppressive effects exerted by the dominant American culture. In attempting to form a symbolic response to the events of the times writers and critics actively sought a synthesis of aesthetics with politics, the most important recurring themes being powerful references to social and class division and to offering support to the demands of the UFW led by César Chávez (Bruce-Novoa 1985: 76). In terms of literary and critical production, this meant that male texts were prioritised over those by women. In the first part of this chapter I explore the implications of this tendency in more detail by highlighting the ways in which dominant trends in early criticism set a narrow precedent in terms dictated by the politics of the movement. The remainder of the chapter explores more recent critical approaches to the study of Chicana/o literature and the ways in which contemporary critics contest the narrow focus of the early years. Rather than attempting exhaustively to distinguish all the different range of approaches which have come to be called Chicana/o criticism, this chapter will instead try to give an introductory sense of some of the most influential approaches adopted by critics since the early years.

Culturalist criticism

A number of studies concerned with the development of Chicana/o literary criticism refer to Joseph Sommers's essay 'From the Critical Premise to the Product: Critical Modes and Their Application to a Chicano Literary Text' (1977) as a first point of intervention into the critical debate (Bruce-Novoa 1990a, Chabram-Dernersesian 1991, Neate 1998). This essay is important and useful because in it Sommers identified what were the three dominant tendencies within Chicano criticism at that time. According to Sommers these were the culturalist, the formalist and the historical dialectical, though during the height of the movement the culturalist approach found most favour. Like the separatist stance of the movement itself, this approach heavily emphasised the difference between Chicano and mainstream critical trends, and practitioners were also adamant about demarcating the limits of the Chicano literary tradition. Arguably it could be said that the deployment of limits is essential to enable the study of a discipline to take place in the first place, but more problematically, the boundaries imposed by culturalist criticism were organised along rigid lines based on limited cultural and racial criteria. As Sommers (1977) points out, the culturalist approach, 'construed race [and ultimately nature and the biological process] as the controlling element in culture, while positing culture as the central determinant of a people's experience' (Romo and Paredes 1977: 57).

Culturalist critics and writers alike tried to negate American or other influences and were more concerned with limitation and demarcation. According to Sommers (1977) their approach was directed towards an idea of 'cultural uniqueness' that selected and emphasised cultural features specific to the Chicano people (Romo and Paredes 1977: 57). Implicit in this argument is the assumption that only Chicanos can understand and interpret Chicano literature, a point made later by Neate (1998) who suggests that 'a politics of experience' was evoked by Chicano critics in order to legitimise or 'authorise' their work (Neate 1998: 25). This tendency, Neate states, promoted the idea that 'descent alone endows one with superior credentials [and] attests to an essentialising and de-historicised view of Chicano identities' (Neate 1998: 25). Certainly many culturalist critics considered that in order to fully understand Chicano literature, the reader had to have 'a knowledge of Nahuatl (Aztec) and Mayan mythology' (Huerta 2000: 15). This was mainly because during the movement pre-Hispanic myths and symbols, and the Jungian theory of the collective unconscious were recalled as strategies to counteract the pejorative perspectives associated with Mexican culture in the USA. These selective aspects of Chicano culture were also favoured by culturalist criticism, and in this sense, as Sommers (1977) points out, culturalist theories tended to be anti-historical and nostalgic:

> A further tendency is to criticise the materialism, racism and dehumanisation of contemporary capitalist society by counterpoising idealistically the values of traditional culture, presenting these values as flawless and recoverable in unchanged form. Needless to say this construes culture as static and separable from the historic process, rather than dynamic, creative and responsive to experience.
>
> (Romo and Paredes 1977: 55–9)

For Sommers the placing of too great an emphasis on the mythic qualities of Chicano literature obscured the real sources of socio-economic exploitation. The tendency to reduce cultural poles to two, Chicano and Anglo, also created a too-rigid dichotomy that suggested a static vision of culture and an absence of cultural elements common to other groups. In these respects culturalist approaches often tended towards the separatist stance advocated by leaders of the movement. Quotations from the main manifesto of the Chicano movement, *El Plan Espiritual de Aztlán* (1969), reflect this tendency. Item 6 of the plan reads:

> Cultural values of our people strengthen our identity and the moral background of the movement. Our culture unites and educates the family of *La Raza* towards liberation with one heart and one mind. We must insure that our writers, poets, musicians, and artists produce literature and art that is appealing to our people and relates to our revolutionary culture.
>
> (Anaya and Lomelí 1989: 3)

This kind of selective focus proved to be insular, and Chicano culturalist criticism as a consequence marginalised itself by setting standards of worth on the basis of the text's usefulness as a form of political activism. Given the masculinist tendencies of the movement's political programme, it also had the effect of avoiding the critical issue of gender altogether.

Such a pattern of gendered exclusion can clearly be seen in Octavio Ignacio Romano-V's influential essay 'The Historical and Intellectual Presence of Mexican Americans' (1969), first published during the heyday of the movement (Hernández-Gutiérrez and Foster 1997: 47–61). In this essay Romano-V (1969) situates the development of Chicano literature firmly within a culturalist paradigm of interpretation. First, the theoretical underpinnings of his essay are clearly separate from mainstream critical trends in that they concentrate in particular on 'the principal historical currents of thought that have gone into the making of the mind of *el Mexicano*' (Hernández-Gutiérrez and Foster 1997: 49). Briefly stated these 'currents of thought', which are 'indianist philosophy', 'historical confrontation', and 'the transcendent idea of the *mestizo*' (or mixed race), all conform to a culturalist paradigm in the sense that they represent the uniqueness of Chicano culture. Second, then Romano-V uses his critical practice as a space for cultural affirmation, highlighting features specific to the Chicano people and emphasising unique cultural attributes such as the Mexican *dicho* or proverb, the Mexican revolution, and José Vasconcelos's theory of *la raza cósmica*. Briefly stated, Vasconcelos, who was the Minister for Education in Mexico during the dictatorship of Porfirio Diaz, developed a theory of a cosmic race or *la raza cósmica*, in which he argued that the mixture of Spanish and Indian races created a superior mestizo race (Juãrez 1972: 69–73). By strategically recalling this text and author Romano-V clearly upholds a politics of cultural affirmation that was integral to both movement discourse and rhetoric. Third, his approach also perceives

Chicano literature and culture as inherently 'revolutionary', again mirroring *el movimiento*'s implicit ideology. According to Romano-V, Chicano cultural production is 'a timeless symbol of opposition to cultural imperialism', and an aid by which to 'avoid the assimilative tendencies and pitfalls of the past' (Hernández-Gutiérrez and Foster 1997: 54). Being both inherently oppositional and ideological, in much the same way as that dictated by the politics of the movement, it is hardly surprising that only those texts which express a specific kind of resistance and foreground acceptable sites of struggle are valued in this analysis. Without fail those texts that conform to this criteria are male authored, and in this sense and much like the movement itself, Romano-V's theory is also inherently masculinist.

Using quotations from selected works by leading movement writers, he explicates his theory of culturalist criticism in overtly patriarchal terms. First, literature is viewed 'internally' from the 'perspectives of multiple philosophies regarding the existence and nature of Mexican American man' (Hernández-Gutiérrez and Foster 1997: 57). Second, the Chicano cultural past is characterised overwhelmingly by the cultural and political works of male authors and by the literary works of Chicano authors such as Alurista, Rodolfo 'Corky' Gonzales and Antonio Villareal, and by the Mexican writers Octavio Paz and Juan Rulfo, among others. Thus the concept of an exclusive Chicano literary canon continues as an authorised set of (male) works which Romano-V considers best represent Chicano culture. Literature and the creation of texts are construed as being uniquely masculine acts, deriving from biological and social analogies. This validates Chicano literature by conferring upon it ideas of procreation, fatherhood and authority. In these respects, Romano-V's essay, like other forms of culturalist criticism, appears to be less concerned with contesting established intellectual hierarchies as the title of his essay would suggest, and more concerned with fostering and emphasising the political and social concerns associated with the dominant and masculinist elements of movement rhetoric.

Jose Antonio Villareal, author of the highly acclaimed novel *Pocho* (1959), refers to the effect that these restrictions, which were imposed by the doctrine of the Chicano movement, had on Chicano literary and critical activity. He states that, 'What resulted then is that an unwritten set of standards began to take form. Codes for Chicano literature were explicit. First and foremost was the fact that we could never criticise ourselves as long as we followed this developing pattern' (Hernández-Gutiérrez and Foster 1997: 33). The 'set of standards' established by movement ideology not only dictated which were legitimate Chicano texts and which were not, but also decided what were acceptable reading criteria and methods of interpretation. This policy of judging Chicano literature according to rigid political criteria also characterised the practices of Chicano publishing houses, which by and large only published those works that they deemed ideologically acceptable. It has been argued that biased readings were characteristic of the publishing policies of the Quinto Sol Press for instance, which in turn influenced the formation of the canon of contemporary Chicana/o literature (Neate 1998: 109). According to Bruce-Novoa, Quinto Sol was to a certain degree responsible for constructing 'a selection that excluded' (Bruce-Novoa 1985: 79). This situation not only led particular groups of critics to attack the literary critical establishment as it was then, and to attempt to redress the exclusions, but also led to reflections on the notion of canonisation itself.

Formalist criticism

The concern with the literary canon characterised the second dominant trend within Chicana/o literary criticism. Sommers (1977) identified this trend as formalist and in his opinion it was exemplified by the critical work of Juan Bruce-Novoa, particularly his seminal essay 'The Space of Chicano Literature' (1975). This was first of all presented as a paper at the National Symposium on Chicano Literature and Critical Analysis in 1974, and in it Bruce-Novoa famously criticised the narrow focus of the dominant approaches to Chicana/o literature, which he later considered were 'incestuous'.[1] According to Bruce-Novoa (1988) the selection of only specific texts threatened to deny the diversity of Chicana/o literary production. During the movement works were excluded on the grounds of a lack of 'ethnic and communal content' or because of issues of gender and sexuality, or because of what was perceived to be a subtext of criticism directed at the movement's centralising ideology (Bruce-Novoa 1988: 147–8). In order to counteract this tendency Bruce-Novoa argued that each and every Chicano work should have a legitimate place.

What he had in mind initially then was the expansion of the Chicano literary canon in ways that would more adequately reflect the diversity of the Chicana/o community and of the Chicano experience. The canon would therefore include the contribution of women and gay writers, as well as the present largely male-authored canonical texts. Additionally this canonical reshaping should not be viewed as a single event but rather as an ongoing process of literary and critical addition. Bruce-Novoa (1978) argued Chicano literary space should not be static but should develop through time and social, cultural and political alteration:

> I proposed in 1974, that we are the space [not the hyphen] between [Mexican and American] the intercultural nothingness of that space. For those reluctant to accept this sense of nothing, I offer a compromise: read the above as the 'intercultural possibilities of that space.'
>
> (Bruce-Novoa 1978: 98)

Here Bruce-Novoa contends that Chicana/o cultural and literary practice derives from the space between its constitutive Mexican and American identities. This is an important point, because it develops his idea of the Chicana/o canon as being 'intercultural', dynamic and ongoing. The lack of a sense of a hierarchy of literary value based on only one kind of reading is also notable in his argument. To approach the study of Chicano literature from this perspective not only transforms the set of texts being read, but also alters the ways in which they are valued, and critically discussed.

The structure of this approach took the form of two different though related modes of phenomenological analyses, involving both a topographical and topological charting. Bruce-Novoa (1988) defines topography as 'a detailed charting of an object/or area in time and space', topology on the other hand is 'the properties of a geometric configuration that remain constant when the configuration is subjected to transformation' (Bruce-Novoa 1988: 146–7). On one level this method revealed that content, structure as well as the analysis of the Chicano situation varied widely from work to work; but on another level his approach also disclosed that despite this degree of diversity, each text also shared a common theme. This deep or hermeneutic structure, the *axis mundi*, stated Bruce-Novoa (1980b), is intimately linked to questions of cultural survival, and provides 'an ordering response to the chaos which threatens to devastate the descendants of Mexicans who now reside in the USA' (Bruce-Novoa 1980b: 114). In order to illustrate his point more specifically Bruce-Novoa selects Raul Salinas' poem 'A Trip through the Mind Jail' as an example of this paradigm. Throughout the poem Salinas places an emphasis on a concern with the disappearance of *la loma*, the East Los Angeles barrio associated with his youth, 'La Loma / Neighborhood of my youth / demolished, erased for ever from the universe':

> Neighborhood that is no more
> YOU ARE TORN PIECES OF MY FLESH!!!!
> Therefore, you ARE . . .
> My loma of Austin
> My Rose Hill of Los Angeles
> My west side of San Anto
> My Quinto of Houston
> My Jackson of San Jo
> My Segundo of El Paso
> My Barelas of Alburque . . .
> Flats, Los Marcos, Maravilla, Calle Guadalupe . . .
> And all Chicano neighbourhoods that
> Now exist and once existed.
>
> (Salinas 1980)

In his reading of this poem Bruce-Novoa (1978) states that 'the centre's destruction flings [the poet's] order into chaos' (Bruce-Novoa 1978: 101). But as the poem progresses both at the narrative and thematic level, Salinas' poetic revisitation of the barrios across the south-west establishes certain 'internal orders' that help him to respond more positively to the chaos of his present-day situation (Bruce-Novoa 1978: 101–2).

As an approach that rejected critical practices that were informed by one ideological perspective, Bruce-Novoa's study provided a valuable contribution to Chicana/o critical debates. There is, however, an underlying assumption in his analysis, which suggests that all Chicano literature can be explained in terms of a general, unified meaning. The *axis mundi* or deep structure is still a centering device, which reinforces an authoritative ideology that aims to explain the meaning of any given text as a whole. By extension it appears to substitute one restrictive mode of analysis, namely culturalist criticism, with another. Taking these factors in to consideration, it would appear that Bruce-Novoa's approach remains consistent with the selective focus of the earlier criticism and by extension with the politics of the movement, and many critics substantiate this claim. Francisco Lomelí in *An Overview of Chicano Letters: From Origins to Resurgence* (1984) charges Bruce-Novoa with attempting to 'impose preconceptions and curtail creativity' (Pérez-Torres 1995: 275). José David Saldívar (1997) on the other hand, more recently has accused Bruce-Novoa of placing too strong an emphasis on the 'epistemological, phenomenological, and anthropological priority of language (literature) over social space' (Saldívar 1997: 78). This is a similar criticism to that of Sommers (1977), who likewise viewed Bruce-Novoa's form of interpretation as tending to elevate Chicana/o literature into 'a separate, non-referential transcendental reality' (Romo and Paredes 1977: 57).

These critics, though vastly different in their critical stances, share a highly sceptical view of the formalist approach, of which Bruce-Novoa is only one example. They consider his approach ahistorical and seem to desire an analysis that will incorporate a greater degree of realism and commitment to the representation of contemporary social issues. However, other critics have responded more positively to the historiographic element in Bruce-Novoa's essay and argue that his method was designed to both 're-evaluate historically situated racial identity as a criterion' as well as restore 'the historical specificity' of the Chicano community (Gutiérrez-Jones 1995: 26). Earlier than this Sommers had called for a more realist and historical mode of analysis, and he had demanded that it should be aligned with a rigid political agenda, a criticism in effect that was 'historically based and dialectically formulated' (Romo and Paredes 1977: 59). But, as Bruce-Novoa (1990a) later pointed out, this approach had the effect of placing the literature in a scale of realism that was linked too closely to ideological principles, and as such it too replicated forms of discursive erasure found in the culturalist criticism of the early years.

Historical dialectical

The concern with the historical and material specificities of Chicana/o literature nonetheless continued to characterise subsequent phases in the development of its related critical activity. In his 1979 essay 'The Dialectics of Difference: Toward a Theory of the Chicano Novel', Ramón Saldívar contends that an attention to 'the sociological, historical, and cultural conditions' of representation is central to his approach (Neate 1998: 42). Likewise, his brother José David Saldívar in *The Dialectics of our America: Genealogy, Cultural Critique, and Literary History* (1991a), goes beyond what he terms 'the naiveté of an old historicism' in order to 'rewrite . . . the history of the Americas' (Saldívar 1991a: xv). Moving away from an exclusively phenomenological analysis and seeking to show how Chicana/o literature is integral to the Chicano experience, both critics placed a much stronger emphasis on Chicano history as being 'the decisive determinant of the form and content of the literature' (Saldívar 1990a: 5).

In *Chicano Narrative: The Dialectics of Difference* (1990a) Ramón Saldívar argues that there is a close link between Chicano narrative and history, and he endeavours to show the ways in which the thematics of individual works provide a framework by which the histories of Chicanos are retold. According to Saldívar there should be no sharp distinction between Chicano narrative and history: '[for] history cannot be conceived as the mere background or context for this literature . . . history itself is the subject of its discourse' (Saldívar 1990a: 5). As he goes on to state, this is not a facile or depoliticised recording of the past, as Chicano narrative undertakes a profound ideological critique of Chicano history. His reading of Chicano narrative as the site of 'conflict rather than resolution' and of 'difference rather than similarity', seeks to maintain and emphasise the importance of conflict and oppositionality as a central literary theme. Consequently any Chicano text that does not overtly express conflictual or oppositional social relations in Saldívar's view automatically 'fails to imagine a critical manner of engaging the sociohistorical context' (Saldívar 1990a: 3–9).

It is largely because of this, arguably didactic approach that Saldívar (1990a) objects to Rudolfo Anaya's prize winning novel *Bless Me Ultima* (1991), with its series of dream sequences and mythical images that implicitly appeal to the collective unconscious. This he considers necessarily parallels a thematic loss of reality. For Saldívar 'reality' resides in 'the conflicts between Spanish colonialism and native Americans, between Mexicans and Anglos and between New Mexican workers and capitalist interests', which he states, are confined to the margins of Anaya's text (Saldívar 1990a: 126). In Saldívar's view these interactions have enormous and far-reaching power and potential towards explaining New Mexico's troubled history. In other words Saldívar considers that race and class struggle provides the key to understanding the whole span of twentieth-century New Mexican history. Accordingly these interrelated antagonisms become the major forces behind all the changes that have occurred during this period, and are formed through a differential access to the means of production. This is an important point, because it develops his idea that Anaya's narrative cannot be successfully interpreted either as a realist fiction or as an accurate historical interpretation of New Mexican society. As he goes on to argue, the 'concrete social contradictions' that exist 'obtain only within the confines of the romance, with its generically constrained requirements of symmetrical closure' (Saldívar 1990a: 123). In other words, Saldívar expresses a desire for a more realistic narrative that will demonstrate the ongoing class and race conflict in New Mexico through a more accurate representation of contemporary social issues. But on closer analysis this is problematic, as from a feminist perspective Saldívar's emphatic focus on class conflict and general labour history simultaneously deletes the economic activity of women.

In *Bless Me Ultima* (1991) a racial and gendered division of labour exists whereby men are seen to embody political and economic agency, while women are the (unpaid) keepers of tradition, morals and spirituality. The protagonist's father is the patriarch of the family who, in theory at least, appears to make the most important decisions as a direct consequence of his position as the main breadwinner. While his wife ostensibly controls the household, her role in the family economy is inferior and subordinate and confined to unpaid housekeeping and domestic duties. In this uncritical use of gender stereotypes, Anaya's text reinforces the politically sanctioned myth of the Chicano *familia*, the heterosexually configured structure within which a distinct gendered and economic hierarchy subordinated women. Arguably in ignoring women's labour in his analysis, Saldívar replicates this tendency, and in so doing by and large represses women's politics within what he terms 'the insular confines of the fetishised family' as much as the subject of his criticism (Saldívar 1990a: 179).

Saldívar does, however, address the exclusion of Chicana writers from previous critical studies. He states that Chicanas are 'building an instructive alternative to the exclusively phallocentric subject of contemporary Chicano narrative' (Saldívar 1990a: 175). Yet his critical methodology is nonetheless predicated on a dominant 'master' narrative that replicates this phallocentric authority. His theory of an oppositional Chicano literary production takes as its source the *corrido* or Mexican ballad, particularly that of 'El Gregorio Cortez', which he considers to be a 'master poem' and 'one of the subtexts for much contemporary Chicano narrative'. However, despite its counter-hegemonic and oppositional qualities, to some critics taking the *corrido* as source signals the collusion of an explicitly phallogocentric authority (Neate 1998: 259). Saldívar himself makes this aspect explicit when quoting from *With his Pistol in his Hand: A Border Ballad and its Hero* (1958), Américo Paredes's folkloric analysis of the ballad of 'El Gregorio Cortez'. He states that 'the *corrido* is chiefly a male performance genre, and in extended family gatherings or in formal ceremonies men were the performers, while the women and children participated only as audience' (Saldívar 1990a: 39). As I go on to argue, when considering the *corrido* as a source for Chicano narrative not only does literary production appear to derive from an exclusively male performative act, it also proposes one set of literary rules that are grounded in a specific context of resistance. The difficulty contemporary writing by Chicanas poses to this critical perspective lies in their refusal to take the *corrido* as their source, and in their ability to critique it as a master narrative. But despite these limiting aspects of Saldívar's mode of criticism, he was concerned like Bruce-Novoa (1990a) to show how Chicana/o works go beyond early readings, and ultimately their extending of previous critical boundaries has ensured that their mode of critical practice continued and continues to exert an influence on subsequent developments in Chicana/o literary criticism.

The postmodern

Much of the contemporary Chicana/o critical debate, like that of Bruce-Novoa and Saldívar, focuses on contesting the selective focus of earlier critical paradigms and attempting to replace these with theories which provide a more liberating critical potential. Arguably, postmodern approaches can more readily account for the differences within Chicana/o literary activity. As Hutcheon argues, postmodernism 'contest[s] the view that the role of criticism is to enunciate the latent or hidden, be it ideological or rhetorical' (Hutcheon 1988: 21). This approach characterises the work of a number of critics currently working on Chicana/o literary and critical production, who rather than conforming to a rigid political agenda, argue that postmodern theories have the potential to exceed externally imposed limitations on meaning. In this sense they support the view that postmodernism may offer a liberating potential as it promotes a critical attitude towards all simple categorisations and 'master narratives', substituting in their place an emphasis on plurality and multiple modes of meaning and interpretation.

In his work the Chicano critic Rafael Pérez-Torres shows how an intersection between multiculturalism and postmodernism is relevant to the study and interpretation of Chicana/o texts as together they form a discourse which is able to 'scrutinise the universal valuation of difference' in ways which acknowledge the heterogeneity of Chicana/o experience. He states that, 'Overlapping the grids of postmodernism and multiculturalism changes their configurations. It brings each discourse into sharper focus so that the diversity and multiplicity of each terrain becomes clearer' (Pérez-Torres 1995: 143).

In other words, as postmodern theories decentre the hegemony of white Western culture, so multiculturalism clears a space from which previously marginalised voices might be articulated. By situating Chicana/o literature within the conjunction of these discourses, the repressed histories of Chicanos becomes known as they both serve 'to reconnect the present to the past in a critical way that highlights absence and dispossession' (Pérez-Torres 1995: 146).

Other critics argue that postmodernism is not inherently radical, liberating or necessarily a critical mode with any particular relevance to Chicana/o literature. For example, José Limón in *Mexican Ballads, Chicano Poems: History and Influence in Mexican American Social Poetry* (1992) constructs a compelling argument about Chicano poetry being the manifestation of a 'modernism of critical difference' (Limón 1992: 164). Chicana critics also consider that when approaching the work of Chicana/o writers the central issue is not one of merely acknowledging difference; rather the more difficult question concerns the kind of difference that is acknowledged and engaged. Tey Diana Rebolledo, for instance, considers that Chicana literature 'has its own characteristics' which problematise the use of overarching theories (Rebolledo 1995: 4).

In her essay 'Chicana/o Studies as Oppositional Ethnography' (1990), Angie Chabram expresses similar reservations concerning the term 'diversity', in that it assimilates Chicana/os and therefore obscures the conditions of their oppression, 'diversity goes hand in hand with cultural pluralism, a construct that erases inequality and the cultural specificity of the Chicano' (Neate 1998: 272). This tendency can be seen in the work of a number of critics who approach Chicana/o texts as 'Third World' literature. From this perspective the fragmentation that Chicano works display can be explained by considering its place within the framework of a much larger fragmenting world and can be read as representative of what Homi K. Bhabha terms our 'human historic commonality' (Bhabha 1994: 6–7). At the same time, this approach tends to ignore the socio-political and historical specificities of marginalised groups in favour of a more generalised analysis. Ultimately, what these somewhat polarised perspectives suggest then is the need for the theoretical and contextual to combine in order to form an understanding of the socio-political representation of meaning in Chicano literature. As I go on to argue, this kind of debate also marks the work of Chicana critics who are also concerned with issues such as these, as well as the more gender-specific concerns of the recovery and reinterpretation of 'lost' and 'recovered' Chicana texts.

Feminist criticism

Largely excluded from mainstream critical attention and from the Chicano canon itself, up until the mid-1980s much Chicana literature faced either negative reception or none at all. In 1985 Lomelí argued that although some gains had been made in bringing Chicano literature into 'some degree of world prominence' there was also 'an alarmingly low number of critical studies devoted to novels by Chicanas' (Rebolledo 1995: 4). He attributed this to external factors such as a lack of publication, but more specifically he suggested that there was 'an underlying implication that issues women writers raise are not of great magnitude or importance' (Rebolledo 1995: 4). This is a highly contentious opinion, as Lomelí appears to be delineating a certain generic code for Chicana/o literature. According to this perspective Chicana/o literature is wholly defined by certain generic definites. But to limit Chicano literature to an unchangeable set of generic codes is restricting and detracts from the achievements of women writers, who have produced innovative reworkings of established socio-political concerns within their work.

Although his critical opinion has modified since Lomelí made this statement, his comments are representative of the prevailing Chicano attitudes towards women's writing at the time. His refusal to position women's texts within the category of 'serious literature' serves as a stark reminder of the extent to which Chicana feminism and Chicana feminist texts continued to be regarded as somehow outside or not part of a 'genuine' Chicano literary canon. During the movement the canon became an issue for feminist critics because it was obvious that it included few women or gay authors. These women argued that it was not enough to assume that the canon preserved the works of the most deserving since the literary institution responsible for the selection was male-dominated, patriarchal and often misogynistic. Many feminist critical projects since then have sought to address this basic issue. Over the past two decades a burgeoning Chicana literary criticism has accompanied the work of such writers as Sandra Cisneros, Alma Villanueva, Bernice Zamora, Ana Castillo, Denise Chavez, Lorna Dee Cervantes, Evangelina Vigil, Gloria Anzaldúa and Cherríe Moraga. Differing critical perspectives and practices, reflected in the diverse works of Marta Sánchez, Rosaura Sanchez, Norma Alarcón, María Herrera-Sobek, and Yvonne Yarbro-Bejarano have also marked approaches to this body of work.

Some of this critical writing, in its concern with gender, draws on relatively conventional ideas of criticism and history. Other critics use an array of ideas from the most recent developments in critical theory. As the critical possibilities in this work also cover an enormous range, for the sake of clarity I shall focus on two prevailing currents of thought regarding Chicana literary criticism. One trend departs from white literary theoreticians in a search for an authentic Chicana critical discourse. The second mode of criticism on the other hand argues for European, American and feminist critical discourses as useful tools in the analysis of Chicana texts (Herrera-Sobek and Viramontes 1988: 37).

Feminist theory

Although the approaches outlined above are different in their political stances, they do share a concern with the oppressive and exclusionary nature of previous critical paradigms. Since the 1980s the study of gender and sexuality has become a central concern. At first the emphasis was on the representation and exclusion of women in literature in various forms. Given the constraints that Chicanas faced, reclaiming a viable and politicised subject position meant forming a radical departure from male-centred movement ideology. In order to do so they enlisted more complex modes of representation that better accommodated their multiple subjectivities. According to Chabram-Dernersesian (1993), among the first strategies employed by Chicanas were substitutions for the term 'Chicano', with the more gender specific terms 'Chicana', 'Chicano/a' or 'Chicana/o'. She states that 'these markers announced the end of the nongendered Mexican American subject of cultural and political identity' (de la Torre and Pesquera 1993: 39). Within Chicana/o discourse the positioning of letters is vital, for whereas the term

Chicano/a 'consciously reinstates the Chicana', the term Chicana/o 'positively privileges' the female subject within group characterisations (de la Torre and Pesquera 1993: 39). Later there were developments in the study of gay and lesbian writing, in gender developments broadly conceived, and in the construction of sexual and gender identities. This set of concerns arose partly as a response to the gender stereotypes, representations, fictions and narratives of identity adopted by the movement and much male criticism. But it also arose through the rise of critical theory and the range of approaches that came to be called feminist criticism.

Much of the Chicana writing studied here in terms of the questions raised, resonates with the issues articulated by the French feminists in the late 1970s and early 1980s. Among Chicana critics Norma Alarcón is perhaps the most purely theoretically based, constructing her theoretical framework from French and American feminist writing. She states that writing by Chicanas is simultaneously 'a complicity with, a resistance to, and a disruption of Western psychoanalysis' (Lavie and Swedenbourg 1996: 52). Chicanas who define themselves primarily as creative writers also readily incorporate a critical engagement in their writing. In the 1980s Anzaldúa's text *Borderlands/ La Frontera* (1987) and Moraga's *Loving in the War Years/Lo nunca pasó por sus labios*, (1983) epitomise this tendency; likewise in the 1990s Moraga's collection of prose and poetry *The Last Generation* (1993), Pat Mora's *Nepantla* (1993), and Ana Castillo's *Massacre of the Dreamers* (1994b), articulate a blurring of the creative and critical that mixes theoretical discourse with literary texts.

The perspective in these texts is political, ideological and critical, incorporating many of the principal ideas of feminist thinkers, at the same time as Alarcón (1990b) points out, they also problematise the theoretical subject of their discourse (Anzaldúa 1990: 356–69). Most obviously concurring with mainstream feminism in the sense that they address the political motives behind male constructions of female sexuality, Chicana writers reveal the binary oppositions and stereotypes that have served to alienate and disempower them. Anzaldúa's *Borderlands/La Frontera* (1987) critiques binary logic, particularly the subject–object dichotomy, in a way that has resonance with the theoretical work of Hélène Cixous. Like Anzaldúa (1987), Cixous argues that a patriarchal Western philosophical tradition has consistently organised conceptions of the world into binary oppositions, such as light and dark, man and woman, logos and body (Marks and de Courtivron 1980: 366–71). Within this system these terms are never equal but are 'hierarchised' within patriarchal culture, resulting in the privileging of one side of the opposition (male) at the expense of the other (female). Cixous (1980) goes on to argue that the underlying structure of a phallocentric symbolic order is therefore geared towards securing meaning through the repression of the feminine. The patriarchal imaginary and its symbolic register is organised around the privileging of the phallus and so implicitly inscribes the female as an absent and passive second term. In this structure of differences the female is only present in such a way as to confirm the primacy of the male (Marks and de Courtivron 1980: 366–71).

Movement ideology can be strongly related to the ideas of phallo-gocentrism and suppression outlined above. López (1977) acknowledges the 'existence of a hierarchy within the Movement which gave Chicano men superior status' (Saldívar-Hull 2000: 31). Likewise, del Castillo (1980) recalls how Chicanas were expected by 'their male peers to involve themselves actively but in subordination' (Saldívar-Hull 2000: 29). Chicana writing from the 1980s questions this hierarchical ordering, and ultimately seeks to subvert its assumptions. Chicana works both reveal and deconstruct cultural constructions of female identity particularly the restricted gender roles defined through the binary logic of masculine/feminine, active/passive, subject/object. As I go on to discuss, in the Chicano context this logic is expressed more specifically through the *virgen/puta* (virgin/whore) and *chingón/chingada* polarity.

These opposed pairs were basic to gender distinction during the move-ment, and serve to reinforce a general sense of the masculine as that which always desires to dominate, to categorise, and to limit with set terms. Cixous (1980) suggests that something in the dominated side of the couple could escape from this hierarchisation. She states that 'either the woman is passive or she doesn't exist. What is left is unthinkable, unthought of' (Marks and de Courtivron 1980: 366–71). Here the first sentence refers to the logic of patriarchy and has resonance with the ideology of the movement, in the sense that Chicana subjectivity was confined by its doctrine to passive stereotypes. The second sentence suggests that there may be something in the feminine which is not passive, an argument that in turn has resonance with Chicana feminism, which endeavoured to liberate Chicanas from this kind of repres-sion. According to patriarchal logic, this could not exist, it is left 'unthink-able, unthought of'. Cixous (1980), however, goes on to argue that this logic is threatened by the 'bringing forth' of possibilities within the term of feminin-ity itself. Any discrepancy in the circularity of this logic (the masculine is always superior because the feminine is always inferior) will bring about its collapse (Marks and de Courtivron 1980: 366–71).

At the level of representation Chicana writing initiates an unsettling and a reconfiguration of patriarchal ideology in terms of the hierarchy of the man-woman dyad outlined above. In many Chicana literary works representations of sexuality are played out against normative models of sex, gender and associated social roles and qualities. Both Moraga's and Anzaldúa's represen-tation of the lesbian subject involves a radical challenge to the traditional construction of gender in psychoanalytic terms which is usually constituted through ideas of contrasting male and female imaginaries. In the Freudian paradigm female sexuality is viewed and defined in relation to or in oppos-ition to male sexuality, and coded in terms of reproduction that are linked to male pleasure and desire. In contrast, lesbian sexuality exposes the contra-dictions in heterosexual models of femininity and reveals the control that phallocentric systems of thought exert upon women. Thus the introduction of lesbian sexuality into modes of representation reserved traditionally as the arena for male desire also destabilise the gender constructs entrenched within Chicano culture. As Anzaldúa suggests:

> Culture (read males) professes to protect women. Actually it keeps women in rigidly defined roles . . . women are at the bottom of the ladder one rung above the deviants [and] for the lesbian of colour the ultimate rebellion she can make against her culture is through her sexual behaviour.
>
> (Anzaldúa 1987: 16–17)

Both Anzaldúa and Moraga refuse to align lesbian sexuality with either masculinity or femininity, but employ it to expose the artifice of the division between the two, and to problematise the categories of sex and gender as defined by a heterosexually based Chicano culture.

As previously stated, during the movement one of the main tools for the transmission and maintenance of the hierarchies within Chicano culture was the family, a model that replicated Freud's Oedipal economy shaped by the father as transcendental signifier. Subsequent Chicana writing and interpret-ation disrupts this model by subversively exposing the gaps and contradic-tions in heterosexual structures and systems of thought in ways that have recast the form and function of *la familia*. In later chapters I explore this tendency with particular reference to *The House on Mango Street* (1991) by Sandra Cisneros and *Giving up the Ghost* (1986) by Cherríe Moraga, both of which articulate a controversial use of the Freudian Oedipal complex to yield an image of family pathology.

Chicana feminist theory

While these psychoanalytically based strategies of textual analysis have proved to be useful tools in the analysis of writing by Chicanas, many Chicana critics also recognise the limitations of mainstream feminist criticism in dealing with their specific concerns. These scholars argue that American feminist criticism fails to wholly account for the concerns of women who are marginalised by factors not only of gender but also race, class and language. Yarbro-Bejarano (1988), for example, believes that perhaps the most import-ant principle of Chicana feminist criticism 'is the realisation that the Chicana's experience as a woman is inextricable from her experience as a member of an oppressed working-class racial minority and a culture that is not the dominant culture' (Herrera-Sobek and Viramontes 1988: 214). She goes on to state that the critic's task 'is to show how in works by Chicanas, elements of gender, race, culture and class coalesce' (Herrera-Sobek and Viramontes 1988: 214). As Chicana literature is inextricably linked to spe-cific experiences in the USA, critical approaches cannot be a duplicate of white feminist theories or subject to 'academic abstraction' but should adequately represent the diverse social locations of the Chicana experience.

The work of Rebolledo (1988) is perhaps the most overt example of this kind of critical debate. She seeks to articulate a 'native' theory and insists critics ought to abandon Western terms of analysis in favour of a more appropriately Chicano approach. When texts by Chicana/os are forced to occupy a theoretical space created through liberal self–other experiential, and post-structuralist paradigms, Rebolledo considers that the diverse socio-symbolic formations, positionalities, and heterogeneous histories of Chicana/os are either ignored or assimilated. Thus Rebolledo (1988) argues that Western modes of analysis ignore culture-specific concerns:

> I personally find it difficult to have theory (male oriented, French feminist, post-structural or whatever) be what dictates what we find in our literature. I prefer to have the literature speak for itself and as a critic try to organise and understand it . . . rather than finding the theory first and imposing it upon the literature.
>
> (Herrera-Sobek and Viramontes 1988: 208)

Like Bruce-Novoa (1990a) her approach relegates the literary critic to the role of hermeneutic 'organiser', and 'facilitator', 'reproducing and making known' the works of Chicano authors (Herrera-Sobek and Viramontes 1988: 206). Arguably, this is more comparable to earlier forms of culturalist criticism, as Rebolledo aims to authorise the work to speak for itself and for the people it represents, rather than have Western modes of theory legitimate its place in existing canons of American literature. In this respect her approach tends to focus on understanding and evaluating works within the same conventions that the earlier modes of analysis used. She favours the 'indigenous' over what she terms a mainstream or an imperialising theoretical framework in ways that resonate with the earlier critical paradigms proposed by the movement. Unlike the politics of the movement, however, Rebolledo (1988) recognises women's exclusion from education and writing and so she discusses Chicana literature in terms of contextual, cultural and historical knowledge from a feminist perspective, wherein the oral epistemology of the Hispano tradition is privileged, including the songs, recipes and folk sayings of women (Saldívar-Hull 2000: 46).

Saldívar-Hull in *Feminism on the Border: Chicana Gender Politics and Literature* (2000) likewise questions the hegemonic power of Eurocentric feminist critics who do not recognise either Chicanas or Chicana theory. For Saldívar-Hull the problem is that 'Chicanas ask different questions which in turn ask for a reconstruction of the very premise of theory' (Saldívar-Hull 2000: 220). In place of more traditional critical paradigms she proposes the 'non-sanctioned sites of theory' including anthologies, autobiographies and a range of cultural theorists from both sides of the US–Mexico border (Saldívar-Hull 2000: 46). Included here are collectively edited texts by

Moraga and Anzaldúa such as *This Bridge Called My Back: Writings by Radical Women of Colour* (1983), as well as their individual works such as Moraga's *Loving in the War Years/Lo nunca pasó por sus labios* (1983); Anzaldúa's *Borderlands/La Frontera: The New Mestiza* (1987), as well as the Latin American *testimonios* of Domitila Barrios de Chungara, Rigoberta Menchú and Elvia Alvarado. She also insists that her theory of border feminism is a 'lived and shared experience' that moves between local processes as well as the more explicit 'global concerns of Chicana cultural workers' (Saldívar-Hull 2000: 54–5).

This strategy of material and feminist engagement is employed by Saldívar-Hull in order to direct critical attention towards 'the specific socio-political issues that Chicana feminist texts display'. The literature, situated firmly within the province of Chicana oppositional politics and acts of resistance, is considered as 'a practice of intervention' with a complex agenda that takes on board both the internal domination as well as the external repression of the Mexican American woman (Saldívar-Hull 2000: 125). Taking some of the movement poetry of the Chicana activist Angela de Hoyos as her starting point, Saldívar-Hull goes on to highlight the subaltern political aesthetics and identity politics which are developed in a number of Chicana literary works, including those of Gloria Anzaldúa, Sandra Cisneros and Helena María Viramontes.

This kind of research and associated critical activity has been receiving a great deal of emphasis in the past decade. Both Yarbro-Bejarano and Rebolledo include as an essential part of a Chicana literary feminist agenda, the recuperation and construction of a woman's literary tradition. Clara Lomas, Rosaura Sanchez and Erlinda Gonzales-Berry are among the literary critics examining the work of women authors who were writing before the Chicano movement. Among the first of such publications that recovered marginalised Chicana texts was the Paso Por Aqui Series in New Mexico, Volumes I, II and III of the series *Recovering the US Hispanic Literary Heritage* in Texas, and *Infinite Divisions: An Anthology of Chicana Literature* (1993) edited by Tey Diana Rebolledo and Eliana S. Rivero. Among those women writers rediscovered are Maria Amparo Ruiz de Burton, Jovita Gonzalez, Leonor Villegas de Magnon, Maria Christina Mena, Cleofas Jaramillo and Fabiola Cabeza de Baca.

Chicana cultural critique

Mexican cultural icons and historical figures associated with female subjectivity which were incorporated into the master narrative of identity promoted during the movement decades, have also been reclaimed and refigured by subsequent Chicana feminist discourse (Neate 1998: 19). The Virgin of Guadalupe, la Malinche and *la llorona* are the most often cited figures in this respect. In *Borderlands/La Frontera* (1987) Anzaldúa addresses the political motives behind male constructions of these figures, revealing the binary oppositions and stereotypes that have historically alienated and disempowered Chicanas. Anzaldúa states that, 'The true identity of all three has been subverted . . . Guadalupe to make us docile and enduring, *la chingada* (*Malinche*) to make us ashamed of our Indian side, and *la Llorona* to make us long suffering people' (Anzaldúa 1987: 31).

Traditionally, the Virgin of Guadalupe, the Patroness of Mexico and of all indigenous people in the Americas, has been portrayed as 'a one-dimensional figure', 'pure and free from sin', her central role being that of a mother and a helper to those in need (Rebolledo 1995: 52). During the 1960s she became one of the major signifiers of nationalist identity and was often used in movement demonstrations both to verify this identity and in order to attract new members and good publicity. Her image often made the activism of César Chávez and the UFW more acceptable to many moderate or conserva-tive Mexican Americans and 'imbued his movement with a moral dimension that transcended traditional labour-union politics' (Gutiérrez 1995: 196). Conversely, according to the leading Chicano playwright, Luis Valdez, the appearance of the Virgin in UFW demonstrations was the first hint to farm workers that the policies of the UFW 'implied social revolution' (Chávez 1984: 135). This was because the peasant armies of Emiliano Zapata during the Mexican revolution had also carried her image. The response, Valdez states, was similarly 'immediate and reverent' (Chávez 1984: 135).

Through the Virgin, Chávez and the Chicano farm workers also linked their struggle to their indigenous past. According to tradition the Virgin appeared to Juan Diego, an Indian, on 9 December 1529 at the site where there had once stood a temple in tribute to the earth goddess Tonantzin. Two hundred years after her appearance to Juan Diego a papal bull declared the Virgin to be the Patroness and Protectress of New Spain. Later the Mexicans used her image during the Mexican revolution as part of their rallying cry for freedom, and during the events of the 1960s her image became strongly associated with many of the movement's most fundamental issues.

Yet, according to Chicana feminist writers and critics, while Guadalupe was associated with ideas of resistance, she also embodied the characteristics desired by patriarchy. In the eyes of many Chicanas this meant that Guadalupe functioned as a feminine (and often negative) ideal rather than as a symbol of militant women's rights. The ethic of *Marianismo* or the veneration of the Virgin simultaneously inculcates the oppression of women in the name of religion:

> The powerful example of Mary . . . impels the faithful to become like the Mother . . . to treasure the Word of God . . . praise God, serve God and neighbour faithfully and offer themselves generously; to act in all things with mercy and humility.
>
> (Trujillo 1998b: 215)

Marianismo thus forces women into acceptable sexual and social roles, as a virgin, as a saintly mother, or as a wife and martyr. By extension if a woman were to put into practice *su libertad* (her freedom) and independence, according to Nieto Gomez (1995) it would lead to whoredom, the negative alternative to *Marianismo* (A. Garcia 1997: 49).

In response, Chicana activists and writers began to redefine the previously configured dualistic interpretations of the icon. Trujillo (1998b) argues that a number of Chicana lesbian artists and writers recreate Guadalupe in sexualised likeness to themselves. In this way, 'they radically resanctif[y] the representation of the body, specifically [their] sexuality within it' (Trujillo 1998b: 225). This kind of reconstruction is considered to be instrumental in 'the transfigurative liberation of the icon' (Trujillo 1998b: 227).

Two of the major Chicana writers of the 1980s, Moraga and Anzaldúa, also resexualise Guadalupe in ways that redefine her patriarchal inscription, as well as the more orthodox codifications of church and state. In their work Guadalupe is no longer the Catholic Virgin imported and constructed through male rule as part of the *puta/virgen* dichotomy, but a multiply valanced and syncretic figure that emerged from indigenous and maternal religious systems of thought.

In the third chapter of *Borderlands/La Frontera* (1987), Anzaldúa resituates the Virgin within a genealogy of indigenous and powerful female deities dating from the older pre-Cortesian figure of Coatlicue, the serpent goddess of life and death, and Tonantsin her subsequent incarnation (Anzaldúa 1987: 27). This perspective of Guadalupe has a firm basis in a female-centred indigenous religion, and provides an alternate religious experience to the patriarchal tradition celebrated by leaders of the movement. Alarcón (1996) argues that Anzaldúa's rewriting of Guadalupe is both an attempt to rein-scribe what has been lost through colonisation as well as an attempt to reinscribe the repressed feminine in the symbolic order (Lavie and Swedenbourg 1996: 52). The line of descent from Guadalupe to Tonantsi and Coatlicue represents, 'a re-establishment of the non (pre)-oedipal (in this case non [pre] Columbian) mother, who displaces . . . the "phallic mother", the one complicitous in the Freudian "family romance" '(Lavie and Swedenbourg 1996: 50).

The reconstruction of a female genealogy and the representation of Guada-lupe in more complex ways are integral to the political praxis of Chicana writers of the post-movement years. She is, however, not the only figure explored for the previously limited configurations of female subjectivity. The role of women in pre-Columbian society and their representation in political and cultural production during the decades of the movement also serves as an important point of intervention for contemporary Chicana feminist criticism (Neate 1998: 17–18). The macho reinscription of the indigenous heritage during the movement decades effectively legitimised the oppression of women and ignored questions related to gender difference. This repression worked by situating Chicana subjectivity in a way that left the complexities of their identity unarticulated (Neate 1998: 17–18). The historical figure variously known as Malintzin Tenepal or Dona Marina or la Malinche clearly falls into this category and has become one of the most contentious sites of female subjectivity of the post-movement decades.

Often seen as the Virgin of Guadalupe's 'monstrous double', according to Alarcón (1989) Malinche first entered Chicano discourse as a female embodiment of betrayal and treachery (McClintock et al. 1997: 278). Chicanas who married American men were often derisively termed *malinches*, as were those Chicanas who left the community to seek higher education, a move commonly regarded by Chicano men as a shift towards assimilation. Chicanas who allied themselves to feminism or lesbian sexuality were similarly labelled *malinches*. In *Chicano Manifesto*, (1972) Rendon observes that *malinches* were considered to be:

> In the service of the gringo [they] attack their own brothers, betray our dignity and manhood, cause jealousies and misunderstandings among us, and actually seek to retard the advance of the Chicanos, if it benefits themselves – while the gringo watches.
>
> (Neate 1998: 264)

Historically, Malinche played a key role in the struggle between the Aztec and Spanish empires as the translator and mistress of the Spanish conquistador Hernan Cortes. She is said to have given birth to a son by Cortes and therefore also to have given birth to the mixed race or mestizo nation. This act of procreation however, is viewed from polarised perspectives. Chicana feminists view Malinche as the creator of a new and dynamic race and therefore responsible for a Chicana/o mestiza/o subjectivity. But according to Mexican popular tradition, and many male critics, she was the passive victim of rape and a sexual and political betrayer of her people (Paz 1967). As Mexico became increasingly nationalist after the Mexican revolution, the Mexicanos, who accused her of *'chingando con Cortés'*, knew Malinche as La Chingada (Pérez 1999a: xv). According to Anzaldúa,

> Malini Tenepat, or Malintzin, has become known as *la chingada* – the fucked one. She has become the bad word that passes a dozen times a day from the lips of Chicanos. Whore, prostitute, the woman who sold out her people to the Spaniards are epithets Chicanos spit out with contempt.
>
> (Anzaldúa 1987: 44)

Malinche emasculated the Mexican male by giving herself to the conqueror. According to Pérez (1993), the male, in response compensates by adopting a form of sexuality based on violence and machismo (de la Torre and Pesquera 1993: 62–3). This perspective was entrenched within movement rhetoric in such a way as to construct Chicanas in negative terms as a passive object or *chingada*, the active subject role or *chingon* being traditionally reserved for the male. The Mexican cultural critic and Nobel Prize winning poet, Octavio Paz, has famously analysed the uses of the verb *chingar* which he argues always carries with it a charge of sexual violence. According to Paz (1967) the origins of *chingar* lie in the Aztec words *chingaste* (meaning lies, residue, sediment) and *xinachtli* (garden seed). The idea of breaking or of ripping open is associated with *chingar* and often has violent sexual connotations. In the fourth chapter of *The Labyrinth of Solitude* (1967), titled 'The Sons of La Malinche', Paz poses the question, 'Who is Chingada?' and goes on to answer, 'Above all she is the mother, a mythical figure' (Paz 1967: 77). The *chingada* is one of the Mexican representations of maternity, but unlike the Virgin, the *chingada* is a mother who has been violated. Paz asserted that the passivity of the violated mother, or *la chingada*, found an analogue in Malinche, the violated mistress/ victim of Hernan Cortes.

Adelaida del Castillo's article, 'Malintzin Tenepal: A Preliminary Look into a New Perspective' (1974) was one of the first Chicana feminist critiques to reclaim and rehistoricise this figure (A. Garcia 1997: 122–6). According to del Castillo, Malintzin Tenepal has consistently been misinterpreted and misrepresented. She bases her argument on the work of Bernal Díaz del Castillo, the Spanish conquistador and chronicler of the conquest of Mexico, though interestingly both chroniclers for the Spanish Crown, Bernal Díaz del Castillo and Bartolomé de las Casas, exalted la Malinche as a heroine (A. Garcia 1997: 123). Dona Marina appears in Bernal Díaz del Castillo's *Historia verdadera de la conquista de la nueva España* (*History of the Conquest of New Spain*). As an Aztec woman of noble birth she was a skilled strategist and linguist. According to del Castillo (1974), she was known as 'the angel of the expedition' by the conquistadors primarily because she saved their lives many times (A. Garcia 1997: 123). The indigenous people also at first took her for a *diosa* or goddess because she could speak their language and served in a diplomatic capacity between themselves and the white settlers. According to del Castillo (1974) Malinche was also a very spiritual woman and believed that Cortes was the Aztec feathered serpent god Quetzalcoatl, returned in a human form to save the indigenous peoples from certain extinction (A. Garcia 1997: 125).

From these perspectives, Malinche contradicts the dominant narratives associated conquest and resistance, which are usually based on masculine heroic activities. She also complicates reductive visions of the conquest as a straightforward relation between victims and victimisers. Along with critics such as del Castillo (1974) and Alarcón (1983, 1989), many Chicana writers including Adaljiza Sosa Riddell, Carmen Tafolla, Cordelia Candelaria, Sylvia Gonzales, Alma Villanueva and Cherríe Moraga see Malinche in more positive terms. These writers figure her as a woman in control of her own destiny. Anzaldúa's overriding concept of a mestiza subjectivity and consciousness for example is based on the fact that the Cortes/Malinche sexual paradigm produced a new race, a mestizo people. Or according to Alarcón (1989) Malinche should be viewed as an empowering and enabling figure, providing

Chicanas with a powerful subject position from which to speak (McClintock et al. 1997: 285).

Along with Guadalupe and Malinche, Chicana writers and critics have also reclaimed the cultural figure of *la llorona*. According to tradition *la llorona* is the mythical weeping woman of Mexican and Chicana/o popular culture. She is supposed to have drowned her children in exchange either for eternal life or alternatively for the love of a man, but instead has been cursed for eternity to wander riverbanks and ditches lamenting their deaths by crying out for them. From a slightly different perspective Saldívar's (1997) reading of this figure draws on Limón's suggestion that *la llorona*'s 'insane infanticide' can be said to be 'a temporary insanity produced historically by those who socially dominate' (Saldívar 1997: 106). Many Chicana writers signify on this analysis and rehistoricise or contextualise *la llorona*'s presence. Conversely, in some of the more patriarchal interpretations she signifies the loss of Tenochtitlan (present-day Mexico City) at the hands of the Spanish conquistadors, and also the loss of Aztlán at the hands of American imperialists. However, in the poem 'Malinchista, A Myth Revisited', Alicia Gaspar de Alba writes from a polarised perspective:

> The woman shrieking along the littered bank of the
> Rio Grande is not sorry. She is looking for revenge.
> Centuries she has been blamed for the murder of her
> child, the loss of her people, as if Tenochtitlan
> would not have fallen without her sin. History
> does not sing of the conquistador who prayed
> to a white god as he pulled two ripe hearts
> out of the land.
>   (Gaspar de Alba et al. 1989: 16–17)

According to Rebolledo (1995), as a syncretic image, *la llorona* brings together Indian, Spanish and European folklore and legend and is connected both to Spanish medieval notions of *animas en pena* or spirits in purgatory, as well as to the Medea myth (Rebolledo 1995: 63). In Chicana/o folklore the images and mythology about *la llorona* and la Malinche often merge until in many areas they are transformed into a unitary figure. In male literary production this syncretic figure is more often than not seen in negative terms, and is often associated with a destructive mother image. In other writing by Chicanos and Chicanas *la llorona* becomes synonymous with a *curandera* (healer) or *la bruja* (the witch). Alluding to the gender inequalities inherent to these figures Ana Castillo writes in *Massacre of the Dreamers* (1994b) that whereas in Mexican culture, 'a *brujo* is someone to fear and to revere', a *bruja* on the other hand 'is someone to hate to the point of killing if at all possible' (Castillo 1994b: 157). Such a negative pattern of characterisation can clearly be seen in Anaya's novel *Bless Me Ultima* (1991). In this text female characters are clearly confined to the rigid stereotypes promoted by movement ideology.

The prostitute and the Trementina sisters are patently Malinche figures, who either tempt men away from the community, or are the personification of evil. The Trementina sisters, as *brujas*, very nearly all die by the end of the text, a conclusion that is figured as fitting punishment for being *mujeres malas* (bad women). The old healer and *curandera*, Ultima, one of the major figures in the novel, is also characterised as a *bruja* or witch. Despite her pivotal function in the narrative her duality (as both *bruja* and *curandera*) transgresses the normative societal roles for Chicana womanhood and subsequently she suffers the fate of other ambiguous female characters in the text and is likewise eventually punished with death.

In Anzaldúa's (1987) poem 'My Black *Angelos*' the *bruja* is figured in much more positive terms, and as an empowering mystical force that is overtly connected to *la llorona*:

> *la bruja con las uñas largas* . . . [the witch with long fingernails]
> She crawls into my spine
> her eyes opening and closing,
> shining under my skin in the dark
> whirling my bones twirling
> till they're hollow reeds . . .
> We sweep through the streets
> We roam with the souls of the dead.
>
> (Anzaldúa 1987: 184)

In Anzaldúa's text, *la llorona* is seen as being a derivation of the earth goddess Cohuacoatl from pre-conquest times, and through Cohuacoatl she is connected to empowering pre-Columbian figures such as the Mocihuaquetzque, who were valiant women, held sacred by Aztec warriors (Rebolledo 1995: 63). In being reconnected to this more powerful genealogy *la llorona*'s weeping is more radically interpreted as an oppositional scream against patriarchal inscriptions of womanhood. As Saldívar-Hull points out:

> the Llorona of Chicana feminists' no longer figures as enemy or as victim. Chicana border feminism, *feminismo fronteriza*, narrativizes the weeping woman's hysterical laments into historically based, residual memories of the disastrous encounter between sixteenth century indigenous America and Europe's conquerors.
>
> (Saldívar-Hull 2000: 126)

In other recent Chicana narratives *la llorona* figures as a central figure in more personal and contemporary encounters. In Ana Castillo's novel *So Far from God* (1994a) *la llorona* is not presented in the role usually ascribed to her but is rehabilitated by Sofia, who concludes that,

> Her father had told her, that La Llorona was a bad woman who had left

her husband and home, drowned her babies to run off and have a sinful life, and God punished her for eternity [but] she refused to repeat this nightmare to her daughters.

(Castillo 1994a: 161)

In Sandra Cisneros' short story 'Woman Hollering Creek' (1993), *la llorona's* wailing is associated with a stream, known locally as La Gritona (Woman Hollering), 'though no one could say whether the woman had hollered from anger or pain' (Cisneros 1993: 46). To the newly wed Cleofilas, it seems a strange name to give to 'a creek so pretty and full of happily ever after' (Cisneros 1993: 47). As the reality of her abusive marriage to her macho husband deteriorates, *la llorona/la gritona* appears to call her 'all day and all night' (Cisneros 1993: 51). In Cisneros' story this voice is reconfigured from a *llanto* (a cry) into a *grito* (shout) and a song of freedom and liberation as the protagonist leaves her abusive relationship with the help of female-centred networks. Thus figured, *la llorona* according to Limón 'symbolically destroy[s] the familial basis for patriarchy' and her paternalistic inscription as murderer and purveyor of matricide is challenged in order to accommodate more feminist interpretations of her cultural legacy (J. Saldívar 1997: 106).

In Helena María Viramontes' short story 'The Cariboo Café' (1995a) *la llorona's* presence can be interpreted in a similar way. In this text *la llorona* becomes associated with all the undocumented women and children from central and South America who attempted to cross the US–Mexico border throughout the 1980s. During a climactic scene a nameless woman who is searching for her 'disappeared' son hears the voice of *la llorona* near her:

The darkness becomes a serpent's tongue, swallowing us whole. It is the night of La Llorona. The women come up from the depths of sorrow to search for their children. I join them, frantic, desperate, and our eyes become scrutinisers, our bodies opiated with the scent of their smiles. Descending from door to door, the wind whips our faces. I hear the wailing of the women and know it to be my own.

(Viramontes 1995a: 72–3)

Instead of stereotypical images of Mexican and indigenous women as passive, Viramontes depicts the women as actively resistant, and, similar to Cisneros in *Woman Hollering Creek*, as a collective. While the woman's experiences of the INS (the Immigration and Naturalisation Service), or *la migra*, highlight her displacement by the juridical systems of the US–Mexico border, the rearticulation of *la llorona's* transgressive and ghostly figure during 'the night of the serpents tongue' contradicts and disrupts the symbolic order embedded within their patriarchal legal structures. While Viramontes suggests the socially constructed notions implicit in the legitimation process and the dominant ideology of the border, at the same time through the figure of *la llorona* she offers a critique of this same process that attempts to erase the cultural and political presence of indigenous peoples and contain them in categories that stress their anonymity. Although the woman remains nameless throughout the narrative, her particular history and specific transgression of the law clearly specifies her individuality and thus the existence of differences within the bounded category of 'illegal' or 'undocumented' immigrant. In these ways Viramontes 'displays the concerns that distinguish feminism on the border from other types of Chicana feminism' (Saldívar-Hull 2000: 145). This is achieved through her transnational perspective, a perspective that forms ties between 'men and women of her own blood' and 'peoples across borders who enter the United States in search of political liberation' (Saldívar-Hull 2000: 145).

All of these cultural and historical figures discussed here profoundly influence the epistemology of feminist writing and criticism in contemporary Chicana literary production, but also represent, as this study goes on to explore, an unravelling politics of identity that contests the masculinist legacies of the movement decades.

4 The relationship between Chicano and Chicana literature

Despite the politicisation and mobilisation of large sectors of the Chicana/o community during the events of the movement, gender issues did not figure prominently in the political programme. Chicano identity was primarily presented then as male, and this assertion was in large part supported by mainstream movement ideology. During this time Rendon (1972) states that Chicano identity was symbolised by exclamations of, '*Viva la raza! Viva la causa!* and by the concepts of *Chicanismo, el Quinto Sol* and by the psychological as well as the seminal birthplace of *Aztlán*' (Gaspar de Alba 1998: 126). Symbolically, these expressions of Chicano pride indicate a close correlation between issues of gender and formulations of group identity. As discussed in previous chapters, their function as forms of identification also masked close ties between gender-related attitudes and political ideology. Concepts of *la raza, la causa, chicanismo*, Quinto Sol and Aztlán also shared a perspective which implied that anyone who had an agenda beyond race and class could not be affiliated to the movement or in extreme cases, consider themselves to be a real Chicano. As Rendon (1972) continues, 'we are oppressed because of the colour of our skin and because of the nature of our being' (Gaspar de Alba 1998: 127). In other words, matters of race and class were considered the primary sources of Chicana/o oppression, and issues of gender rather than co-existing alongside these matters were relegated to the margins of movement activism.

Chicanas who deviated from this nationalist political stance were subjected to being labelled *malinches* or betrayers, *vendidas* or sell-outs, and *agabachadas* or white identified. Such social and political sanctions not only prevented them from participating in political activities, but also discouraged them from articulating feminist issues. Although over the course of the next twenty years a self-defined Chicana feminism flowered, mainly in academia in the form of groups such as The National Association of Chicana and Chicano Studies (NACCS) and Mujeres Activas en Letras y Cambio Social, (MALCS, Women Active in Letters and Social Change), during the movement matters of female identity and sexuality were ignored or stereotyped. Gender issues and an official Chicano identity were defined by reference to a male-dominated value system, and as a consequence Chicanas were relegated to the margins of both literary and political representation.

This ideological and gendered exclusion meant that from the mid-1960s onwards Chicano literary discourse was almost exclusively the province of male writers, dominated in particular by the works of José Montoya, Rodolfo 'Corky' Gonzales, Luis Valdez, Tomás Rivera, Rolando Hinojosa, Rudolfo Anaya, Ricardo Sanchez, Alurista, Raul Salinas and others. Their literary dominance has continued to exert a powerful influence into subsequent decades, and by and large these writers feature in anthologies, collections and retrospective studies of the Chicano movement as still the most authentic and representative voices of *la raza*. Chicana feminist writings from the movement decades, published in serials and journals alongside those of Chicano men on the other hand, have been consistently ignored. Although altered in his later publications, this kind of exclusionary practice continued to influence Bruce-Novoa's study of fourteen Chicano authors, *Chicano Authors: Inquiry By Interview* (1980a), as well as his authoritative study *Chicano Poetry: A Response To Chaos* (1982), neither of which integrates women's writing in any significant way. Although a tradition of women's writing had existed since at least 1848, it was not officially recognised until the development of their own small but influential feminist publications such as *Regeneración*, *Hijas de Cuauhtémoc*, and *Encuentro Femenil*, and the publication of the first major collection of Chicana writing, Estella Portillo's *Chicanas en la literature y el arte: El Grito* in 1973 (Rebolledo and Reviro 1993: 23).

The recognition of women's writing as an important literary force first occurred during the middle of the 1980s when larger Chicano publishing firms began to commission their work. This study goes on to explore the intertextual relations between the writing of these Chicana writers and the literary and ideological configurations of the movement. The following chapter introduces some of the issues that are central to this study by providing a comparative analysis between the identity politics developed in Chicano and Chicana poetic production both during and after the movement decades. A broadly deconstructive approach to Rodolfo 'Corky' Gonzales's movement narrative 'Yo soy Joaquín' (1967) forms the basis of my initial analysis and highlights some of the main sources of Chicano identity as defined by nationalist discourse. Selected poetic texts by Chicana writers are then read in terms that disrupt these formulations, in particular the explicitly paternalistic representation of women and the masculinist tendency in movement politics.

Like most literary genres during the 1960s, poetic production developed a reciprocal relationship with Chicano political activity (Neate 1998: 107). Its distribution was largely made possible through the establishment of Chicano publications such as *El Malcriado, El Grito, Aztlán, Con Safos*, and *El Grito del Norte*, and Chicano publishing houses such as Quinto Sol and later Arte Publico. Poetry of all genres was also circulated on a more grass-roots level in the context of political activity. In order to more fully explore the relationship between Chicano poetry and its adoption as a kind of agit-prop form of literature, I intend to move onto a fuller consideration of the *corrido* and its function as a political and cultural form of resistance during the protest decades, before considering Gonzales's text in more detail.

Described as being 'the most inspiring piece of literature written in the 1960s', the epic *corrido* by Rodolfo 'Corky' Gonzales, 'Yo soy Joaquín' (I Am Joaquín), continues to hold social and political importance to the present day (Del Castillo et al. 1991: 141–54). Neate (1998) among other critics considers Gonzales's poem as a 'contemporary ur-text' and a 'reference point for subsequent texts' (Bruce-Novoa 1990a, Del Castillo et al. 1991, Neate 1998). Part of its continued critical significance lies in its distinctive rhetoric, the inclusion of Chicano cultural heroes and its expression of pride in Chicano history (Calderon and Saldívar 1991: 167–80), though arguably its greater significance lies in its taking the form of the *corrido*, as this signified that Gonzales's poem was engaging with a specific set of cultural and political values. Herrera-Sobek and Saldívar argue that the *corrido*'s true significance can be found in its historical status as a 'master poem' which forms 'a substantial part of the folk base of Chicano narrative' (Saldívar 1990a: 42). Although critics such as these now perceive the *corrido* as being 'the central socio-poetic Chicano paradigm', at the time of the publication and distribution of Gonzales's text only a relatively small number of Chicano critics considered the *corrido* to be a central form of Chicano poetics (Calderon and Saldívar 1991: 167–80). Américo Paredes's seminal study *With a Pistol in his Hand: A Border Ballad and its Hero* (1958) was only just beginning to influence some Chicano critics by the late 1960s and early 1970s, but in time it would come to have a profound influence on Chicana/o Studies of the 1980s and 1990s.

In this highly influential work Paredes identified the *corrido* as a dominant mode of Mexican American popular expression. As a musical form the *corrido* first of all emerged in the mid-nineteenth century as an expression of the deep schism between Mexicans and Americans following the US–Mexico war and the creation of the US–Mexico border. The political, social, economic and linguistic transformations brought about by annexation are important factors when considering the formation and development of the *corrido* as they not only created the context for its development, but are also reflected in its content and form. Basing his reading of the *corrido* on Paredes' analysis, Saldívar states that structurally the *corrido* has three main elements: a hero or protagonist, 'with whom the audience is meant to identify'; a world in which 'the hero acts and is acted on by antagonistic Anglo centric forces'; and an oral narrative in which 'the interaction of the protagonist and the world is described' (Calderon and Saldívar 1991: 171–3).

As previously stated, the world reflected in the *corrido* is that of the post-annexation south-west when complex and unequal racialised relationships were being forged throughout the region. At that time, a fractured and divisive stratification emerged and was organised into three distinct strata. Gutiérrez (1995) states that the Christianised or detribalised Indians were at the bottom of the hierarchy, smallholder mestizos were next, and the landowners, government and military administrators, merchants and

Catholic Church administrators, who dominated the political economy, occupied the third and highest tier (Gutiérrez 1995: 31). According to this classification, the newly formed Mexican American community was relegated to a subordinate position in the new but changing social and economic hierarchy in the land that was once theirs (Gutiérrez 1995: 21). In California and south Texas racial subjugation and dispossession of Mexican land was often accompanied by violence, some of which took the form of banditry (Gonzales 2000: 88–90). Figures associated with banditry and outlaw activities especially Joaquín Murrieta, Juan Nepomuceno Cortina (1824–92) and Gregorio Cortez (1875–1916) feature in *corridos* and are significant heroes in Chicano folklore and history. Gonzales (2000) states that as Chicano nationalists condemned the historical injustices of their past, they constructed a pantheon of oppositional heroes from these figures whose activities they interpreted as a response to hostile American actions (Gonzales 2000: 88).

Paredes's work on 'El corrido de Gregorio Cortez' led the way in forming what was to become this widespread opinion. According to Paredes, the ballad of Gregorio Cortez vividly displays the theme of conflict and injustice emblematic of the *corrido*. Typically these facets provide a key example of the *corrido*'s ability to express socio-cultural resistance and to 'dismantle the opposition upon which much of white supremacy was based' (Saldívar 1991b: 173). Gonzales's *corrido* 'Yo soy Joaquín' (1967) follows this model closely in the sense that the speaker of the poem, Joaquín Murrieta, the infamous Californio bandit, offers resistance to an Anglo enemy who steals his land and rapes his wife. This perspective of Chicano literature as resistance literature and as inherently oppositional has subsequently exercised a marked and continuing influence on developments both within Chicano writing and Chicano literary criticism. Limón (1992) similarly argues that during the events of the movement, despite certain deviations from the traditional ballad form, 'as a significant form of symbolic redressive action' and 'as an active residual practice', the *corrido* continued to exert this kind of counter-hegemonic influence (Limón 1992: 42). Working on a number of levels, 'Yo soy Joaquín' conforms to this model of literary and cultural resistance. Initially Gonzales introduces Joaquín as an anti-hero who states that he is 'lost', 'confused' and 'suppressed' by the chaos of America. The dilemma he faces in the USA mirrors that facing the Chicano people. He must not only resolve the socio-political struggle for self-determination in a 'gringo' society, but also more importantly come to terms with the contradictory identity politics involved in becoming part of that society:

> I look at myself
> and see part of me
> who rejects my father and my mother
> and dissolves into the melting pot
> to disappear in shame.
> (Hernández-Gutiérrez and Foster 1997: 215)

Joaquín's dilemma revolves around the central question of identity and the conflicts associated with the retention of cultural integrity within a hegemonic white American society. Historically, American society has been structured around assimilation and ideas of the melting pot, which promoted the merging of immigrant cultures and groups into a unified whole. This process, as many critics have observed, is characterised by a contradictory dynamic of inclusion and exclusion, which involves homogenisation and a stripping away of cultural differences and historical specificities. Neate (1998) concurs with this view and states that:

> The melting pot has been an allegorical-ideological mechanism which conceals the reality of its socio-politically oppressive effect derived from a fundamental act of repression. Its method of inclusion is inextricably linked with a dynamic of exclusion as the ethnic pluralism that it ostensibly guarantees, belies a practice of internal colonisation and liminalisation of those bearing the marks of difference.
>
> (Neate 1998: 86)

From a slightly different perspective Rosaldo (1993c) has famously argued that assimilation and the melting pot are responsible for the creation of 'a curious kind of hybrid invisibility' whereby 'immigrants and socially mobile individuals' appear 'culturally invisible' primarily because 'they are no longer what they once were and not yet what they could become' (Rosaldo 1993c: 209). The melting pot, he goes on to state, 'strips individuals of their former cultures' in order that they may become American citizens (Rosaldo 1993c: 209).

This process has also helped to ensure a subaltern status for Mexicans in the USA and has underwritten Anglo representations of Mexican Americans and their history. The speaker of the poem recognises the dangers of assimilation, and the sacrifices which are a necessary part of becoming part of white American society. Conversely, later revisions of the assimilation paradigm in the poem echo those of the movement itself which largely advocated a militant separatism and considered that Chicanos were 'the social and cultural product of a racial and cultural [process] of deranged assimilation' – a process which effectively 'produced a monstrous distortion of [the] true past' (Gutiérrez 1993: 528–9).

In order to avoid assimilation and to reconstruct a positive identification with the Chicano past, the movement proposed a politics of separation that involved a quest for origins and an authentic Chicano identity. In the poem this is represented through a withdrawal to an hermetically sealed space, 'to the safety within the / Circle of life / MY OWN PEOPLE' (Hernández-Gutiérrez and Foster 1997: 208). Beginning in pre-Cortesian times, Gonzales commences a genealogical tracing of his family circle with the idealisation of the Aztec emperor Cuauhtémoc (the last emperor of the Aztecs) who he states was a 'civilised beyond the dreams / of the *Gachupín Cortez*'

(Hernández-Gutiérrez and Foster 1997: 208). Gonzales (1967) then extends this line of descent to include Nezahualcoyotl, a famous Aztec poet and '[g]reat leader of the *Chichimecas*' (Hernández-Gutiérrez and Foster 1997: 208). This construction of family from indigenous pre-Cortesian tribes reflects the accepted position between most Chicano groups at that time which tended to glorify Indian contributions and to denigrate the Spanish. His description of Cortes as the '*Gachupín*' or stranger at this point, mirrors the anti-imperialist sentiments of the movement, which in large part also sought to decolonise their heritage. In subsequent stanzas the Spanish are overtly related to 'gun and flame' and therefore to conquest, bloodshed and weaponry (Hernández-Gutiérrez and Foster 1997: 211). Conversely, Aztec tribes are associated with more organic symbols such as the eagle and serpent and other indicators of Mexican cosmology and the Chicano homeland (Candelaria 1986: 53). Although Gonzales extols the miscegenation process and later Joaquín claims a Spanish lineage, equal value is not given to these constitutive elements of mestizo identity at this point in the poem. Instead Gonzales opens with a series of powerful cultural assertions that overwhelmingly reinforce an association between Chicanos and the elite rulers of the Aztecs and Mayans from the past.

This tendency is reflected in other Chicano literary productions of the movement years. Alurista's poetry embodied this influence most overtly in the collections *Floricanto en Aztlán* (1971) and *Nationchild Plumaroja* (1972) where he writes:

> leaving no tracks
> or marcas in the wind
> music is born
>   and la fiesta del silencio [the festival of silence]
> permeates our hearts
> and our blood pounds a beat
>   to reach the point
> where and when, rhythmically
>   we know ourselves
> to be
>   Chicanos de colorada piel [Chicanos with red skin]
>   de espirito guerrero [with warrior spirit]
> hunting in our own land
>   nuestra tierra [our land].
>   (Arteaga 1997: 97)

Joaquín's retreat to a cultural space inflected by an indigenous past reflects the same tendency in Alurista's poetry and movement politics, particularly the ideological notion of ownership of 'nuestra tierra' and a separate state, Aztlán.

The concept of the homeland, Aztlán, was derived from two main sources:

first, it drew heavily on the legendary symbolic homeland of the Aztecs, situated to the north of the Aztec empire in pre-conquest times, and, second, it represented the lands lost to the USA after the US–Mexico war of 1846–8. Chicano nationalists aimed to reclaim this land both symbolically in literature and the arts and literally through concerted political effort. In a similar move Gonzales repeatedly seeks to locate Chicano identity in a series of cultural co-ordinates that include ownership or a strong relationship with the land:

> I owned the land as far as the eye
> could see under the crown of Spain
> and I toiled on my earth . . .
> THE GROUND WAS MINE.
> (Hernández-Gutiérrez and Foster 1997: 208–9)

Despite the fact that this strategy of reclamation is not tied to any specific geographical location, the accumulative effect of naming and claiming different geographic and social landscapes does create a unification between the land and a sense of identity. These sentiments were also later recorded in *El Plan Espiritual de Aztlán*, first announced at the Denver Youth Conference in 1969, which also reaffirmed ownership of a Chicano identity based on the land:

> In the spirit of a new people that is conscious not only of its proud historical heritage but also of the brutal *'gringo'* invasion of our territories, we, the Chicano inhabitants and civilizers of the northern land of *Aztlán* from whence came our forefathers [are] reclaiming the land of their birth.
>
> (Anaya and Lomelí 1989: 1)

The concept of Aztlán is not only figured as a continuation of the indigenous past but is also conceived of as a separate state with a separate political system. Although it is not mentioned in concrete terms, in the poem Gonzales also creates a counter-state that is reclaimed from a history characterised by violence and racial persecution. Historically, it was racial and cultural differences between Anglos and Mexicans that legitimised the unequal treatment and status of Mexicans in the USA. Essentially Mexicans were viewed as intellectually and culturally inferior (Pesquera and Segura 1993: 298). Cultural nationalist ideology countered this pejorative perspective by symbolically reclaiming their geographic and cultural heritage, and asserting an identity based on this legacy.

The emphasis placed on neo-indigenist thought and culture by movement leaders was not only a quest for an authentic identity but also a strategy designed to instil a sense of pride and strength among Chicanos. Gutiérrez (1971) recalls how, 'by seeking strength and inspiration in a heroic Aztec past ... Chicano men, a largely powerless group, invested themselves with images of power' (de la Torre and Pesquera 1993: 588). In the poem the reconstruction of a heroic mythology derived from pre-Columbian leaders mirrors these aims and functions as an intensely symbolic and empowering presence in the process of Chicano identity formation. A large part of this process involves looking retrospectively not only to leaders of entire empires, but also to those who had helped incite revolution. This again mirrored movement philosophy and discourse, which similarly endeavoured to culti- vate revolutionary motive and ideology largely through the construction of a resistant cultural tradition rooted in pre-Cortesian times and figures from the Mexican revolution (Pérez 1999a: 9). But despite the emphasis placed on these 'indigenous elements', it would be inaccurate to suggest that Chicano identity is viewed wholly in these terms in the poem. Instead, Gonzales views a paradigmatic Chicano identity as mestizo following the conquest by Hernan Cortes in 1521. In another reassertion of his ancestry Gonzales (1967) claims that Joaquín is also, 'Yaqui', 'Tarahumara' as well as 'Mestizo' and 'Español' (Hernández-Gutiérrez and Foster 1997: 213). The logical outcome of this synthesis of a number of Indian tribes while initially appearing to be mestizo or mixed race, in the final analysis becomes *Español* or the Spaniard. In this sense Gonzales' mixed-race discourse resembles the racial theories of Vasconcelos first expressed in *La Raza cósmica* originally published in 1925. Here he argued that the mixture of Spanish and Indian races created a superior and transcendent mestizo race, 'a new type of race to which the white man would have to aspire with the object of achieving synthesis', a race that was in effect the only hope for the future of the world (Juãrez 1972: 70). This theory later appealed to some leaders of the Chicano move- ment who also considered *mestizaje* or the mixing of races to be superior to monogenistic ideas of racial purity. But significantly, as Juãrez (1972) argues, the inspiration behind Vasconcelos' theory was in large part based on his personal reaction to a prevalent set of Western racial ideas based on principles of biological racism (Juãrez 1972: 51). This meant that in the last analysis, the racial composition of *la raza cósmica*/the cosmic race was overwhelmingly determined not by the desire to have the racial traits of all peoples blended together but rather by Vasconcelos' own Hispanic preferences (Juãrez 1972: 70).

Gonzales' mixed-race theories are less didactic than this but nonetheless strive to achieve a racial synthesis within accepted ethnic boundaries. Thus a dialectical process of oppositions and syntheses between Indian and Spanish antecedence characterise later sections of the text (Candelaria 1986, Bruce- Novoa 1990a, Neate 1998). According to Gonzales (1967), Joaquín is both 'the sword and flame of Cortez / the despot' as well as being 'the Eagle and the Serpent of / the Aztec civilisation', he is therefore 'both tyrant and slave' (Hernández-Gutiérrez and Foster 1997: 208–9). From lines such as these, Cortes, it would seem, despite being a 'despot', a murderer and 'Gachupín', is also part of Joaquín's quintessential Chicano identity as much as his indigenous roots. These lines not only illustrate the mestizo process in the construction of Joaquín's identity, but also reify blood, as several literary critics have observed, as the central image associated with this process (Candelaria 1986, Bruce-Novoa 1990a, Neate 1998).

Certainly, masculine violence and bloodshed characterise much of Gonzales' review of Chicano history, so that the altars of 'Moctezuma' are said to be stained 'a bloody red', the backs of Indian slaves are likewise 'stripped crimson', and revolution is perceived as being inherently 'bloody' (Hernández-Gutiérrez and Foster 1997: 216). At the same time, the poet attends to the *mestizaje* or subtypes of blood that constitute this process. Thus 'Part of the blood that runs deep' in Joaquín 'Could not be vanquished by the Moors'; while another 'part of blood has laboured endlessly five-hundred / years under the heel of lustful / Europeans' (Hernández-Gutiérrez and Foster 1997: 220). Equally, during the course of the narrative Joaquín also claims that he was part of the village priest Hidalgo who began the war of independence against Spain in 1810 with a loud *grito* (shout) (Hernández-Gutiérrez and Foster 1997: 210). In the construction of the mestizo subject, a variety of blood types therefore mix, though interestingly the mixing is not confined to inter-racial processes alone but also extends to matters of class and social position. Thus the blood of priests, kings and those who have fought in battle or revolution, is readily mixed with that of arguably less noble antecedents such as that of Chicanos who bleed 'in some smelly cell' or from 'the vicious gloves of hunger' (Hernández-Gutiérrez and Foster 1997: 217). Blood as the carrier of Chicano identity therefore cuts across classes, histories and social formations; Chicanos bleed, as the speaker states, 'in many ways' (Hernández-Gutiérrez and Foster 1997: 216). Through repeated association blood and bloodshed thus become the pre-eminent symbols associated with the evolution of Chicano identity.

Significantly, the emphasis placed on the ritual spilling and mixing of blood forms a direct link with the masculinist politics forwarded during the movement decades. *El Plan Espiritual de Aztlán* (1969) also bases the Chicano claim to the US south-west on biology and history, and states that political affiliations arise automatically from the 'blood' that is 'our power, our responsibility, and our *inevitable* destiny' (Anaya and Lomelí 1989: 1). Yet this is obviously problematic, as the only political affiliations that blood significantly enables in the plan appear to be exclusively male. Like many political documents produced during the movement decades, the plan repeatedly asserts that 'Brotherhood unites us, and love for our brothers makes us a people' (Anaya and Lomelí 1989: 1). The poem in large part reiterates this economy, as bonding through blood only forms fraternal relations between male Mexicanos. This kind of discursive projection of *carnalismo* or Chicano brotherhood circulated extensively throughout the movement and facilitated a system of brotherly relations that maintained male privilege and excluded women from any form of political empowerment.

Gutiérrez-Jones (1995) argues that Eve Sedgwick's reading of homosocial bonding in *Between Men: English Literature and Male Homosocial Desire* (1985) and *Epistemology of the Closet* (1990) bears resonance with Chicano *carnalismo* or systems of brotherhood (Gutiérrez-Jones 1995: 132–3). In his opinion homosocial bonding was a key element of *carnalismo*, and together they created 'a great variety of partially covert relations', including 'sexism and its sharing' (Gutiérrez-Jones 1995: 132–3). This ultimately means that during the movement *carnalismo* was based on an economy of homosocial bonding that explicitly maintained male privilege and denied Chicanas any form of political empowerment (Gutiérrez-Jones 1995: 132–3). In the poem, male bonding and blood relations are likewise defined in relation to the sexist marginalisation of women. Appearing as passive and silent onlookers, women do not appear as autonomous subjects but bear witness to a parade of male heroes who forge history through the ritual of blood and toil. They function to underscore the primacy of the male subject and the importance of forming brotherly bonds. In a similar manner to Lee's (1999) analysis of women's roles and depictions in other nationalist move-ments, women do not contradict the all-male collective, but rather function to secure bonds even as they remain marginal to that bonding (Lee 1999: 17–43). In these terms Chicano history is founded and maintained by the activity of fathers and brothers while women are supplementary to the nationalist cause.

The gendered nature of the *corrido* underscores and substantiates this kind of masculine bias. Limón (1998) argues that the *corrido* is male engendered, not only in terms of imagery, subject matter and the 'principally male-defined performative context', but also in 'the *corrido*'s form . . . [I]ts rigid, repetitive quatrains, [and] its linear, hard driving narrative style' (Limón 1998: 116). Along with these matters of form, the content of Gonzales's narrative also reinforces values and systems of male dominance. On one level this is achieved through the articulation of a male narrator and a masculinist historical tradition. Chronologically, after reconnecting to an indigenous past, Gonzales's text also follows the time frame that Pérez (1999a) considers emphasises the 'great events' of Chicano history at the expense of other sig-nificant occurrences (Pérez 1999a: 8). The series of 'great events' begin with the Spanish conquest of 1521, then the US–Mexican war of 1846–8, followed by the Mexican revolution of 1910 and the Chicano movement of the 1960s. According to Pérez (1999a) this linear 'structure of historical meaning' mani-fests dominant, masculine modes of historical interpretation in a way that subordinates women's politics under a nationalist paradigm (Pérez 1999a: 7–27). By implicitly constructing Chicano identity as predominantly male, and by casting the present and the past as an Anglo–Chicano dichotomy the poet conforms to this logic and consequently disregards other sites of Chicana/o oppression.

During the movement it was not only the writing of history that displayed this pattern of representation but also literature and the modes of thought that underpinned Chicano political activism. In a famous speech made by Gonzales in 1972 he states this ideological positioning more clearly, 'Nationalism is a common denominator', he proclaimed, and nationalism is a 'tool for organisation [that] transcends all boundaries; religious, financial, social, political, and class' (Esquibel 2001: 64). In this and other speeches and writings from the movement years, issues of gender are absent or not addressed except when seen in a negative light. These gendered ideologies were not confined to speeches given by the leaders of the movement alone, but also substantially inform more generally the literary production of the movement decades. In 'Yo soy Joaquín', as a number of literary critics have observed, women are almost wholly excluded, repressed or dehistoricised (Candelaria 1986, Limón 1992, Neate 1998). Confined to stereotypical roles as wife or mother and wearing the traditional black *rebezo*, Gonzales (1967) describes women as being 'faithful [and] humble' (Hernández-Gutiérrez and Foster 1997: 214). At other times in the poem this paternalistic logic is reinforced through the casting of women as cultural icons who were considered to embody these attributes, the Virgin of Guadalupe, or the goddess Tonantsin for example. This definition of women is also characteristic of movement politics, which as I go on to discuss similarly relegated women symbolically to the margins of the nationalist cause.

As previously stated, movement ideology can be strongly related to ideas of phallogocentrism and suppression. According to Cixous the underlying structure of a phallocentric symbolic order is geared towards securing meaning through the repression of the feminine. The patriarchal imaginary and its symbolic register is organised around the privileging of the phallus and so implicitly inscribes the female as an absent and passive second term. In this structure of differences the female is only present in such a way as to confirm the primacy of the male. These phallogocentric modes of thought and ideology have sought to 'ensure for masculine order a rationale equal to history itself' (Marks and de Courtivron 1980: 366–71). Gonzales's poem strongly adheres to this logic as the gendered definitions of the poem reflect and reinforce a discursive order that binds women to culturally sanctioned roles. When women are represented they are done so in terms of traditional gender positions, 'sheltered beneath / her shawl of black / eyes / that bear the pain of sons long buried / or dying / on the battlefield or on the barbed wire / of social strife' (Hernández-Gutiérrez and Foster 1997: 219). In these lines the masculinist bias is mainly evident in the representation of woman as a suffering mother, her anonymity being further accentuated by the traditional black *rebezo* she wears. But male bias is also made manifest in the construction of masculine enterprise as work and in the simultaneous omission of working women. Later in the poem those who 'toil on the earth' and 'work, sweat, bleed' are all exclusively male. As in other nationalist movements, women are not only unrecognised as labour, but, as Lee (1999) suggests, in fact appear the 'other' of labour to the extent that women are 'the abject identity against which male labour defines itself' (Lee 1999: 27).

Despite these gendered ideologies, at one point Gonzales does attempt to construct an androgynous sense of self, suggested by the lines, 'I am in the eyes of woman, / And I am her / and she is me / we face life together in sorrow / anger, joy, faith and wishful thoughts' (Hernández-Gutiérrez and Foster 1997: 220). But despite these overtures towards female positionality, ultimately this is not a transgressive manoeuvre, but instead merely recapitulates woman's objectification. It is noticeable that only the male speaker of the poem is active in any ordinary sense, the woman is seen in terms of passive poses and roles. Within this world of stasis, although both man and woman appear to be fixated on looking, there is an implicit power differential between the two. The male looks and the woman is looked at; she is the object of the male gaze. Thus the Chicano subject in Gonzales' poem can only be fully realised through the reinscription of the gender binary, wherein men and women are created as mutually defining opposites. In this scheme of things, the masculine is associated with activity and the feminine with passivity. Female subjectivity as a consequence merely serves as the ground for the figure of active masculinity, and emerges in second-class terms as the necessary opposite to man.

In recent writing by women, feminist issues often combine with the themes expressed by their earlier male counterparts, including the issues associated with cultural conflict, racial oppression, alienation, and the search for identity expressed in Gonzales' text. At the same time they dispute the fiction of an exclusively male subject and the limited conceptions of female identity promoted by movement discourse. Initially this response took the form of an aggressively asserted oppositional Chicana identity, as in Lorna Dee Cervantes' 'Para un revolucionaro' where she writes,

> You speak of your love of mountains,
> freedom,
> You speak of a new way,
> a new life . . .
> Pero your voice is lost to me, carnal,
> In the wail of tus hijos,
> in the clatter of dishes
> and the pucker of beans upon the stove . . .
> but my hands will be left groping
> for you and your dream in the midst of la revolución.
>   (Rebolledo and Reviro 1993: 151–2)

Further revisions of movement paradigms of female identity can also be found in the work of Alma Villanueva, particularly 'Witches Blood' from the poetry collection *Bloodroot* (1982). Whereas Chicana sexuality and the female body were traditionally repressed by movement ideology, Villanueva celebrates their potential as subversive areas of Chicana identity. Unlike the male bonding effected in terms of bloodshed and violence in Gonzales text, in

'Witches Blood' (1982) Villanueva celebrates the female-to-female bonding effected through menstrual blood:

> Power of my blood, your secret
> wrapped in ancient tongues
> spoken by men who claimed themselves
> gods and priests and oracles – they
> made elaborate rituals
> secret chants and extolled the cycles,
> calling woman unclean.
> men have killed
> made war
> for blood to flow, as naturally
> as a woman's
> once a month.
>   (Rebolledo and Reviro 1993: 219–20)

This section of the poem in one sense parallels the review of Chicano history provided by Gonzales in 'Yo soy Joaquín'. Beginning in 'ancient' times, Villanueva appears to map a similar space and time. The past is characterised by 'cycles', 'rituals', 'gods and priests and oracles', and war. These symbols, traditionally associated with Chicano identity, are recast by the poet and are implicitly associated with the gendered oppression of Chicanas. 'Gods and priests', patriarchy and patriarchal systems are responsible for creating a cosmology that implicitly encodes the subordination of women. Within this system women are labelled 'unclean', thus marginalised they are implicitly positioned as outsiders. Villanueva, in an ironic twist, juxtaposes this assertion with the declaration that 'men have killed', that they have 'made war', in ways that construct a counterargument to the masculinist heroics associated with the blood and bloodshed forwarded during the movement years. In contrast to this male-dominated ideology, menstruation represents the female body's creative possibilities rather than the death and destruction associated with the male blood rights of Gonzales' text. Implicitly, this argument asserts that women's blood is 'natural' and by association that the bloodshed of men is unnatural. In so doing it challenges the narratives of identity presented in 'Yo soy Joaquín' and more generally in movement discourse by positing a more 'natural' and explicitly feminised bloodline and antecedence.

In this and other ways Villanueva presents a reversal of paternalistic logic and movement ideology on a number of different levels. In narratives of identity promoted during the movement years, such as 'Yo soy Joaquín', men and blood are the main progenitors of Chicano identity, while simultaneously symbolically signifying war and death. Villanueva (1982) likewise affirms this connection, but in a critique of this logic she conversely associates women's blood with strong vaginal imagery, such as reproduction, 'birth' and 'power' (Rebolledo and Reviro 1993: 219–20). These images project a wholly subversive function to women's bleeding that subliminally exists as a counterdiscourse outside of the patriarchal inscriptions that open the stanza. Rather than a carrier of cultural material that implicitly encodes the suppression of Chicanas, Villanueva recontextualises and reverses the significance of blood into an ideological expression of cultural and political resistance. Julia Kristeva observes in *Pouvoirs de l'horreur* that menstrual blood is one of the primary forms associated with the abject, which she characterises as 'that which perturbs an identity, a system, an order. That which does not respect limits, places, rules' (Browdy de Hernandez 1998: 247). Villanueva's resignification of women's blood as a source for Chicana identity conforms to this feminist logic. In 'Witches Blood' (1982) she disrupts dominant discourses normally associated with Chicano subjectivity and supplements these with an empowered transgressive Chicana identity. This means that like other Chicana writing, Villanueva's text effectively 'deconstructs and exceeds the individuating narrative of phallocentrism characteristic of movement politics' (Neate 1998: 131).

Among the women writers so far discussed, Anzaldúa (1987) is arguably the most influential regarding these radical transformations in conceptions of Chicana identity. In much the same way as Gonzales in 'Yo soy Joaquín' (1967), in *Borderlands/La Frontera: The New Mestiza* (1987) she often re-asserts a sense of identity through historical associations. In the opening chapter titled 'The Homeland, Aztlán: *El otro México*' she recounts the familiar events of Chicano history, beginning with the migration of Aztec tribes, the founding of the Aztec empire, and the conquest, before proceeding towards a consideration of the annexation of Mexican land following the treaty of Guadalupe Hidalgo. Like the earlier writers this assertion of historical primacy serves to emphasise the land and the mixed race in the construction of Chicana/o identity:

> The *mestizos* . . . founded a new hybrid race and inherited Central and South America. *En 1521 nació una nueva raza, el mestizo, el mexicano* [people of mixed Indian and Spanish blood], a race that had never existed before. Chicanos, Mexican-Americans, are the offspring of those first matings.
>
> (Anzaldúa 1987: 5)

Anzaldúa then appears to initially reaffirm the claims of movement rhetoric implicit in this historical trajectory particularly when she asserts that, 'Today we are witnessing *la migración de los pueblos mexicanos*, the return odyssey to the historical/mythological Aztlán' (Anzaldúa 1987: 11). Yet as the text progresses, this migration does not represent either the same search for, or the perpetuation of origins expressed in the earlier writing.

In the poem 'Sus plumas el viento', it is women's rather than men's history that functions as a signifier for the larger history of the Chicana/o experience in south Texas. Set explicitly within the political and social contexts of the agricultural worker's life, Anzaldúa implicitly positions Chicanas as a transnational labour force within the economies of mercantile, monopoly and, finally, corporate capitalism, 'Swollen feet / tripping on vines in the heat, / palms thick and green-knuckled, / sweat drying on top of old sweat. / She flicks her tongue over upper lip / where the salt stings her cracked mouth' (Anzaldúa 1987: 116). In contrast to Chicano writers of the 1960s and 1970s, whose work was dominated by references to the troubled relationship between male Mexican labour and an American economy, Anzaldúa here presents the material effects experienced by the female workforce. In these lines, the physical being of the Chicana worker demarcates the mutually overdetermining restrictions of race, class and gender as violence done to the female body. The intense itemising of the woman's features emphasise the deeper social implications of labour whereby the body is fractured into a series of component parts by the sheer toil of working in the fields. Yet, in later sections of the poem this partial figuring is effectively challenged by contrasting images of women workers bonding through the singing of *corridos* as they labour on the land, 'She listens to Chula singing *corridos* / making up *los versos* as she / plants down the rows / hoes down the rows / picks down the rows / the chorus resounding for acres and acres / Everyone adding a line' (Anzaldúa 1987: 116–19). By providing a critique of the *corrido*'s entrenched masculine bias through a reappropriation of its content and form, Anzaldúa allows Chicanas to emerge as political subjects in much more dynamic, participatory and antagonistic ways. In subsequent stanzas the juxtaposition of the material conditions of existence in the present with the evocation of Nahua and Mexica cultures from the past, performs a similar function:

> She looks up into the sun's glare,
> *las chuparrosas de los jardines*
> *¿en dondé están de su mamagrande?*
> [Where were the hummingbirds from her grandmother's garden?]
> but all she sees is the obsidian wind
> cut tassels of blood
> from the hummingbird's throat.
>
> (Anzaldúa 1987: 118–19)

Many Chicana writers like Anzaldúa reclaim the indigenous heritage in order to counteract movement discourse as it approached the indigenous past in ways that legitimised the oppression of women. 'Yo soy Joaquín' (1967) as a master narrative of identity served to further entrench this ideology. In a counter-movement Anzaldúa deviates from this by returning to a period in pre-Columbian history prior to the emergence of male dominance as a parallel source for Chicana identity (Neate 1998: 23). Anzaldúa argues that the Aztec legacy idealised by the movement was patriarchal and based on military power and the suppression of the maternal, 'the male dominated Azteca-Mexica culture drove the powerful female deities underground by giving them monstrous attributes and by substituting male deities in their place' (Anzaldúa 1987: 27). She goes on to state that Coatlicue, the serpent goddess of life and death was substituted for Tonantsin, a move that severed the older deity from her darker attributes. Tonantsin, after the Spanish conquest, became Guadalupe, a shift that effectively extracted the essence of Coatlalopeuh or the serpent, and therefore her sexuality from her literal and political representation. Subsequent colonisations by the Spanish completed the deracination and desexualisation of these figures. According to Anzaldúa (1987) this colonial imaginary has created a rigid dichotomy whereby the syncretic Virgin of Guadalupe has become synonymous with the Virgin Mary and thus a chaste and submissive figure, whereas Tlazolteotl/ Coatlicue/*la chingada* have become synonymous with *putas* (whores) (Anzaldúa 1987: 27–8).

Anzaldúa's critique in this section of the text demonstrates how alterations to certain foundational myths were transformed by the politics of the movement into a discourse that denigrated women's gender and sexuality. By resurrecting the older Meso-American symbology Anzaldúa reinscribes an empowered Chicana identity through what Alarcón (1996) terms 'a reinscription of gynetics' (Alarcón 1996: 48). In the poem 'Sus plumas el viento' the reinscription of the mother performs a similar function. The mother, figured as a continuation of the indigenous past, together with the vision of women workers bonding through the singing of *corridos*, is a strategy that allows Chicanas to emerge as political subjects in much more dynamic, participatory and antagonistic ways.

Providing a critique of the *corrido*'s patriarchal ideology through a reappropriation of its content and form, Anzaldúa deconstructs the gender roles and subject positions assigned to women by movement discourse. In her other writing this reconfiguration is more obviously expressed as a new and more radical perspective on the dynamics of interracial mixing in the construction of Chicana/o mestiza/o identity. As we have seen prior representations of *mestizaje* and the mestizo subject contained differences within selected racial identities that presupposed a confluence based on equal mixtures of Spanish and Indian blood. Anzaldúa complicates this model of identity in a number of different ways. In the poem 'To Live in the Borderlands Means You' the relations between races are figured as fluid, making the mestiza subject neither Hispanic (hispana), Indian (*india*), black (*negra*), Spanish (*española*) or white (*gabacha*), but a 'half-breed' mixed race that moves outside of the prescribed racial parameters of nationalist ideology, 'you / are neither *hispana india negra española / ni gabacha, eres mestiza, mulata,* half-breed' (Anzaldúa 1987: 194). The components of this 'mulatta' identity, particularly the inclusion of the white race, clearly contradicts the Chicano–Anglo dichotomy of the movement years, when whiteness was openly repudiated and most often associated with ideas of conquest and colonisation. Such representations of whiteness also interrupt the racist power structure that conditions the beliefs and practices surrounding miscegenation and whiteness in both the Mexican and US contexts. Referring to the *afromestizo* roots of Chicano ancestry through the inclusion of the black race also constitutes a substantially different perspective on Chicana and Chicano identity from that of the earlier texts.

Ultimately, this more racially inclusive vision while having the effect of disrupting existing anti-miscegenation and racialised power hierarchies, simultaneously extends the possibilities of Chicana/o identity by developing what Anzaldúa terms a 'new species' that has a 'skin tone between black and bronze' (Anzaldúa 1987: 202). Significantly, this 'new species' bears comparison with the identity politics forwarded by *El Plan Espiritual de Aztlán* (1969) which also stated that the Chicano people were 'a bronze people with a bronze culture' (Anaya and Lomelí 1989: 1). Tactically the adoption of the colour bronze was meant to emphasise the pride in racial mixture and to offset the majority's pride in racial purity. Arguably Anzaldúa's 'new species' that has a 'skin tone between black and bronze' represents a similar strategy. Yet in spite of this, her use of the term 'half-breed' in her description of the borderlands subject is problematic, as the new mestiza appears to be progressing towards this as a logical outcome or synthesis of its various racial parts. On the one hand reclaiming the derogatory term 'half-breed' repudiates the racialised power relations embedded in the history of colonisation in both Mexican and US history. While on the other hand the term 'half-breed', as Yarbro-Bejarano (2001) states in another context, also 'relies heavily on a biologised, genetic discourse of race and racial purity' (Yarbro-Bejarano 2001: 11). In this sense Anzaldúa appears to base Chicana identity on limited biological criteria in a way that produces a dichotomised mixed-race subject along the lines of earlier discourse. The descriptions of the new mestiza clearly bears comparison to the synthetic racial composition illustrated in Gonzales's text. The new mestiza, she states, is someone who 'copes by developing a tolerance for contradictions, a tolerance for ambiguity. . . . Not only does she sustain contradictions, she turns the ambivalence into something else' (Anzaldúa 1987: 79). The mixing of races is thus figured, like that of the earlier writers, as a process during which racial contradictions converge and are transformed into a higher or more enlightened *mestizaje*.

Any seemingly definitive statements made on this issue are, however, immediately undermined by further modifying or qualifying factors. The multiple constitutive elements of the 'new mestiza' are never in stasis but move between and across categories of race, sexuality and gender, in ways that clearly subvert the masculinist and racially dichotomised subject of the movement years. In the following chapter I explore this response in more detail by discussing Chicano and Chicana dramatic production. As a genre that has traditionally lent itself to protest, drama also readily evolved in conjunction with movement ideology and produced didactic representations of Chicano identity. Following an analysis of Luis Valdez's *Zoot Suit*, the chapter traces how in the decade of the 1980s, drama developed alternative perspectives and provided an arena for the articulation of far more radical conceptions of Chicana/o identity.

5 Mexican American theatre and the politics of Chicana/o identity

In the following chapter I read the play *Zoot Suit* (1992) by Luis Valdez as a reflection of movement politics, particularly in its gendered representation of identity. The play is contextualised in terms of its radical critique of historical events as well as some of the more dominant concerns of the movement. I then go on to read Cherríe Moraga's *Giving up the Ghost* (1986) as a counter-discursive critique of *Zoot Suit's* political configuration. As I go on to show, it is important to place Moraga's text in this context in order to more fully explore its disruption of Chicano theatrical canons as well as dominant narratives of identity proposed during the movement decades.

Chicano drama evolved in conjunction with the more militant activities of the movement, and so overtly reflected its political ideology (Neate 1998, Xavier 1999). At that time the most important and influential theatre was the political drama of Luis Valdez and his oppositional group the Teatro Campesino (Farm Workers' Theatre). From 1965 to 1967 Valdez's theatre group was directly linked to the farm workers' struggle in California, and his satirical skits known as *actos* focused solely on farm-labour problems. But by 1967 the bond between Teatro Campesino and the UFW was severed, first, by the leader of the farm workers, César Chávez, who made it clear that the UFW did not support Valdez's leanings towards Chicano nationalism, and, second, by Valdez himself, whose own ambitions led him to move away from the struggles associated with farm workers and towards other sites of oppression. As the Chicano movement gained momentum, activism from other quarters suggested that the content of the plays had to be expanded, and Valdez was also aware that the vast majority of Chicanos lived in cities and that it was this urban-based audience who were most likely to be sympathetic to his politics and forms of cultural expression.

In Los Angeles the politics of the times were characterised by organisations such as the Brown Berets, the Chicano Moratorium Committee and the Centro de Acción Social Autónomo, or CASA, by student walkouts, or 'blowouts' as they were called, and by mass protests such as the Chicano Moratorium Against the Vietnam War. A climate of political surveillance by agents of the FBI and other intelligence agencies, and of government harassment through their paid informants and provocateurs also dominated the events (Muñoz 1989, Chávez 2002). According to Chávez (2002), the Brown Berets, were 'plagued by harassment from law-enforcement authorities and weakened by infiltrators' (Chávez 2002: 60). The reason being 'the FBI's belief (shared by other law enforcement agencies) that the Berets were controlled by "rabble rousing" Mexican Americans who were apt to incite "racial violence", [and] pose a threat to national security' (Chávez 2002: 60). Yet it was during this turbulent period that Valdez began to play a pivotal role in the formation of Chicano identity politics. He founded the theatre group TENAZ and contributed a prolific dramatic output, including a screenplay for the movement epic, *Yo soy Joaquín* (an adaptation of 'Corky' Gonzalez's poem, 'I Am Joaquín'), which also won Valdez a national film award in 1971. It was *Zoot Suit* in 1974, however, which became his most commercially successful play to date.

Zoot Suit is a play in two acts divided into twenty sections. Like much movement writing it returns to a decisive phase in the Mexican American experience for its sources. The Sleepy Lagoon murder trial of 1942 and the subsequent zoot-suit riots that erupted in East Los Angeles, and other cities a year later, profoundly affected the community of the east side barrios and represent one of the many miscarriages of justice in Chicano history. Gutiérrez (1995) states that,

> The Zoot Suit Riots referred to a period of violence between American servicemen and Mexican American youths that took place between June 3 and June 13 in downtown and east Los Angeles . . . [T]he events were widely publicised in the local and national press as yet another example of Mexicans' inherent barbarity, hooliganism, and questionable loyalty.
> (Gutiérrez 1995: 124)

In keeping with the intense paranoia of wartime America, the media allegations inevitably linked the wearers of the zoot suit (termed *pachucos*) with a complicated international conspiracy to overthrow the USA. As one member of the prosecution in the play puts it:

> The City of Los Angeles is caught in the midst of the biggest, most terrifying crime in its history. We are dealing with a threat and danger to our children, our families, our homes. Set these pachucos free, and you shall unleash the forces of anarchy and destruction in our society.
> (Valdez 1992: 62)

In the Sleepy Lagoon trial, which one character in the play describes as 'the largest mass trial in the history of Los Angeles county', twenty-two youths were tried on sixty-six charges and were wrongfully indicted for the murder of another gang member, Jose Diaz, and sent to prison. The riots, which emerged as a result of the trial, consisted of the mass beating and stripping of young Mexican Americans wearing zoot suits by groups of US servicemen exuding patriotic fervour. Conversely, general opinion as to what had occurred almost unanimously blamed the riots on the Mexican American youth (Vargas 1999: 302–3).

The young Mexican Americans who wore zoot suits embodied all the characteristics of second-generation Mexican urban working-class immigrants. Sometimes called *cholos*, but more often called *pachucos*, they were characterised by their sense of alienation from mainstream America, most obviously by their use of hybrid slang known as *calo*, by their tattoos and by their distinctive suits. These over-exaggerated business suits expressed the complexity of Chicano positioning at a transitional historical moment. During the 1930s the continued immigration of Mexicans into the USA contributed to the creation of a distinctive barrio culture in Los Angeles, particularly in Belvedere and Boyle Heights, which became important settings for the definition of Chicano identity (Sanchez 1993, Griswold del Castillo and de León 1996, Ruiz 1998, Gonzales 2000). These areas were also distinguished by racial restrictions, class barriers, poor and congested housing, and police repression. Encountering such racial discrimination only strengthened the quest for identity among the Mexican American youth and in effect provided a unique context for the development of the *pachuco* gang (Sanchez 1993: 272).

Rather than disguise their sense of alienation from this set of circumstances, the *pachucos* openly flaunted their difference, and the zoot suit by its very oppositional nature became the means by which that difference was most visibly encoded. The suits consisted of the *tacuche* or finger-length jacket with padded shoulders and wide lapels, the *tramos* or trousers with pegged pant legs, the *calcos*, thick or triple-soled shoes with metal taps, and the *tando* or wide-brimmed pancake hat worn over a ducktail haircut. This distinctive dress style exacerbated racial tensions in Los Angeles, which since the events of Pearl Harbor had been especially volatile. Within such a political climate it represented a subversion of US authority on a number of economic, cultural and national levels. In an attempt to cut back on the use of fabric, the War Production Board announced the production of what *Esquire* magazine called 'streamlined suits by Uncle Sam' (Vargas 1999: 318). In this sense, as Mazón (1984) states, 'It was iconoclastic, taunting; a statement of narcissism, omnipotence, and over compensation. It represented a state of being popularly perceived as unrestricted and uninhibited' (Mazón 1984: 64). Significantly, Paz (1967) in a similar manner to this also considered the *pachucos'* appearance and stance as being 'an empty gesture' and 'a failure of identity' (Paz 1967: 5–7). In *The Labyrinth of Solitude* he considers them to be between national and cultural identities, neither 'authentic Mexicans' nor 'inauthentic Americans' but 'existential casualt[ies]', who were 'without parentage' (Paz 1967: 5–7). He goes on to state that 'they were sheer negative impulse, a tangle of contradictions . . . saying nothing and saying everything' (Paz 1967: 5–7).

By contrast, in the play Valdez reinvests *pachucos* with subversive characteristics. The lead figure 'El Pachuco' is an almost constant presence; he serves as a continual commentator on the action and provides the incarcerated gang leader, Henry Reyna, with inner strength during his trial and sub-sequent solitary confinement. El Pachuco's opening speech, delivered in a mixture of *calo* and English, clearly articulates his central importance to the forthcoming action, and simultaneously inscribes a particular form of *pachuco* identity politics:

> ¿Que le watcha a mis trapos ese?
> ¿Sabe qué, carnal?
> Estas garras me las planté porque
> Vamos a dejarnos caer un play, ¿sabe?
> *(HE crosses to center stage, models his clothes.)*
> Watcha mi tacuche, ese. Aliviánese con mis calcos tando lisa, tramos, y carlango, ese.
> (Pause.)
> Nel, sabe qué, usted está muy verdolaga. Como se me hace que es puro square.
>
> (Valdez 1992: 25)

Although more widely used now, *calo* originally signified a particular form of *pachuco* self-referentiality, being a mixture of different languages including archaic Spanish slang, thought to derive originally from the conquistadores, Aztec or Nahuatl languages, Portuguese, and corruptions of English and contemporary Spanish (Sanchez 1994). El Pachuco's prologue, together with the directions for the stage settings clearly sets the tone of the play and foreshadows much of the action:

> SETTING
> The giant facsimile of a newspaper front page serves as a drop curtain.
> The huge masthead reads: LOS ANGELES HERALD EXPRESS Thursday, June 3, 1943. A headline cries out: ZOOT-SUITER HORDES INVADE LOS ANGELES. US NAVY AND MARINES ARE CALLED IN. A switchblade plunges through the newspaper. It slowly cuts a rip to the bottom of the drop. EL PACHUCO emerges from the slit. HE adjusts his clothing, HE tends to his hair, with infinite loving pains. Then HE reaches into the slit and pulls out his coat and hat. Now HE turns to the audience. HE proudly, slovenly, defiantly makes his way downstage. HE stops and assumes a pachuco stance.
>
> (Valdez 1992: 24)

In his analysis of the play Huerta argues that the setting and prop design indicate the degree to which the Los Angeles newspapers and the national media contributed to the hostilities by demonising *pachucos* during the trial and subsequent riots (Valdez 1992: 15). Indeed several scenes substantiate this claim and have actors and actresses moving towards the audience holding sensationalised front-page headlines and editorial accounts that emphasise Mexican immigration, delinquency and gangsterism. These headings are at the same time juxtaposed with contrasting accounts of allied activities in the war effort, which are infused with fifth-column rhetoric and increasingly depict the *pachuco* youth as the 'enemy within'.

Gutiérrez-Jones (1995) on the other hand interprets these scenes from a slightly different perspective. He states that by highlighting the media's racial bias in this way, Valdez counterbalances the widespread belief that the zoot-suiters were guilty of deviating from what was an otherwise fair and democratic society (Gutiérrez-Jones 1995: 44). The fact that the trial is presented as a breach of legitimate judicial procedures further emphasises this point. Despite the lack of any concrete evidence, an all-white jury indicts seventeen gang members for first-degree murder during courtroom proceedings that were clearly racially biased. This is most obviously reflected in the uncompromising efforts of the prosecution to stigmatise and pathologise the defendants. During the interrogation it is suggested that the young Mexican Americans are 'greasers', 'animals', and 'monkeys' (Valdez 1992: 32). Additionally it is suggested that they have 'twisted minds' and are capable of 'assault [and] more violence' (Valdez 1992: 62). The prosecution lawyer also manipulates evidence, openly intimidates the defendants, and draws attention to their zoot suits as evidence of guilt. The fact that the judge at the same time prevents the defendants from changing their clothes adds to this circumstantial evidence (Gutiérrez-Jones 1995: 47). First, this accentuates their 'criminality' making them appear in the words of the gang leader, 'bad [and] disreputable, like mobsters', and, second, it strips them of their identity. In this sense, the court's actions mirror the events of the zoot-suit riots themselves, when the *pachucos* were similarly demonised and 'symbolically annihilated, castrated, transformed and otherwise rendered the subject of effigial rites' (Mazón 1984: 64).

Valdez counters this derogatory perspective with a number of positive assertions related to matters of racial and cultural identity, which are staged in a number of different ways and on a number of differing levels, and it would be fair to say with varying degrees of success. Of these arguably the most successful strategy employed by Valdez concerns the symbolic reclamation of space. In the play the city of Los Angeles is often referred to affectionately as 'los' or 'el lay', 'the brown metropolis', and at one point given its original Spanish name 'el pueblo de nuestra señora la reina de los Angeles de porciúncula' (The town of Our Lady the Queen of the Angels de *porciúncula*) (Valdez 1992: 28). So, one could argue that in response to spatial, cultural and ideological invasion by American forces the east-side barrio is figured by Valdez as being profoundly Chicano. It appears as a mythologised geographic and cultural space that embodies family ties, Chicano music and dance styles. Collectively, these facets of barrio life create a space of ethnic solidarity and a positive assertion of Chicano identity. Its vibrancy and freedom effectively form a contrast to the confinement and repression of various institutionalised spaces that are also figured throughout the drama, such as the courtroom, the prison and the cell. Through this series of oppositions the play's spatial representations establish visual images that effect a symbolic displacement of the ideological basis that legitimised the unequal treatment and status of Mexicans in the USA.

Historically, Mexicans were considered to be culturally predisposed towards certain pathological and antisocial forms of behaviour. One lieutenant of the sheriff's department, Ed Duran Ayers, famously attempted to compound these beliefs. While testifying before the grand jury he overtly linked the *pachucos'* behaviour with that of their pre-Columbian ancestors by presenting a discourse on genetics that supposedly proved their shared disposition towards cold-blooded murder:

> The biological basis is the main basis to work from. When the Spaniards conquered Mexico they found an organised society composed of many tribes of Indians ruled over by the Aztecs who were given over to human sacrifice. Historians record that as many as 30,000 Indians were sacrificed in one day. This total disregard for human life has always been universal throughout the Americas among the Indian population which of course is well known to everyone . . . Representatives of the Mexican colony may be loathe to admit this [but] again let us repeat; the hoodlum element as a whole must be indicted as a whole . . . it is just as essential to incarcerate every member of a particular gang, whether there be 10 or 50, as it is to incarcerate one or two of the ringleaders.
>
> (Vargas 1999: 310)

Perhaps the most effective but also problematic attempt to counter Ayers' disquisition occurs in Act II Scene 6, when El Pachuco is stripped of his zoot suit by a group of sailors and appears not as a beaten gang member but as a god-like descendent of the Aztecs:

> (They fight now to the finish.) EL PACHUCO is overpowered and stripped as HENRY watches helplessly from his position. The PRESS and SERVICEMEN exit with pieces of EL PACHUCO'S zoot suit. EL PACHUCO stands. The only item of clothing on his body is a small loincloth. HE turns and looks at HENRY, with mystic intensity. HE opens his arms as an Aztec conch blows, and HE slowly exits backward with powerful calm into the shadows.
>
> (Valdez 1992: 81)

With this climactic conversion scene Valdez places the *pachuco* within a specific ideological locus. The gesture of ennobling Chicanos with pre-Columbian attributes was a well-used strategy throughout the movement, and instilled a sense of pride, historical identity and provided an antidote to racism. The subject position Valdez creates here, then, is on one level oppositional to the kind of discourse perpetrated by the courts. Rather than signalling a series of pathologies, pre-Columbian attributes instil in the *pachuco* a subliminal power. Thus charged and justified by the identity politics of the Chicano movement, he is able to transcend the barrio hierarchy, from the socially deviant gang member as seen from the perspective of the judge, prosecution and American servicemen, into a god-like and sacrificial entity.

But while redefining the *pachuco*'s place within a larger framework of the 'social drama' of emancipation and self-determination of the 1960s and 1970s, *Zoot Suit* itself reinscribes a repressive ideology. Much of its rhetoric, like that of the movement, contains an underlying dynamic that aims to recover manhood. Neither the monumentalised and phallicised figure of the *pachuco* or the indigenous spirituality of the male Aztec warrior presents a balance of power in gendered terms, but instead upholds a patriarchal discourse that fed into the identity politics of the movement during its most influential years. At this time myths of descent were inflected by a perception of the cultural past as a privileged site where configurations of masculinity and identity merged. The hagiography of the pre-Columbian past served to endorse a cultural legacy that embraced machismo and paternalism as unifying facets of Chicano identity. The combined effects of male domination and Chicano nationalism that shaped *el teatro*'s productions effectively replicated these tendencies.

One of the most overt expressions of this ideology can be seen in the way that *Zoot Suit* mirrors the emphasis placed on the interlinking systems of *carnalismo* (brotherhood), machismo and *familia* (family) by movement politics. During the movement displays of *carnalismo* cemented the relations between men, while culturally organising gender in such a way as to facilitate women's exclusion. Ideologically then, *carnalismo* worked to define all gender in relation to a clear and unambiguous male identity. At the same time *carnalismo* worked towards defining the Chicano community 'as a social group consensually unified around a reverence for machismo' (Gutiérrez-Jones 1995: 134). Rendón, author of the highly polemical *Chicano Manifesto* (1972), stated this connection more explicitly. Machismo, he explained 'is in fact an underlying drive of the gathering identification of Mexican Americans . . . the essence of *machismo*, of being *macho*, is as much a symbolic principle for the Chicano revolt as it is a guideline for family life' (de la Torre and Pesquera 1993: 41). Yet claiming machismo as the fundamental dynamic of the movement was problematic, and set into motion a system of gender differentiation designed to maintain a form of male power over women's subjugation. A significant proportion of male literary production both during and after the movement decades reinforced this notion, the family figuring prominently in its representations as a paternalistic and largely conservative unit.

In many ways *Zoot Suit* overtly illustrates this point. Huerta argues how in detailing the arrests and subsequent incarceration of Henry Reyna,

Zoot Suit also indirectly depicts a Chicano family in crisis (Valdez 1992: 15). Yet in the play the problems the Reyna's face are also quite deliberately counterpoised by the many allusions to the bonds of *familia*, its strengths and values, and its abiding links with the community. In this sense the Reyna family closely conforms to the politically sanctioned myth of *la familia* as a safe haven and locus of culture. As previously suggested, this myth worked towards masking the heterosexually configured structure within which a distinct gendered and sexual hierarchy subordinated women. Following this logic the father is depicted as being central to the Reyna home; he dominates his wife and daughter; he also silences them and frequently evokes the masculine heroes of, as well as his own experiences of, the Mexican revolution (Valdez 1992: 35). This again mirrors movement ideology, which not only drew heavily on the rhetoric of the Mexican revolution, but also sustained the power of the father in both public and private spheres.

The Reyna *familia* also closely follows the polarities of movement rhetoric in the sense that male and female are locked into symbolically loaded pairings. In relation to the male subject, woman is represented as other (that which is not male) and as an object of male desire. *Zoot Suit* thus tends to reinforce the centrality of male subjectivity at the expense of and in relation to woman's status as object. This means that by and large women are relegated to the roles of reproduction within the organisational structures of the household and the traditional familial order. They are thus organised in a symbolic system that defines the worthiness of the female body in terms of its sexual functioning and reproductive ends.

Within this symbolic system, Henry Reyna's mother Dolores is stereotyped as *una madrecita sufrida* (the suffering mother) who endures the aggression of barrio violence and endless domestic labour. Her labour however, is overridden by her symbolic designation as mother and by implication also her potential as the wellspring of brotherly bonds. Her specificity as a female subject as well as her labour are thus subordinate to her role as mother and nurturer of men. Lupe, Henry's sister is another case in point as she is forbidden to wear the drapes of the zoot suit, and is told by Enrique her father that things are, 'Different for Henry . . . He's a man. *Es hombre . . . Bien macho*! Like his father' (Valdez 1992: 35). Henry's girlfriend Della also offers another instance of this ideology at work as she plays a relatively submissive, even self-sacrificial role and enacts certain cultural ideals that in turn inculcate the legitimacy of gender hierarchies.

These good women are in turn counterpoised by Valdez's representation of the bad women archetypes. These include the highly sexualised figure of the white woman Alice who is described as being 'just a dumb broad only good for you know what', as well as the character Bertha who is the male *pachuco*'s female counterpart (Valdez 1992: 49). She is represented by Valdez in typically limited terms as an exaggerated and hyper-sexed female. This stereotype, as Fregoso points out (1999), effectively prohibits any meaningful interpretation of women's subjectivity and positions them instead as overdetermined figures of libidinal excess (Kaplan et al. 1999: 81).

In *Zoot Suit* then, women are figured in terms that seem to suggest that they are only necessary as counterparts to the full performance of masculinity. In this sense Valdez promotes an exclusively male version of events, and as such a perspective that reflected the essentialising tendencies of movement ideology which dichotomised a 'monolithic' male Chicano identity in response to American domination. Clearly, in such a political climate women's politics faced stiff opposition. Although they had been calling attention to their specific gendered oppression, as previously stated race and class issues were seen as being more important and feminist issues, being closely allied to white feminism, were considered divisive. Homosexual and gay issues were also by and large absent from the political programme of the movement, and attempts to gain recognition were largely ignored. Lesbian sexuality in particular became outlawed and was seen as a disruption of woman's role as reproducer, a function deemed necessary for the reconstitution of Chicano masculinity and culture.

Cherríe Moraga's dramatic output consistently produces an alternative model of gender relations to this male-centred vision. Widely considered to be instrumental in bringing about 'a distinct transitional phase' in the development of Chicano theatre, her 1984 play, *Giving up the Ghost*, suggests the emergence of significantly new representational strategies and modes of performativity that clearly move beyond the confines of movement ideology (Arrizón 1999: 76). While evolving in relationship to the *teatro* of Valdez, Moraga's approach to the representation of women is also clearly informed by Chicana feminism. This effectively disrupts the repressive enactment of female identity in ways that undermine rather than collude with *el teatro's* Oedipal economy and articulation of its own patriarchal law.

The action of *Giving up the Ghost* takes place over a period of years in East Los Angeles. While this urban space resembles that of the earlier play, it is not associated with the *chicanismo* of *Zoot Suit*. There are nonetheless productive tensions between the plays' spatiality as the opening speaker tells us that the action, like that in the earlier play, also revolves around the question of 'prison, politics and sex' (Moraga 1986: 1). Unlike *Zoot Suit*, however, the prison to which the speaker refers designates the repressive coding given to women by movement ideology. Moraga's stage directions emphasise this as the play centres on limited locations within which the female characters move. These locations, which are described as 'the street, a bed, a kitchen', reflect the three main spaces offered to women by movement discourse, and indicate a prescriptive and rigidly defined conception of female identity. As Anzaldúa (1987) states in another context, 'for a woman of my culture there used to be only three directions she could turn: to the church as a nun, to the streets as a prostitute, or to the home as a mother' (Anzaldúa 1987: 17).

The action of *Giving up the Ghost* revolves around these spaces as much as the three female characters and the relationships between them. But in contrast to the conventions and limitations of prior theatrical depictions of Chicana subjectivity, two of the characters are one and the same person. Marisa is a Chicana in her late twenties; Corky, her 'other' pubescent and adolescent self, is a *pachuca* at ages eleven and seventeen years old. The other character Amalia is a middle-aged Mexican woman who is Marisa's lover. Although men are marginal to the narrative, Amalia's past male lovers, Alejandro and Carlos, haunt her, to the extent that they constantly interrupt the development of a fully erotic relationship with her lover Marisa. At the opening of the play Marisa declares that the figure of the male lover 'is a ghost / always haunting her . . . lingering' (Moraga 1986: 3). And again later in Act I when Amalia learns of Alejandro's death she simultaneously feels her womanhood leave her and his ghost being born in her:

> When I learned of Alejandro's death,
> I died too, weeks later.
> I just started bleeding and the blood wouldn't stop,
> not until his ghost had passed through me
> or was born in me
> I don't know which.
> [*pause*] Except since then,
> I feel him living in me
> Every time I touch *la Marisa*
> I felt my womanhood leave me.
> Does this make sense?
> And it was Alejandro being born in me.
> (Moraga 1986: 27)

Judith Butler might call the reappearance of Amalia's lovers 'the normative phantasm of a compulsory heterosexuality', which in the play re-emerges like the 'return of the repressed' to haunt Marisa and Amalia's relationship (Arrizón 1999: 137). The sense of entrapment within this symbolic order is contextualised through the strong association established between heterosexuality and loss and melancholia. Amalia later refers to the men who have used her sexually as a river of dead bodies, and through repeated allusions the predominant tone associated with heterosexuality becomes one of silence, trauma and death.

If the men represent the ghosts that Amalia must give up, then the ghost Marisa must relinquish is her younger self, Corky, who is a young *pachuca*. When she appears she is dressed in the *chuca* style of the 1960s, she also speaks in *calo* and is generally depicted as a streetwise, defiant, and dangerous character:

> the smarter I get the older I get the meaner I get tough . . .
> sometimes I even pack a blade no one knows

I never use it or nut'ing but can feel it there
there in my pants pocket
run the pad of my thumb over it
to remind me I carry some'ting
am sharp secretly.

(Moraga 1986: 4)

Despite this cool and tough exterior, Corky and her experiences of rape and oppression is one of the ghosts to be given up in Moraga's play. The memory of these experiences as a young girl haunt her older self Marisa in the form of a pain that disables her, making her legs feel 'like they got rocks in em' (Moraga 1986: 7). In tracing the events that lead to this disablement, chronology in the sense of a teleological narrative and normative temporality are largely displaced from the plot action. Despite running contemporary to Corky's adolescence, the history and politics of the Chicano movement are decentred from the action because they don't enter the protagonist's world. As a young gay Chicana, Corky's connection to the Chicano movement would have at best been slim or non-existent. Instead Moraga displaces an overarching historicising narrative such as that presented in *Zoot Suit* with several personal narratives, which instead present multiple interpretations that subvert established masculinist interpretations of the Chicano experience and of Chicano identity politics.

The juxtaposition of past and present narratives and subjectivities also fragments the essentialised female subject of movement discourse (Neate 1998: 201). Throughout the drama, the social roles of women and men are constantly undermined through complex and ironic manipulations of normative expectations about sexuality and gender. At one point during Act I, Corky's older self Marisa declares that, 'It's not that you don't want a man, / You just don't want a man in a man. / You want a man in a woman. / The woman-part goes without saying. / That's what you always learn to want first' (Moraga 1986: 29). These gender transgressive positions can be read as a radical critique of designations of female sexuality by movement ideology, which promoted a binary logic that legitimised the oppression of women. Marisa's viewpoint in contrast is not conventionally dichotomised by movement dogma, but sexualised in a way that undermines normative expectations. The interchangeably butch–femme relationship between Amalia and Marisa present sexualities that are crucial to Moraga's unsettling of the 'violent hierarchy of the man–woman' dyad on a number of different levels. In one sense they enact a performance that parodies the entrenched inequalities of the phallic economy represented by the traditional heterosexual partnership. But in a more culturally specific sense their relationship, based as it is on 'wanting the woman first', is also a symbolic inversion of the Chicano cultural mandate of 'putting the male first' within Chicano families. Within this economy the mother is the betrayer of the daughter by loving the males in the family more than the females, thus bearing responsibility for the daughter's subordination and abandonment. In her essay 'A Long Line of Vendidas' (1983) Moraga states this more explicitly, 'You are a traitor to your race if you do not put the man first. The potential accusation of "traitor" or "vendida" is what hangs above the heads and beats in the hearts of most Chicanas' (Moraga 1983: 103). Under the pressure of the conflation of her sexuality with betrayal, the Chicana must prove her fidelity through commitment to the Chicano male, thereby initiating what Moraga famously terms 'A Long Line of Vendidas'. By putting women first in her dramatic productions, by excluding men from representation, and by imaging women as desiring subjects, Moraga represents the possibility of liberation from this 'prison of sex'.

Her strategies of female representation are an inherent part of this liberating project. Among the most significant is the simultaneous appropriation and critique of the symbolism associated with Mexican Catholicism. Inverting the church's inherently patriarchal ideology, it becomes an important source for a Chicana lesbian identity (Yarbro-Bejarano 2001: 90). During the play women and women-centred relationships are often expressed in religious terms as a site of worship or as a 'liberating angel' and are said to offer 'salvation' and 'redemption'. At one point during the second act titled 'La Salvadora' Marisa declares that 'Sí. La Mujer es mi religion', and later she places her mother at its centre, '"n' it was so nice to hear her voice / so warm like she loved us a lot / 'n' that night / being cath-lic felt like my mom / real warm 'n' dark 'n' kind' (Moraga 1986: 13). In this scene Moraga shifts the relations of power from the patriarchal conventions normally associated with Mexican Catholicism, to Marisa's mother who is instead figured as the source of religiosity. This feminisation of religion subverts the macho ethic of *aguantar* (forbearance) and subservience normally associated with the church. The connection between the mother's faith and the daughter's faith in a vision of women bonding also disrupts the usual hierarchies established between God and the priest who exercises the secular control of religious power. By implication this also severs the ties that are normally established between the church's institutionalised authority and its enactment through daily sexual domination.

Closely related to this positive identification between women and religion are the passages that describe the love between the female characters. In these scenes the relations between women are often figured as fluid and in opposition to the gendered binaries of movement logic. As Yarbro-Bejarano states (2001), Moraga's characters represent 'non-binary giving and taking in sex within a butch-femme erotics' (Yarbro-Bejarano 2001: 89). These erotic exchanges occur particularly in the scenes where Marisa and Amalia are collectively remembering the discovery of their shared desire for each other. At one point Marisa asks Amalia, 'was the beautiful woman / in the mirror of the water / you or me? / who do I make love to? / Who do I see in the ocean of our bed?' (Moraga 1986: 27). The breaking down of physical borders and the merging of one self with another represents a link between a lack of boundaries and female sexuality that undermines dominant narratives of identity promoted during the movement years. In keeping with this logic, when the action switches to the movement period, we are shown how as a younger woman, Marisa's sexual identity then was also multiple, complex and subversive. At times this complexity is revealed through the performance of what she calls her 'movie capture games' (Moraga 1986: 9). These 'sick little fantasies' ultimately disclose an identity that problematises the dominant interpretations of female subjectivity in movement discourse:

> When I was a little kid I useta love the movies
> every Saturday you could find me there
> my eyeballs glued to the screen
> then during the week my friend Tudy and me
> we'd make up our own movies
> one of our favourites was this cowboy one
> where we'd be out in the desert
> 'n' we'd capture these chicks 'n' hold 'em up
> for ransom we'd string 'em up 'n'
> make 'em take their clothes off . . .
> strip we'd say to the wall
> all cool-like
> in my mind I was big 'n' tough 'n' a dude
> in my mind I had all their freedom
> the freedom to really see a girl
> kinda the way you see
> an animal you know?
>
> (Moraga 1986: 4–5)

Within Chicana/o discourse American movies are often presented as symbols of the US colonial legacy. Within this economy representations of Mexicans have traditionally been stereotyped and limited (Fregoso 1993, Limón 1998, Benjamin-Labarthe 2000, Tonn 2000). The domination of the cowboy in the narrative of the American West is a particularly clear indicator of the ways in which US cultural imperialism has historically operated. The cowboy has effectively erased the presence of the *vaquero* and substituted that historical figure with a colonising figure who eventually came to preside over the south-western landscape. Corky's fantasy fails to acknowledge this fact and therefore displays none of the traditionally vexed intersections between Hispano, American, Indian and Mexican cultures normally associated with this process. Instead, Corky appears to conform to the logic of colonialism in a number of different ways.

Before considering the implications of this tendency in further detail, I want to turn first to an analysis of how film has impacted on other constructions of *pachuco* identity. In particular, I want to consider Jose Montoya's elegy to a dead *pachuco* titled *El Louie*, which was published in 1969, as it also turns to American cinema as a source for self-representation:

> En Sanjo you'd see him
> sporting a dark topcoat
> playing in his fantasy
> the role of Bogart, Cagney
> or Raft.
>
> And Louie would come through—
> melodramatic music, like in the
> mono – tan tan taran! – Cruz
> Diablo, El Charro Negro! Bogart
> smile . . . He dug roles, man,
> and names – like 'Blackie,' 'Little Louie . . .'
> Ese Louie . . .
> Chale, call me 'Diamonds!' man!
> (Hernández-Gutiérrez and Foster 1997: 224–6)

As both Montoya's and Moraga's quotations illustrate, *pachuca/o* identity is formed through a process of negotiation between real and imagined, Mexican and American cultures. It was largely because of this process that Montoya's poem provoked extensive argument concerning questions of authenticity, resistance and identity both during and after the movement years (Limón 1992: 106–9). Bruce-Novoa (1985) considers that *El Louie* 'serves as an excellent paradigm for Chicano literature' (Bruce-Novoa 1985: 81). Yet Limón (1992) disagrees with this and states that *El Louie* is 'diminished as [a] socio-political statement[s] . . . for little is said or even implied . . . about a political "life-struggle" against a racist society' (Limón 1992: 107). Moreover, as Limón goes on to state, there are no 'imperatives for social resistance', within the work, instead the poem depicts 'a world of intracommunity violence, which while socially conditioned is nonetheless also self-generated and certainly self-inflicted' (Limón 1992: 107).

Certainly *El Louie* appears to embody none of the pre-Columbian attributes of nationalist discourse, but instead in the main relies on American heroics as a source for self-identification. To what extent this presents a critique of, or recapitulation towards white identification remains ambiguous. Critical opinion over the role of popular culture in the construction of Chicano identity is deeply divided. Within the Chicana/o context, some critics consider that mass entertainment is ultimately a form of oppression that manipulates the audience into complacent acceptance of the status quo (Gaspar de Alba 1995: 108), while others see it as inherently subversive, providing an opportunity for Chicana/o writers to 'construct a form of political agency for subjects that occupy multiple subject positions' (Garcia 2002: 64). These polarised perspectives can be seen in both Moraga's and Montoya's work.

As the quotation above indicates, El Louie's identity frequently merges with media images in ways that enable him to adopt various roles and personas for his own political ends. Corky's fantasises on the other hand indicate an internalisation of the modes of social control mediated through film and mass culture.

What differentiates El Louie's role play from Corky's fantasy most overtly, however, is the affirmation of stereotypical images of women that re-enact the legitimacy of gender hierarchies. Forced through lack of positive portrayals of Mexicans to turn to consumerised images of white male bravery in order to define herself, Corky further entrenches herself in the domination against which Chicanas stand. Her female 'captives' signal a profound lack of personal liberty, whereas freedom is equated with masculinity and the penetrating force of the male gaze. Feminist criticism, especially psycho-semiotic film criticism, has concentrated on the spectatorial position women occupy both on and off the screen. Corky's 'captives' share the quality of 'to-be-looked-at-ness', a phrase coined by Laura Mulvey in order to analyse systems of representation which position women as objects to be watched, gazed upon and the source of spectatorial pleasure (Mulvey 1989). In Corky's fantasy women possess no power and agency over their bodies, but occupy passive recipient positions. She simultaneously objectifies these women while identifying with the male subject of the action.

As the drama unfolds it becomes clearer why Corky adopts an identity that necessitates the repression of her own femininity, as at the centre of the second act are graphic descriptions of her earlier rape that are retold through a mixture of comedy and pathos. Corky's speeches here, performed in opposition to the sanctity of patriarchal culture and religion, in effect restage a kind of secular confession that presents a radical shift in gendered power relations. Within Catholicism the vows of chastity and obedience function as church laws and any infringement of them has to be confessed to the father. As God's corporeal substitutes and emissaries, this father or the priest is invested with the power to mediate, punish or absolve. A mainstay of this power is the ritual of confession, which, as Michel Foucault explains, unfolds within a power relationship in which 'the agency of domination does not reside in the one who speaks ... but in the one who listens and says nothing' (Trujillo 1998a: 148). Moraga disrupts the patriarchal nature of these relations, as the point of address is not the symbolic father of the church or the priest, but the audience who act as Marisa's confessor (De Lauretis 1994: 57–8). The following quotation clearly illustrates this point:

> Got raped once.
> When I was a kid.
> Taken me a long time to say that was exactly what happened.
> but that was exactly what happened.
> Makes you more aware than ever that you are one hunerd percent

female, just in case you had any doubts
one hunerd percent female whether you act it or like it or not.
(Moraga 1986: 36)

Corky's speech poses fundamental questions about constructions of gender identity in the Chicana/o context. Her insight into gender as a performative mode during her confession underscores this. Up until the moment of rape she thought that it would never happen to her because of her appropriated masculinity and denied femininity. But the guilt and shame the rape mobilises is also strongly associated with the myth of Malinche, a central cultural icon that contributed to what Alarcón (1989) calls 'the extensive ideological sedimentation of the [silent] good woman and the bad woman archetypes that enabled the cultural nationalistic and paternalistic "communal modes of power"' (McClintock et al. 1997: 278). According to movement rhetoric Malinche was the *mujer mala* (the bad woman), whose sexual union with Hernan Cortes made possible the defeat of the Aztec nation. Moraga states that she is thus viewed not '[as] innocent victim, but [as] the guilty party . . . ultimately responsible for her own sexual victimisation' (Moraga 1983: 118). Each Chicana inherits and transmits this cultural legacy that situates her as *la india*/the whore, *la vendida* (sell-out/betrayer) and *la chingada* (the fucked one).

Paz (1967) was one of the first to note the link between Malinche and the epithet *la chingada*. He asserts that the verb *chingar* is masculine, active and cruel, 'it stings, wounds, gashes, stains' and 'provokes a bitter, resentful satisfaction' (Paz 1967: 77). The object who suffers this action is passive, *la chingada*, in contrast to the active, aggressive subject who inflicts it. Paz asserted that the passivity of the violated, or *la chingada*, found its analogy in Malinche. This passivity accordingly causes her 'to lose her identity, to lose her name / she is no-one / she disappears into nothingness / she is nothingness' (Paz 1967: 77). Taking these factors in to consideration, it is particularly significant that Corky states after the rape that 'HE MADE ME A HOLE!' and Marisa later comments in reflection that 'He only convinced me of my own name' (Moraga 1986: 43).

Analysing the stereotyping tendencies of this discourse, Pérez (1993) argues how the contempt for Chicanas began with the Oedipal conquest triangle, within which the indigenous male was castrated and lost his language to that of the white rapist father (de la Torre and Pesquera 1993: 57–71). It is significant then that Corky's violator is white, rapes her while speaking both English and Spanish, and is associated with an Oedipal subtext that clearly demonstrates his paternal signification:

'n' I kept getting him confused in my mind this man 'n' his arm
with my father kept imagining him my father returned
come back
I wanted to cry '*papá papá*' . . .

'*¿Dónde 'stás papá?*'
'*¿Dónde 'stás?*'
'n' finally i imagine the man answering
'*aquí estoy. soy tu papá*'
'n' this gives me permission to go 'head
to not hafta fight.

(Moraga 1986: 41)

Subliminally imaging these paternal relations, Corky's experiences establish their point of origin in the primal scene of colonial rape. Rather than suggesting a continuum in the economy of the masculinist myth that effectively silenced and marginalised women, her very speech disrupts the previously repressive coding given to Malinche's cultural legacy. This successfully enables a reconciliation of self and past experience for her older self, Marisa. According to de Lauretis (1994), this 'performance' 'Enacts her simultaneous recrossing of the "stages" of psychic development toward subjectivity and subjecthood . . . from primary narcissism and autoeroticism to the disavowal of castration and a new body ego' (de Lauretis 1994: 57–8).

In this sense Moraga's elaboration of gender and body politics in *Giving up the Ghost* forces a reconsideration of the explicitly masculinist underpinnings of Chicano identity promoted by Valdez through the performance of *Zoot Suit*. Displacing the binary logic that repressed women's self-representation within the Virgin/Malinche polarity, the multiple facets of her characters clearly challenge the repressed female identity of their productions. Given *el teatro's* nationalist tendencies, by extension this redefinition simultaneously critiques the homophobia, sexism and oppressive gender definitions of the movement more generally. In the following chapter this analysis is extended to include prose writing in order to focus in particular on representations of the family and the associated identity politics associated with *familia* ideology in contrasting Chicano and Chicana novelistic production.

6   Women, confinement and *familia* ideology

This chapter first of all situates the work of the Chicano novelist Tomás Rivera in relation to the identity politics of the movement by exploring the ways in which he conceives of family in the novel, *Y no se lo trago la tierra/ And the Earth Did Not Devour Him* (1987). During the movement it was in terms of the textual representation of issues associated with family and community that the quality of literature was often evaluated and published or conversely, excluded from both Chicano literary and publishing canons. Those works that did not represent what was considered to be an accurate portrayal of Chicano ideology, or were somehow inappropriate to movement dogma, were as a consequence overlooked or consciously repressed. *The House on Mango Street* (1991) by Sandra Cisneros, although published after the protest decades, received similar treatment, its reception being tainted by the substantive effects of a residual nationalist ideology (Saldívar-Hull 2000: 84–5). In the following chapter I aim to show how *The House on Mango Street* (1991) problematises and subverts the patriarchal imaginary of Rivera's text, and ultimately produces a more consciously complex and expository account of the politics of *la familia*.

The ideology of home and community overlapped in much movement politics. This is in large part due to the central importance traditionally placed on the function of the Chicano family. Many sources indicate that a strong sense of family has enabled Mexican immigrants to survive in a discriminatory American society and has contributed greatly to the formation of a sense of community within that society (Segura and Pierce 1993, Sanchez 1993, Gutiérrez 1995, Ruiz 1998, Saldívar-Hull 2000, Gonzales 2000). This can be observed in several ways, first of all, for example, by the establishment of *mutualistas* (mutual-aid societies) in the nineteenth century following annexation; by the high value placed on family unity and solidarity; by the presence of multigenerational and extended households; and by the level of interaction between family and kin networks (Segura and Pierce 1993: 73). Systems of family relations within the Mexican American group such as *compadrazgo* refer to relationships within families but also create 'fictive kin' among the people in the community. People who are chosen as godparents by the immediate family, become *padrinos* and *compadres* (godparents and parents who become co-parents). These relationships that create connections between families, simultaneously enlarge the scope of family ties and serve as important strategies for cultural survival and resistance (Segura and Pierce 1993: 73–4).

The ideological commitment to the intertwined notions of *familia* and community was placed at the centre of the movement's oppositional politics. By and large the Chicano family was promoted then as a vital force in the conservation and reproduction of cultural identity and as a 'bastion of raza defence' in what was perceived to be a hostile American society (Saldívar-Hull 2000: 128). Rodolfo 'Corky' Gonzales, author of the proto-nationalist poem 'Yo soy Joaquín' (I Am Joaquín) (1967), leader of the Crusade for Justice and one of the main articulators of cultural nationalism and political separatism promoted the belief that 'Nationalism becomes *la familia*. Nationalism comes first out of family' (Esquibel 2001: 40). Similar sentiments also came from the poet Alurista's *El Plan Espiritual de Aztlán* (*The Spiritual Manifesto of Aztlán*) put forward at the Youth Conference in Denver in 1969, which similarly conceived of Chicanos as 'the family of *la raza*'. Item 6 of the plan, which Rudolfo Anaya has termed 'the ideological framework and concrete political program of the Chicano movement', states this more explicitly (Anaya and Lomelí 1989: 5). It reads as follows:

> Cultural values of our people strengthen our identity and the moral background of the movement. Our culture unites and educates the family of *La Raza* towards liberation with one heart and one mind … the cultural values of life, family and home will serve as the powerful weapon to defeat the gringo dollar value system and encourage the process of love and brotherhood.
>
> (Anaya and Lomelí 1989: 3)

Clearly, movement groups and politics coalesced around the 'cultural values of life, family and home' in ways which ensured that the family and by extension also *la familia de la raza* became a safe site against capitalist and American domination. At the same time it is also clear that the Chicano family and what the plan terms 'the process of love and brotherhood' served as a response that solidified male dominance. Although many Chicanas recognised the need to struggle against this deeply entrenched male privilege, many were equally reluctant to embrace a feminist position that appeared anti-family. Nieto Gomez (1974) stated that the male leadership of the movement considered that if they were 'anti-family' then it followed that they must also be 'anti-cultural, anti-man and therefore … anti-Chicano' (A. Garcia 1997: 88). To be an *adelita* or a loyalist a Chicana could not adopt feminism as a strategy for liberation. According to Pesquera and Segura (1993), those Chicanas who did express an interest in feminism and who fought against gender as well as class and race oppression were considered to be *malinches* (betrayers) who were destroying the most basic bonds of *chicanismo*, which were the patriarchal bonds of *la familia* and *carnalismo* (brotherhood) (A. Garcia 1997: 294–307).

In her essay 'The Cartographies of Bonded Space' Gayatri Spivak names the family as 'the machine for the socialisation of the female body through affective coding' (Spivak 1993: 77–95). By and large the Chicano family structure mirrored this kind of socialisation, reproducing traditional gender roles and male dominance, and attributing to women moral and spiritual attributes most suited to the private, domestic arena. In his influential essay 'Chicano Literature: Fiesta of the Living' (1975), published soon after the main events of the movement, Rivera presents a theory of Chicano writing in which he explicitly upholds this familial ideal (Rivera 1975: 439–52). Chicano literature is, according to Rivera, based on three simple images, 'la casa [the house], el barrio [the community or neighbourhood], and la lucha [the struggle]' (Rivera 1975: 439–52). While on the one hand these themes represent a fairly accurate synthesis of some of the major concerns in both Chicano and Chicana literature, Rivera's theory is also inherently masculinist. Using quotations from Alurista's poem 'La casa de mi padre' and selected works by leading movement writers such as *Recuerdo* by Ricardo Sanchez and 'La jefita' by Jose Montoya, Rivera goes onto explicate his theory of *la casa* in overtly patriarchal and oedipal terms. '*La casa*', he states, 'evokes the constant refuge, the constant father, and the constant mother. It contains the father, the mother and the child' (Rivera 1975: 441). For Rivera, the house/la casa, and the family/*la familia* are intertwined. Together they offer the possibility of what he considers to be 'refuge . . . intimacy [and] privacy', providing both the individual and the family with identity and security (Rivera 1975: 441). Yet in Montoya's poem 'La jefita', while the mother is rendered central to the family home, she is also silent and subordinate to others needs, in effect the stereotype of *la madre sufrida* (the suffering mother) found in much movement rhetoric and discourse:

> *Y la jefita* slapping tortillas.
> *Prieta*! Help with the
> *lonches*!
> *Calientale agua a tu 'apa!*
> *(Me la rayo ese! My jefita*
> never slept!)
> [And my little boss slapping tortillas.
> Dark one! Help with the
> lunches!
> Heat up the water for your dad!
> (I'll be damned! My little boss
> never slept!)]
>
> (Rivera 1975: 441)

This portrayal of mothers as silenced and good women by male authors was not uncommon during the movement years. Rivera's description of the family in 'Chicano Literature: Fiesta of the Living' (1975) also incorporates this perspective, and like other male writers he appears to celebrate both *la familia* and the claustrophobia of domesticity from a distinctly masculinist bias.

From a different and more feminist perspective his reading of *la casa* can be seen as being heavily dependent on the interrelated concepts of what Alarcón (1996) terms the 'Chicano holy family romance', as well as Freud's Oedipal triad (Alarcón 1996: 43–8). In this sense, in Rivera's work the house and that which it contains necessarily becomes the site where both religious and psychoanalytic texts combine and collude. From a feminist perspective these competing ideological discourses problematise the sense of well-being within *la casa* that Rivera initially describes. One of the central tenets of early Chicana feminist theorising about the Chicano family was that it was not simply a 'haven in a heartless world' but was the 'locus of struggle' and the source of psychological oppression of Chicanas (Segura and Pierce 1993: 78). As one Chicana feminist argued:

> Some Chicanas are praised as they emulate the sanctified example set by [the Virgin Mary]. The woman par excellence is mother and wife. She is to love and support her husband and to nurture and teach her children. Thus, may she gain fulfilment as a woman. For a Chicana bent upon fulfilment of her personhood, this restricted perspective of her role as a woman is not only inadequate but crippling.
>
> (A. Garcia 1997: 6)

Rivera's 1971 novel, *Y no se lo trago la tierra/And the Earth Did Not Devour Him* (1987) also reproduces this inherent hierarchical and rigidly patriarchal family structure. Published shortly after the politicisation of Chicano labour struggles and the emergence of a broad-based Chicano movement, Rivera's text implicitly parallels movement ideology through its emphasis on *la familia*, its depictions of migrant farm workers' lives, and through its sense of group solidarity. Commonly referred to 'as a major document of Chicano social and literary history', Rivera's text holds a special place within Chicano letters (Saldívar 1990b: 74). It was the first novel published by the newly established Quinto Sol Press, which, under the new artistic and political imperatives of the movement, judged works by their degree of social function. The ethnic and communal content, anti-establishment political ideology and readily identifiable socio-political aesthetics make apparent the novel's social function and clearly also thematically links Rivera's text with the political ideology of the movement (Saldívar 1990: 74).

For a period of time the activism of César Chávez and his union of farm workers dominated the movement, and many literary and artistic works produced during this time readily engaged with the farm workers' cause. Set explicitly within the political and social contexts of the post-Second World War agricultural workers life in south Texas, Rivera's text recalls and parallels these issues. It was during the post-war decades that over five million Mexican nationals were brought into the USA as wartime contract labour under the terms and conditions of the Bracero programme. Despite the fact that this bilateral agreement was a compromise between factions in the USA and the Mexican government's attempting to regulate the treatment of its citizens abroad, migrant farm workers were primarily seen as existing outside of the social order at the same time as being a necessary part of it (Gutiérrez 1995: 153–60).

Organised through the state, the Bracero programme yearly imported thousands of Mexican workers for seasonal work in the fields of US agribusiness. When the *braceros* completed the harvest, they were sent back to Mexico until the next season. The poor communities from which they originated and returned bore all the costs of developing and reproducing this migrant labour force. When as a direct response to the fluctuations in the domestic economy the bounty of cheap Mexican labour increased dramatically, the Department of Labour began to initiate a massive deportation drive code-named 'Operation Wetback' (Montejano 1987: 273).

In south Texas the climate of racism propelled by Operation Wetback and other US initiatives provided popular ideological support for Texan white supremacism and its attendant theories of racial continuums and hierarchies (Montejano 1987: 220–34). The historian David Montejano (1987) points to the ways in which ideas of white racial superiority were supported by ideas of monogenism whereby the higher evolutionary progress of whites was assumed (Montejano 1987: 220–34). Mexican inferiority was taken for granted by most Anglos, and fears of miscegenation took shape within an ideological system that inscribed a hierarchy of types. As one Texan farmer put it:

> They [the Mexicans] are a mixture, a mule race or cross breed. The Spaniard is a cross between a Moor and a Castilian, and the Indian is a cross with them. By intermarriage you can go down to their level but you can't bring them up to yours ... when you cross five races you get meanness.
>
> (Montejano 1987: 221)

In constructing racial identities as inhuman, by suggesting that Mexicans are a 'mule race' and 'alien', this 'Texas legend' proved to be a common and long-lasting justification for anti-Mexican prejudice in the state. Through this discourse Mexicans were defined as 'other' and as the enemy that 'Texans had fought in several official and unofficial wars throughout the nineteenth century' (Montejano 1987: 223–4). Continuing bitterness over the battle of the Alamo, when the Mexican army led by Santa Ana defeated the Texans meant that certain myths and legends continued to be evoked in order to facilitate the denigration of the Mexican people. According to Montejano the legend and subsequent prejudice effectively 'mut[ed] the presence of indigenous peoples' yet simultaneously 'se[t] the context for the formation of "races" ' (Montejano 1987: 309).

Although the demographic mix of south Texas had by the setting of the time of the novel (the post-Second World War years) become complex and apparently unordered, the underlying logic of racism nonetheless continued to exert a significant and powerful residual influence on American perceptions of Mexican Americans in the state. Montejano (1987) in his discussion of the 'Logic of Repression' in South Texas alludes to 'Horsewhipping, chains, armed guards, near-starvation diets . . . vagrancy laws, local pass systems and labour taxes' as indicators of American labour controls (Montejano 1987: 201). In the text Rivera depicts this logic and the overt efforts of whites to solidify economic and racial domination through various forms of juridical, political and social discrimination. Indeed, many of the novel's vignettes reflect the repressive and violent manner by which the organisation of the Mexican labour market was regulated. Some restrictions appear as individual attempts as in the chapter titled 'The Children Couldn't Wait' which details the shooting by an American farm owner of a migrant child who stops work to drink from a cattle trough. Other restrictions appear to be a collective effort and point to a more institutionalised dimension as in the chapters which detail school segregation and racism. Historically, as Muñoz (1989) points out, 'Schools have been central institutions in perpetuating ideological hegemony in the US' (Muñoz 1989: 191). In this way the Mexican American youth 'have been subject to a socialisation process that reinforces the dominant ideology and undermines competing ideologies' (Muñoz 1989: 191).

But it is not only through vignettes such as these that Rivera reveals 'the complex patchwork of exploitation' in south Texas in the post-war years (Montejano 1987: 201). Throughout the narrative the design of segregation-ist policies, from educational programmes to residential codes and other social distinctions, are the primary language in which Rivera expresses the racial and economic separation endemic to the area. Throughout the narrative Anglos are portrayed as aggressively prejudiced individuals, as in the chapter titled 'It's that it Hurts' where a childhood friend of the narrator tells him candidly that, 'some old ladies told mama that Mexicans steal and now mama says not to bring you home anymore' (Rivera 1987: 94). Alongside this kind of discrimination, the text also demarcates in a highly visible way the distinct social standing of each racial group. The physical appearance of the Mexican townships and American neighbourhoods express the contrasts in social hier-archy in very dramatic ways. American neighbourhoods are distinguished by their commercial centres, theatres, houses and paved streets, and therefore stand as a stark contrast to the material realities of Mexican *colonias* where the prevalence of sickness, sunstroke, lice, TB and other poverty-related diseases, clearly mark them out as being primarily 'labour camps'.

Amid this planned and systematic segregation there are also several other practices that extend, and preserve the American social position. For example, all contact between American and Mexican follow explicit rules so that movie houses, drugstores and schools all have definitions of the 'proper place of Mexicans'. This can be seen in the following extract which details the protagonist's own experiences of this kind of segregation:

> The barber told him again he couldn't cut his hair . . . furthermore he told him that it would be better if he left . . . he crossed the street and stood there waiting for the theatre to open, but then the barber came out and told him to leave. Then it all became clear to him.
>
> (Rivera 1987: 103)

Several Chicano critics point to the ways in which debilitating scenes such as these are counterpoised by other crucial scenes, which establish and identify a more positive common ground for a collective unity (Saldívar 1990b: 98–113). Movement ideology likewise established criteria whereby acceptable literary works were those that reflected and prioritised collectively oriented articulations of resistance to the oppressive influence of the dominant white power structure. In Rivera's text these are chronicled in an implicit critique of economic, religious and racial formations, rebellious thoughts or actions, and through the formation of a communal oral history and voice (Saldívar 1990b: 75, Calderon 1991: 102).

This oppositional perspective was typical of many male authors who were associated with movement ideology. The literature of Rolando Hinojosa, Rivera's contemporary, can be referenced here as he similarly reconstructs a communal oral history and 'voice' which reflects the experiences of the Mexican American inhabitants of Belken County in south Texas (Saldívar 1985). Hinojosa's *Klail City Death Trip* series details the accelerating marginalisation suffered by the Mexican American community in an increasingly reified Texas world.[1] His project, like that of Rivera, subverts racist ideology and stresses the importance of relationships between the community and the land. Unlike Hinojosa's work, which has evolved into a history of land claims closely woven with family relations, Rivera's narrative is concerned with itinerant people. Tracing what he terms 'the utopian dialectics' in Rivera's text, Saldívar (1990b) cites Fredric Jameson, and has termed Rivera's oppositional narratives 'the anticipation of the logic of the collectivity which has not yet come in to being' (Saldívar 1990b: 83). He goes on to illustrate how they implicitly recreate 'the dawning sense of solidarity with other members of [his] class and race' (Saldívar 1990b: 83). Yet while these oppositional narratives enable the reader to see the emergence of a group identity, it is a group identity wholly based on male subjectivity, and as such implicitly reinforces the paternalism of much movement discourse. Writing in another context, the Chicano critic Genaro Padilla (1993) would seem to substantiate this claim. He states that within Chicano narrative, 'Th[e] displacement of a self-absorbed "I"-centred narrative by a narrative in which the cultural subject is refigured within a collective matrix may be regarded as a filial act' (Padilla 1993: 29).

In Rivera's text such acts of 'filiation' emerge in a number of different ways, but most obviously in his depictions of female subjectivity and in the submerged but nonetheless idealised Chicano myth of *la familia*. One particular example of this can be seen in the vignette that documents the preparation and ceremony of a local wedding:

> throughout the entire week prior the groom and his father had been busy fixing up the yard at the bride's house and setting up a canvass tent where the couple would receive the congratulations of family and friends . . . after they were married in the church the couple strolled down the street followed by a procession of godmothers and godfathers and ahead of them a bunch of children running and shouting . . .
>
> (Rivera 1987: 123)

The image of the conjugal union of woman and man in the text provides an effective example of communal solidarity. Significantly, marriage was also an institution located at the heart of movement rhetoric. During this time marriage was seen as strongly upholding the politics of *la familia* and therefore of the movement. As Pesquera and Segura (1993) point out, 'the Chicano movement exalted marriage and reproduction as integral to the politics of cultural reaffirmation' (A. Garcia 1997: 296). In the text the Chicano wedding ceremony functions in a similar way. It is depicted primarily as a rite of unity, for the families of the bride and groom are joined in each other's extended family and become not merely hyphenated in-laws but actual relations, that are termed *suegros* and *cunados* (Segura and Pierce 1993: 62–91).

Within the Chicano community marriage as an institution has traditionally functioned as the primary vehicle in the formation and sustaining of the unequal relations between genders, and maintains and upholds the complex set of social relations defining male and female, masculinity and femininity. In the Mexican family these hierarchies are further entrenched through the mechanisms of the large extended family structure in which gender roles are strictly separated and reinforced by stern parental discipline and community pressure (Segura and Pierce 1993: 62–91). The wedding depicted here is thus a ritual that primarily marks the woman's passage from being her father's property to being that of her husband. The territorial actions of the groom and his father indicate this transition, and are clearly acts that empower the man and disempower the woman.

Clearly, it is also depictions such as these that highlight the most ambiguously negotiated site in the text, which is that of female identity. In the predominantly masculine world of the novel, women's experiences are cast in ways that reinforce the cultural stereotypes of the movement. Following entrenched patterns within Mexican culture which characterised women either as the good woman or the bad woman, Chicano discourse similarly situated women within limited subject positions either as *la madre abnegada*, the suffering mother and the passive virgin, or as the embodiment of female treachery and sexual promiscuity sublimated into the figure of la Malinche, or *la puta* (the whore) (A. Garcia 1997: 49).

By and large Rivera's portrayal of women follow this schematisation. De la Fuente (1986) argues that women contribute a muted, and often inconsequential background to the male experience in Rivera's text (Olivares 1986: 81–9). Certainly, mothers are stereotyped as self-sacrificing, passive and eager to serve men's needs. Generally they are confined to gendered environments and incorporated within strategies that bind them to a subordinate position within the family home. As the representatives of domesticity, they have to remain what Irigaray (1985a) calls 'an unrecognised infrastructure', and in keeping with the iconography of the movement which labelled them as transmitters of the religious/family past, they are also cast in ways which further stress their anonymity (Irigaray 1985a: 84).

In the text, women's lack of subjectivity is further reinforced through their association with particular cultural representations, imagery and symbols. Folklore and religion are particularly associated with female subjectivity, as in the first vignette, which offers a typical example of this association, as well as the author's indirect characterisation of woman as an absence:

> One thing his mother never found out was that every night he would drink the glass of water that she left under the bed for the spirits. She always believed that they drank the water and so she continued doing her duty.
>
> (Rivera 1987: 85)

Here the mother is represented as being bound by superstition, gullibility and by 'duty'. Within the Chicano familial structure, organised by the sexual division of labour, women's duty signifies a series of endless and infinitely repeatable chores. For the Mexican American mother the family is the site of the affirmation and replenishment of others at the expense and through the erasure of the self. The narrator's comments reveal the inequality of her position within *familia* politics as well as reinforcing male dominance. The mother does not challenge this status quo but rather reinforces her own culturally gendered role. In short she represents the paradox of the silent complicity of women who are contained by the patriarchal family structure, and in their enforced passivity also help to sustain it.

In much the same way as Moraga describes mothers as 'sell-outs' to male ideology in her essay *A Long Line of Vendidas*, in Rivera's text the narrator's mother must prove her fidelity through commitment to Chicano men by 'putting the male first' in the family (Moraga 1983: 90–144). Segura and Pierce (1993) argue that the consequence of this ideology on gender identification differs radically for the young Chicano as opposed to that of the young Chicana (Segura and Pierce 1993: 76). From an early age the male is encouraged to identify with machismo in order to 'become masculine' and so to confirm patriarchal privilege ideologically and interpersonally (Segura and

Pierce 1993: 77). In much the same way, from an early age the narrator of *Y no se lo trago la tierra* must repress his identification with women and at the same time strive to achieve masculine gender identification with his father and other men. This repression engenders a highly ambivalent stance towards women, and in the narrative is suggested through strong feelings both of longing and disdain (Segura and Pierce 1993: 77).

In several vignettes the mother's subjection is manifested through her devotion to her family and religion, seen here in an extract that tells of a Chicana who anxiously waits for her son to return home after fighting in Korea:

> Dear God, Jesus Christ protect him, that they may not kill him. Please, Virgin Mary, you too, shelter him. I have made a promise to the *Virgen de San Juan* to pay her homage at her shrine and to the *virgin de Guadalupe* too . . . Jesus Christ, Holy God, *Virgen de Guadalupe* bring him back alive. I promise you my life for his. I sacrifice my heart for his. Bring him back alive and I will give you my very own heart.
>
> (Rivera 1987: 90)

Throughout the text, the narrator is seen to develop a growing spiritual poverty and to question the ability of Catholicism to fill that void. As Bruce-Novoa observes, the narrator 'constantly finds himself suspended between rejection by the American system and the impossibility of accepting Mexican superstitions and rigidity' (Bruce-Novoa 1990a: 117). Yet Rivera constantly equates women with these latter attributes. The mother is strongly associated with all the trappings and dogma of the church including sacramentals, rosaries and devotions. *La Virgen* as both cultural and religious representation also frames this mother's gendered and ethnic sense of self. It is through the figure of the Virgin, who Anzaldúa claims to be 'the single most potent religious, political, and cultural image of the Chicano/*mexicano*', that Rivera most strongly associates women with suffering and enslavement (Anzaldúa 1987: 30). These values, which are effectively fostered by the church, are usually translated through the Virgin into love and devotion. At the same time they reinforce woman's subordinate position and servitude within a rigidly proscribed patriarchal hierarchy. As a desexualised image used by the church and community, the figure of the Virgin enforces this repression, most often being used symbolically as 'a role model for a feminine ideal' based on 'the virtues of passivity, obedience, unswerving love, and an endless capacity to endure suffering and pain' (Trujillo 1998b: 219). In religious terms, the Virgin is the good woman who symbolically steps on the serpent, turning down temptation and living in virtuous service to God (Trujillo 1998b: 215). In more secular terms she also reinforces the centrality of family in the Chicano community, and this can be seen in Rivera's own triadic conceptualisation of *la familia* within which the Virgin is caught forever in an Oedipal relationship with her son Jesus Christ and the father God (Trujillo 1998b: 221).

Contemporary Chicana feminist texts actively reclaim the figure of the Virgin as a source of female power and therefore affirm themselves as 'subjects in a female-gendered frame of reference' (Trujillo 1998b: 221). Trujillo (1998b) points out that 'the Virgin is often regarded differently by men versus women . . . Men seem to place [her] importance into that of a relation-ship to a man' (Trujillo 1998b: 221). Rivera likewise places the Virgin always in relation to, and also always displaced by, men. Clearly then, the Mexican Catholicism reinscribed by Rivera and embraced by movement dogma implies a patriarchal structure and a traditional familial order. This reconsti-tutes the subordination of the mother through a selective interpretation of the Virgin, so that ironically, what is valued is her absence or lack. The mother figures prominently in Rivera's text in a similar way, and ultimately as some-one who is denied positive womanhood. As a verifier of masculinity, she is the negation that defines maleness to itself and makes it signify, and in this respect she also resembles the mythic and dispersed figure described most famously by Paz in *The Labyrinth of Solitude* (1967) as *la chingada* or 'a nothing' (Paz 1967).

In Rivera's portrayal of the other category of women, the fallen woman, an already problematic sense of womanhood becomes even more unstable. American women often appear in this category, and are generally positioned as destructive forces that threaten the Chicano community. An American wife 'drinking in a bar out of sadness because her husband had left her' is later responsible for the deaths of sixteen Mexican farm workers on a truck (Rivera 1987: 129). A second example illustrates a similar pattern of nega-tive characterisation, whereby American women are seen as temptresses who lure men away from the safety of the community. A seventeen-year-old 'little gringa' is responsible for the imprisonment of a compadre who also contracts a life threatening 'nasty disease' (Rivera 1987: 141). A minister's young American wife, employed as a translator like an inverted Malinche figure, commits adultery and in so doing also 'betrays' the community (Rivera 1987: 107).

This pattern of negative characterisation takes on a slightly different perspective in the chapter titled 'The Night the Lights Went Out', where it is the Mexican American woman who is the *mujer mala* (the fallen woman). This story deals with two adolescent partners, Ramón and Juanita, who for economic reasons have to be separated for four months. She has to leave Texas and go with her parents to work in the fields of Minnesota. Once there she meets another man described as being 'all duded up [with] orange shoes and real long coats' (Rivera 1987: 125). Ramón's subsequent suicide is an extreme response to Juanita's independence, as the sexist comments of the community reveal:

> somebody told me that she'd been going around with some dude out there in Minnesota. And that she still kept on writing to Ramón. Kept lying to him . . . I think she liked to fool around, otherwise she wouldn't

have been unfaithful [. . .] what was bad was her not breaking up with him . . . that woman left behind nothing but pain.

(Rivera 1987: 125)

Juanita's fight for independence against this kind of repressive social and religious mores, transgresses tradition, violates the sanctity of the family unit and ultimately subverts the dictates of community. In much of her writing Cherríe Moraga elaborates upon this risk. 'The woman who defies her role as subservient to her husband, father, brother, or son by taking control of her own sexual destiny', Moraga writes,

> is purported to be a 'traitor to her race' by contributing to the 'genocide' of her people-whether or not she has children. In short . . . she is *una malanchista*. Like the Malinche of Mexican history, she is corrupted by foreign influences that threaten to destroy her people.
>
> (Moraga 1983: 113)

Juanita's position in a culture that completely devalues women who stray from the community and male-defined roles, mark her out as la Malinche and by extension also the *puta* (whore), and therefore an essentialised and sexualised object of male desire. Men are exclusively interested in Juanita's physical being and in conquering and possessing her. In effect it is male desires, as in Rivera's other portrayals of women, which serve as the basis to define what is supposed to be a female character. In keeping with movement ideology Rivera depicts female sexuality as needing to be controlled, whether it is through the church, through the institution of marriage or through the structures of the family.

Subsequent Chicana narratives challenge these limited constructions of female subjectivity and with them women's containment by *familia* ideology. Recent research on Chicano families confirms that 'patriarchal privilege, structurally, ideologically, and interpersonally' continues to affect Chicanas in a number of different ways (Segura and Pierce 1993: 78). Fuelled by the support for family values by neo-conservatives during Reagan's presidency in the 1980s, Chicana writers and activists openly moved away from the alienating gender politics and rigidly delineated boundaries of *familia* ideology. As Moraga writes in *Loving in the War Years* (1983) it is imperative that Chicanas no longer invoke, 'the family, as the righteous *causa* without linking themselves with the most reactionary, and by definition, the most racist political sectors of this country' (Moraga 1983: 117). Chicana writers such as Moraga questioned and redefined the traditional notion of *la familia* and proposed wholly different paradigms that clearly went beyond the confines of what is understood and accepted as family, according to both the conservative and Chicano ideal. In challenging this construction as the desired and dominant configuration, her text *A Long Line of Vendidas* became an important cornerstone in the development of a Chicana feminist analysis of sexuality and gender. In effect it helped to significantly establish what over the course of the 1980s became the clear-cut agenda for Chicanas, namely the articulation and deconstruction of what both Moraga and Anzaldúa termed 'the many headed demon of oppression' which afflicts Mexican American working-class women's lives (Moraga and Anzaldúa 1983: 195).

A year later, in 1984, this programme took concrete political form when the conference of the NACS adopted the theme 'voces de la mujer' which addressed the critical question concerning the nature of oppression experienced by Chicanas. Sandra Cisneros reading from the text of the *House on Mango Street* (1991), during the conference overtly developed this critique. The recipient of two fellowships for poetry and fiction, Cisneros is the author of the novel *House on Mango Street* (1991), *Woman Hollering Creek and Other Stories* (1993), the poetry collections *My Wicked Wicked Ways* (1987), *Loose Woman* (1994) and more recently the novel *Caramelo* (2002). She is also winner of the Lannan Literary Award (1991), the PEN Center USA West Literary Award (1991), QPB New Voices Award in Fiction (1992) and the Anisfield Wolf Award (1992).

Unlike Rivera's text, which was well received by publishing houses in the 1970s, *The House on Mango Street* suffered from various misreadings before being awarded the Before Columbus Foundation's American Book Award in 1985. There were many objections to the narrative's generic status, a substantial majority emanating from male critics. In foregrounding the house and more specifically female domestic space as a legitimate and largely unrecognised site of struggle, Cisneros was accused of selling out to the American dream. Juan Rodríguez vehemently asserts that *The House on Mango Street* indicated Cisneros' desire to, 'move away from her social/cultural base to become more "anglicised", more individualistic [and therefore] more "problematic" to the serious reader' (Saldívar-Hull 2000: 84). These comments made by Rodríguez, editor of the Chicano newsletter *Carta Abierta*, are representative of the prevailing male attitudes towards women writers at the time. As I previously stated, Francisco Lomelí also suggested that there was 'an underlying implication that issues women writers raise are not of great magnitude or importance' (Rebolledo 1995: 4). Generally these critiques were based on previous and largely masculinist paradigms of literary interpretation. Their refusal to position Cisneros' text within the category of 'serious literature' largely because of its innovative narrative strategies serves as a stark reminder of the extent to which Chicana feminism and Chicana feminist texts continued to be regarded as somehow outside or not part of a 'genuine' Chicano literary canon. Yet Cisneros shares this subject matter with several other Chicana writers including Helena María Viramontes in the novel *Under the Feet of Jesus* (1995b) and *The Moths and Other Stories* (1995a), among many others. *The House on Mango Street* like these texts closely explores *familia* ideology and the migrant experience and therefore can be said to present a 'legitimate' and 'serious' focus, in much the same way as movement writing.

During the Bracero programme in the 1940s and 1950s many Chicano farm workers migrated to the mid-west and other areas of the USA in order to secure higher paying jobs in the industries that were developing over this period of time (Acuña 1988: 408). It was then that people established distinct Chicano barrios in the Back of the Yards and the Pilsen area of South Chicago, bringing with them a desire to recreate and perpetuate the communal familiarity that characterised their former rural lives. These unique familial considerations and the diasporic configuration of Chicano communities are reinscribed in Cisneros' text. Mango Street's neighbourhood of African Americans, Puerto Ricans and Latinos demonstrate its ethnic complexity as well as the mobile nature of the immigrant experience:

> We didn't always live on Mango Street. Before that we lived on Loomis on the third floor, and before that we lived on Keeler. Before Keeler it was Paulina, and before that I can't remember . . . what I remember most is moving a lot.
>
> (Cisneros 1991: 3)

The initial movement of Esperanza Cordero's family from home to home is typical of the Mexican immigrant experience in the USA (Sanchez 1993: 198–201). Mango Street, however, is not so much a typical zone of social mobility but rather is an area of economic instability. Poor housing is reflected in the number of boarding houses, rented rooms and third-floor flats, while the presence of unscrupulous landlords, substandard plumbing facilities and overcrowding reveal the material and social realities of migrant lives. As Esperanza points out, 'We had to leave the flat on Loomis quick. The water pipes broke and the landlord wouldn't fix them because the house was too old. We had to leave fast' (Cisneros 1991: 4). These conditions of social oppression and their socio-economic relationships form an integral part of Cisneros' representation of *familia* politics. Like the narrator of Rivera's text, Esperanza is aware that social, cultural and political distinctions operate in ways that segregate her from the other sectors of the society in which she lives. She is aware, for instance, that racial and economic segregation work to circumscribe the neighbourhood, 'Those who don't know any better come into our neighbourhood scared. They think we're dangerous. They think we will attack them with shiny knives. They are stupid people who are lost and got here by mistake' (Cisneros 1991: 28). She also remembers how a nun from her school observes the Cordero house on Loomis in a way that made her 'feel like nothing' (Cisneros 1991: 5).

These social distinctions ultimately make home-ownership the valued goal of the Cordero family. As Esperanza says, 'I knew then I had to have a house. A real house. One I could point to' (Cisneros 1991: 5). Within the social and economic roles delineated for Mexican Americans buying a house is considered to be an act of defiance and a form of self-assertion. It signifies adaptation to and permanent settlement in a hostile American society and serves as a metaphor for success and escape from the limitations of poverty (Sanchez

1993: 198–201). Yet Esperanza explains that the house on Mango Street is 'not the house we'd thought we'd get'. Instead:

> it's small and red with tight steps in front and windows so small you'd think they were holding their breath. Bricks are crumbling in places, and the front door is so swollen you have to push hard to get in.
>
> (Cisneros 1991: 8)

In contrast to the material realities of the house on Mango Street, Esperanza has always dreamt of owning a house that stands as the quintessential product of contemporary American society. By reading the codes by which it is described, 'white with trees around it, a great big yard and grass growing without a fence', it is possible to assess the fundamental values of American society (Cisneros 1991: 4). The house she dreams of is a model of the mainstream American family home and is not representative of the cultural others who dwell in America. From a semiotic perspective it communicates both the basic structure and fundamental value of mainstream culture, that is the famous American dream based on individual landownership. The house Esperanza dreams of thus depicts her internalised oppression, a state of mind prompted by her belief in the American dream and her desire for the escape which assimilation offers.

Whereas on an ideological level Esperanza appears to dream the American dream, on a material level like the rest of her community she remains excluded from it. While home-ownership allows Esperanza's narrative to develop a quality of permanence, security and belonging, it does not imply moving up the social ladder. Owning the house on Mango Street in fact masks the family's increasing social inequality. Owning homes in Mango Street, unlike other forms of property wealth, does not necessarily translate into 'the social form of capital' (Sanchez 1993: 2000). Indeed, owning the house on Mango Street actually inhibits Esperanza's family and any dream they might have had for further integration and mobility out of the neighbourhood, because of their lack of means to secure higher priced housing outside of the barrio.

In these respects both *Y no se lo trago la tierra* and *The House on Mango Street* share a similar sense of privation and discrimination. However, for Cisneros, economic and racial oppression are not the only forms of discrimination and consequently different narratives emerge from these comparable barrio and *colonia* spaces. These differences are most obviously encoded within the forms of narration and the narrative voice. According to de la Fuente (1986), *Y no se lo trago la tierra* includes two competing gendered narratives, whereby narrative authority is coded as masculine and silence as feminine (Olivares 1986: 81–9). The sections dealing solely with the young male protagonist, such as 'El ano perdido' (the lost year) and 'Debajo de la casa' (under the house), provide the overall frame of reference for the twelve tales and thirteen fragments which make up the narrative (Calderon and Saldívar 1991: 104).

The narrator of the forty-four vignettes that make up *The House on Mango Street* on the other hand is clearly a female child. In this way, Cisneros self-consciously foregrounds the relations of gender and power in inherited types of discourse.

Whereas Rivera's text implicitly reinforces values and systems of dominance through a male narrator and the articulation of Catholic belief, mythology, history and tradition, Cisneros counters this authority with fairy tales, children's games and rhymes as well as the female-to-female tradition in her narrative. Traditionally the fairy tale is a form that arrives via the mediation of generations of strongly ideologically motivated readings and interpretations. As a primary source of socialisation, especially female socialisation, it functions as a cipher for a particular description of female behaviour, especially passivity, dependency and gullibility. But Cisneros' use of the fairy tale goes beyond the standard reading and instead offers a potentially radical fictional space in which she can unravel and reimagine existing power relations. While the tendency within *Y no se lo trago la tierra* was to idealise the home as the sacred abode of the *familia*, through the form of the fairy tale, *The House on Mango Street* exposes the configurations of power which haunt these gendered spaces.

In contrast to its depictions in Rivera's text, marriage in *The House on Mango Street* is represented in order to reject the social conventions of that institution, particularly its inherent containment of women. Physical and psychological abuse are dealt with overtly by Cisneros, and are clearly illustrated in the story 'Rafaela who drinks coconut and papaya juice on Tuesdays'. Trapped in an implied phallic tower, Rafaela is the epitome of the silent (or silenced) good woman inherent to movement discourse. We are told that:

> She leans out the window and leans on her elbow and dreams her hair is like Rapunzel's. A long time passes and we forget she is up there until she says kids go to the store and buy me something. She throws a crumpled dollar down and we send it up to her in a paper shopping bag she lets down with clothesline.
>
> (Cisneros 1991: 79–80)

Here the fairy tale of Rapunzel is recast by Cisneros in order to evoke the darker undercurrents of the Chicano home as the form of the fairy tale allows for the juxtaposition of images of innocence with those of monstrous brutality. Imprisoned in the domestic space by patriarchal and cultural constraints, and effectively separated from social networks, Rafaela represents the repression of female subjectivity by the structures of *familia*. Her husband's manipulation and containment is first and foremost about male control. It is a macho response that symbolises his paranoid projections. Machismo, while clearly performing an organising principle for the family according to dominant narratives of the movement, is here translated as men's hostility, aggression and containment of women. Rather than providing a vital source for activism and interaction, machismo in fact transforms the home into the domain of hatred and control.

The chapter titled 'There was an Old Woman She Had So Many Children She Didn't Know What to Do' continues to present the problematic of the 'family romance':

> They are bad those Vargas, and how can they help it with only one mother who is tired all the time from buttoning and bottling and baby-ing, and who cries every day for the man who left without even leaving a dollar for *bologna* or a note explaining how come.
>
> (Cisneros 1991: 29)

Unlike the socialising function usually associated with the fairy tale, which provides either a symbolic learning experience or strives to emphasise appropriate mothering roles, the fairy tale here functions to unmask the myth of mothering. As an abandoned single mother her place is one of domestic confinement, of 'waking up with the tortilla star for the making of lunchbox tortillas', and not one of liberation and choice.

Apart from women like Rosa Vargas who are the sole heads of their house-holds and as a consequence are too 'tired of being worried about kids', the Mango Street neighbourhood is also full of mothers who reproduce their own exploitation. For instance, the chapter titled 'Minerva Writes Poems' scrutinises the perpetuation of mother-to-daughter exploitation and eco-nomic dependency. Minerva, who is only a few years younger than Esperanza, 'has two children and a husband who left' (Cisneros 1991: 80). As a single parent she duplicates her mother's situation who also 'raised her kids alone and it looks like her daughters will go the same way too' (Cisneros 1991: 80). In this sense the women of Cisneros' text also resemble the mother's situation in Ana Castillo's *So Far from God* (1994a) of whom it is said:

> Sofia had not left her children, much less drowned them to run off with nobody. On the contrary, she had been left to raise them by herself. And all her life, there had always been at least one woman around her, left alone, abandoned, divorced, or widowed, to raise her children, and none of them had ever tried to kill their babies.
>
> (Castillo 1994a: 161)

In contrast to the masculine myth of *la llorona* who murdered her children for the sake of a man, most Chicanas in these stories are the sole parent and source of *familia* solidarity. In opposition to Rivera's depiction of *la familia* as warm and nurturing, and as an environment of support in times of stress, much contemporary Chicana fiction envisages a version of home as a site of contestation and disruption. Home life in these stories is generally not as Rivera suggests, a place of 'refuge . . . intimacy [and] privacy', but is overwhelmingly unhappy and dysfunctional; a place where the social-sexual relations between women and men are inherently unhealthy and destructive.

Within this escalating economy of male violence, the home of Esperanza's friend Sally is the exemplar of the phallocentric effacement of women. Sally is the girl 'with eyes like Cleopatra and nylons the colour of smoke' who is restricted and defined by the rules of the father. Sally's codes of dress indicate the extent to which she has learnt to symbolise herself through a sign system specifically geared towards the reproduction of patriarchal values. Obsessed with her sexualised appearance her father beats her 'like a dog . . . like . . . an animal' (Cisneros 1994a: 85). Her bruises signify her painful entrance into what Irigaray terms ironically the 'reasonable' discourse of his [sexual] law' (Irigaray 1985b: 81). As a response invoked in order to rationalise his own incestuous desire, the father adopts a form of sexuality based on violence, the belt he uses to beat her signifies the phallus and asserts male sexual power. This psycho-social complex is fundamental to machismo and is used as a justification for sexism within the Chicano community. In the chapter titled 'Red Clowns', this damaging aspect of machismo ideology is extended to include Esperanza's own experiences of sexual assault and attempted rape, 'Sally, make him stop. I couldn't make them go away. I couldn't do anything but cry. I don't remember. It was dark. I don't remember. I don't remember. Please don't make me tell it all' (Cisneros 1991: 93). Rape and sexual assault are not isolated acts of course, but are part of the greater imbalances of power between genders. According to Herrera-Sobek (1988), rape in a patriarchal society 'insure[s] continuation of phallocentric rule' (Herrera-Sobek and Viramontes 1988: 243). This statement is readily substantiated in the story titled 'The Family of Little Feet', a Chicana version of *Little Red Riding Hood*, as Esperanza and her friends enter a symbolic system that simultaneously objectifies and sexualises them. As they walk through the neighbourhood in borrowed high-heel shoes, their newly sexualised selves evoke a paedophiliac and fetishistic response from the men they encounter. The girls are suddenly dangerous, their bodies commodified and sexualised, they require policing.

Cisneros thus portrays women's confinement and powerlessness within patriarchal systems of power, while simultaneously exploring the ways in which given social codes govern and regulate their bodies. This perspective of the socially and symbolically conditioned female self also informs other chapters in the text. In the fourth story, 'My Name', it becomes clear that Esperanza wants to reinvent herself in order to transcend the limitations that result from her ethnic and gendered identity. In this story Cisneros recognises the place of cultural transmission within the family yet simultaneously problematises the ideological terms and function of that process. Generally within Chicano family life, grandmothers and great grandmothers signify the symbolic matriarchal handing down of cultural traditions. In this story though, the figure of the great grandmother represents traditional cultural values as confining and debilitating:

My great grandfather threw a sack over her head and carried her off. Just like that, as if she were a fancy chandelier. And the story goes she never forgave him. She looked out the window all her life, the way so many women sit their sadness on an elbow. I wonder if she made the best with what she got or was she sorry because she couldn't be all the things she wanted to be.

(Cisneros 1991: 12)

Esperanza's name is linked to this tradition via her great grandmother. But this does not necessarily mean that she must continue to suffer male oppression, as she emphatically states, 'I have inherited her name, but I don't want to inherit her place by the window' (Cisneros 1991: 11). Esperanza prefers a name that is not culturally embedded in a dominating, male-centred ideology such as 'Esperanza as lizandra or maritza or zeze the x. Yes. Something like zeze the x will do' (Cisneros 1991: 11).

Esperanza's quest for a culturally uncoded new name gives way to the realisation that, unlike the collective and filial coding given in Rivera's text, there is no fixed 'I'. This pluralistic notion of self contests the terms of the patriarchal imaginary, and as Alarcón argues (1989) this kind of multiple identity serves as a radical point of departure for dismantling the confines of 'the community's socio-symbolic system and contract' (McClintock et al. 1997: 286). This includes the challenging of woman's 'proper' (heterosexual) place in the sex/gender system as Esperanza refuses to be like other women who 'lay their necks on the threshold waiting for the ball and chain' (Cisneros 1991: 88). Instead she would rather 'leave[s] the table like a man, without putting back the chair or picking up the plate' (Cisneros 1991: 89). This dual sense of self undermines traditional stereotypes of women and the confinement of patriarchal paradigms of female identity. Against societal and cultural codes Esperanza usurps male privilege, she refuses to acknowledge her proper place.

In an echoing of Virginia Woolf's plea for a 'room of one's own' she also refuses to acknowledge her father's house as her home, but searches instead for her own house and space, 'Not a man's house. Not a daddy's. A house all my own . . . a space for myself to go, clean as paper before the poem' (Cisneros 1991: 108). With the displacement of the father as patriarch, Cisneros finally disrupts the Oedipal family romance promoted by movement discourse. Whereas Rivera's depictions of female subjectivity and the myth of the Chicano family reflect movement ideology in a number of ways, Cisneros on the other hand portrays a dysfunctional unit dominated by the macho male who subjugates his wife and children. Recent statistical evidence supports this view. Alongside factors such as urbanisation and discrimination, machismo continues to rank as one of the major causes of family problems within the Mexican American community (Gonzales 2000: 239). Opinion over *familia* ideology, however, is deeply divided and an idealised view of the Chicano family continues to coexist alongside studies that view it less favourably (Gonzales 2000: 237–8).

In rewriting the myth of *la familia* Cisneros reveals the unequal gender and sexual relationships that have maintained its stability and rigid ideologies for many generations of Chicanas. In the following chapter I explore this tendency in more detail in relation to narratives of homeland and nation. By examining the differences between male and female narratives, I show how recent Chicana writing calls into question and redefines existing Chicano constructs of these spaces in much the same way as it problematises and subverts movement formulations of *familia* ideology.

7 The search for Aztlán

The Chicano nation

During the movement, conceptions of a homeland began to coalesce specific-ally around the idea of a separate Chicano nation, which was called Aztlán. The myth associated with this homeland, argues Chávez, 'is central to Chicano/a consciousness' (Chávez 1984: 1). Its importance can be seen in the repeated allusions to Aztlán during the 1960s and the rapid spread of the concept throughout the south-west following the Denver Youth Conference in 1969. From this time onwards its use as a literary symbol also multiplied and books in whose titles the word Aztlán appeared were numerous. During the spring of 1970 the first edition of the journal *Aztlán* was published and in it *El Plan Espiritual de Aztlán* was reproduced in both English and Spanish. In the following year Alurista had an anthology, *El Ombligo de Aztlán*, published and a year later his poetry collection *Nationchild Plumaroja* (1972) appeared. At the same time a bibliography by Ernie Barrios published in 1971 bore the title *Bibliografía de Aztlán*; and in 1973 Luis Valdez and Stan Steiner edited a work called *Aztlán: An Anthology of Mexican American Literature*. The novels *Peregrinos de Aztlán* (1974) by Miguel Mendez and *Heart of Aztlán* (1988) by Rudolfo Anaya followed soon after. More recently the publication of *North to Aztlán: A History of Mexican Americans in the US* (1996) co-authored by Griswold del Castillo and de León indicates that Aztlán continues to hold a significant symbolic significance for the Chicano people.

In order to more fully explore the shaping of Aztlán and its relation to movement politics, in the following chapter I first consider its representation in the political manifesto *El Plan Espiritual de Aztlán* (1969) before moving on to assess its depiction in Anaya's novel *Heart of Aztlán* (1988). Both of these texts perpetuate the paternalistic ideology of the movement in the sense that they formulate Aztlán in overtly masculine terms, thereby excluding women from its borders. Before exploring this gendered polarisation more specifically, it is first appropriate to discuss the myth of Aztlán itself in more detail.

Although the contemporary use of the myth emerged from the found-ational document of Chicano nationalism, *El Plan Espiritual de Aztlán*, its origins lie with the Aztláneca Mexica or Aztec people. According to Pina (1989), the myth was recorded in a number of colonial-era chronicles including the *Crónica Mexicáyotl* (1609) by Don Fernando Alvarado Tezozómoc, the *Historia de las Indias de Nueva España e Isla de Tierra Firme* by Fray Diego Duran and *Historia de las cosas de la Nueva España* by Fray Bernadino de Sahagun, with some degree of historical accuracy (Anaya and Lomelí 1989: 16). But the myth of Aztlán also has a protean quality and is therefore the subject of multiple interpretations (Anaya and Lomelí 1989: 16). As a definite geographic territory it has yet to be identified with any degree of precision or certainty, and there are a number of conflicting perspectives concerning its original location. Leal (1989) argues that some of these range from Lake Chapala in the state of Jalisco, Mexico, to the island of Mezcaltitlan in Nayarit, Mexico as well as to the south-western states of America (Anaya and Lomelí 1989: 10). Generally, these differing geographic and literary interpretations form a consensus in their descriptions of Aztlán, which are by and large lush and paradisiacal. Home to exotic birds, trees, and floating gardens, Aztlán was distinguished by a central hill surrounded by water, and on its slopes were several caves where the Chicano forefathers were said to have lived. This in turn has given rise to the multiple naming of the Chicano homeland, as 'the place of whiteness or herons' (Aztlán), 'the land of seven caves' (Chicomostoc), and 'the place of the twisted hill' (Colhuacan) (Pérez-Torres 1995: 229).

Despite its multiple signification, lack of geographic certainty and idealisation, the myth is not devoid of ideological function. Aztlán's central importance lies in its being the Chicano homeland and the land from which their Aztec ancestry began their migrations southward towards the central plateau in AD 820. On exit from this earthly paradise, the Aztecs were considered lowly Chichimecas (literally translated as 'sons of dogs' or 'barbarians'), a generic term given to the tribes of the north. Yet they were not leaving Aztlán as a dejected or demoralised people, but rather they left in pursuit of a destiny that was filled with promise and anticipated glory (Anaya and Lomelí 1989: 19).

According to the myth, Huitzilopochtli, the sun god and warrior, instructed the Aztecs to leave Aztlán. The all-powerful deity endowed them with a warrior spirit and promised them victory in any campaign that they undertook. Under his divine guidance the Aztecs appeared in the Valley of Mexico, which they called Anahuac, sometime in the thirteenth century. According to his prophecy, the sight of an eagle perched on a cactus with a serpent in its mouth would signal the spot where they were to stop, build a capital, and inaugurate their quest for hegemony. Apparently this event came to pass and they began to build Tenochtitlan (present-day Mexico City) in the midst of lake Texcoco. Distinguished by an advanced civilisation and imperial power, the Aztec ruled militaristically in this location until the arrival of the conquistadores and the fall of Tenochtitlan in 1521.

The divine intervention of Huitzilopochtli into the narrative of the Chicano homeland was also emphasised by movement ideology, mainly in order to counteract the eventual destruction of the Aztecs with the view of themselves as a people favoured with divine guidance. Pina (1989) states that viewed from a nationalist perspective Huitzilopochtli was instrumental in the shaping of Aztec identity, thought and culture (Anaya and Lomelí 1989: 24–6). Using this native ancestry as a resource in their search for origins, certain sectors of the movement claimed that Chicanos were descendants of Ollin Tonatiuh (the Nahuatl name for the fifth sun) who had 'come in fulfilment of a cosmic cycle from ancient Aztlán, the seed ground of the great civilisations of Anahuac, to modern Aztlán, characterised by the progeny of our Indian, Mexican, and Spanish ancestors' (Anaya and Lomelí 1989: 77). According to this myth of descent, Aztlán and the mestizo heritage are intertwined in a way that suggests that Chicano subjectivity is the product of the transcultural processes of blended Spanish and indigenous roots. In much the same way, *El Plan Espiritual de Aztlán* (1969) also presents the idea of constructive miscegenation and mestizo identity as a renewing force, asserting that Chicanos 'are a bronze people with a bronze culture' (Anaya and Lomelí 1989: 1). In an effort to unify the heterogeneous Chicano group, the different racial and ethnic markers that traditionally and historically comprise the Mexican American community (such as the Hispanos and Nuevo Mexicanos of New Mexico, the Californios and Tejanos of their respective states) are subsumed under one collective identity, a 'bronze people with a bronze culture'. Recognising one another as bronze constituted a way of asserting racial representation and rallying cultural resistance. It also recreated a sense of national cultural uniqueness and differentiated *la raza* from other ethnic groups as cultural nationalists sought to assert the legitimate place of their culture in the face of dominant American hegemony.

It was the land and Aztlán, however, which acted as the primary symbol for movement ideology. Although Aztlán had Edenic features and utopian qualities, activists were concerned to convert that idealism into pragmatic goals and a present-day nation where they hoped to actualise political, economic and cultural autonomy. Rodolfo 'Corky' Gonzales in his 'Message to el Congreso on Land and Cultural Reform' (1972) states this more explicitly:

> There is no greater issue in any social, economic or political struggle than land. Land is the base on which our cultural values are created. Land then is necessary to create a nation with a political philosophy constructed on unity, unity of a total people based on our common history, our culture and our roots.
>
> (Esquibel 2001: 239)

The overt nationalistic discourse of this statement was first introduced to Chicano consciousness with *El Plan Espiritual de Aztlán*, at the Denver Youth Conference in 1969. Sponsored by the Crusade for Justice, the conference attracted more than 200 delegates representing Chicano students, community organisers and political organisations from across the country. Through the plan, the conference endeavoured to galvanise the Chicano community into collective action. It advocated the reclamation of the lost land following the Texas– and US–Mexico wars and the signing of the treaty of Guadalupe Hidalgo in 1848. In an act of restoration it follows the logic of a nativist philosophy and rejects the division of the land from the people by openly declaring that Chicanos 'do not recognise capricious frontiers on the bronze continents' (Anaya and Lomelí 1989: 1).

Concurring with these ideological sentiments, Chicanos were considered to not only 'regard the boundary as an impertinence', but also to consider that the south-western USA and northern Mexico 'compose a single geographical and cultural entity' (Pérez-Torres 1995: 91). The notion of historical and cultural primacy in the south-west and of previous ownership of the land is also central to the plan's ideology:

> In the spirit of a new people that is conscious not only of its proud historical heritage but also of the brutal 'gringo' invasion of our territories, we, the Chicano inhabitants and civilizers of the northern land of Aztlán from whence came our forefathers, reclaiming the land of their birth and consecrating the determination of our people of the sun, declare that the call of our blood is our power, our responsibility, and our inevitable destiny.
>
> (Anaya and Lomelí 1989: 1)

The image of the Chicano homeland presented by the plan is that of a land settled by an indigenous and 'civilised' people who were subsequently conquered and divested of their territory. In order to symbolically reclaim this territory the point of view is reoriented from dominant American perspectives, so that what is commonly known as the south-west of America becomes 'our northern land' from a Mexican perspective (Arteaga 1997: 13). The plan also rejects the brutal 'gringo' invasion of these territories, and states that 'Aztlán belongs to those who plant the seeds, water the fields, and gather the crops and not to the foreign Europeans' (Anaya and Lomelí 1989: 1). Leal (1989) points out that the emphasis placed on the tactics of land occupation, the role of land and labour in historical change, as well as the recognition that the land belongs to those who work it, clearly situates the plan in a Mexican revolutionary tradition (Anaya and Lomelí 1989: 11). Indeed, part of its dynamics lie in the power of this counter-discourse and the strong case it makes for railing against the American, the *gabacho* (a derisive term for Anglo-Saxon), whose intervention led to the loss of Mexican land after US annexation (Anaya and Lomelí 1989: 11).

The American conquest, having severed the region from the control of Mexico City and the local Mexican elites, effectively detached the resident Mexicans from their economic base and social position, thus damaging the prestige of Mexican culture in the region. The failed promises of the treaty of Guadalupe Hidalgo served to strengthen these injustices. Under Articles 8 and 9 of the treaty, Mexicans living in this area would become US citizens (if they so desired) and their civil and property rights would be protected. But because of the historic failure to guarantee these rights, Mexicans began to see themselves repeatedly as 'foreigners in their own land' and were increasingly excluded from participation in the larger American society (Gutiérrez 1995: 18). But it was not only the conflict over landownership that encouraged the perception of Mexicans as a 'foreign element'. As in other American wars, enemies of the USA were perceived as evil and unworthy of respect and anti-Mexican sentiment during the second half of the nineteenth century was ubiquitous. Religious difference was another source of anti-Mexican prejudice, and finally there was the crucial element of race. Collectively these distinctions were sufficiently powerful to justify the confinement of Mexican Americans to the most menial positions in the emerging capitalist economy (Gutiérrez 1995: 18–28).

The idea and theory of internal colonialism which fed into the politics of the movement and which informed *El Plan Espiritual de Aztlán*'s perspective developed logically from this interpretation of the Chicano experience in the south-west. Serrano (2000) states that, 'Internal Colonialism arises from the necessity of studying new types of subordination not included in traditional colonialism or in neo-colonialism . . . traditional colonialism (oppression among separate nations) d[oes] not explain why some ethnic or racial minorities were discriminated in countries where they had full citizenship' (Lomelí and Ikas 2000: 191). Generally, the common denominator of these studies states that internal colonialism is marked by the forced entry of the colonised into the colonising society (America); the subsequent genocide of the colonised culture; the imposition of external administration by the coloniser, and the perpetration of racist practices by the colonising group (Acuña 1988, Serrano 2000). Accordingly, this model is applicable to the Chicano situation in the south-west, as although Mexican Americans were granted citizenship under the terms of the treaty, they were socially, culturally and economically subordinated and territorially segregated by the colonising forces of America.

Conversely, it was the socio-political aims generated by the movement that marked a key moment in the proposed emancipation of Chicana/os from what was considered to be colonial rule. An integral part of *El Plan Espiritual de Aztlán* is the 'programme' section that outlines a series of resolutions designed to achieve these kinds of goals. Promising the redress of past grievances, it demanded restitution for past 'economic slavery, political exploitation, ethnic and cultural psychological destruction and denial of civil and human rights' (Anaya and Lomelí 1989: 3). It stated that 'our struggle then must be for the control of our *barrios, campos, pueblos*, lands, our economy, our culture, and our political life' (Anaya and Lomelí 1989: 2). And 'lands rightfully ours will be fought for and defended. Land and realty ownership will be acquired by the community for the people's welfare' (Anaya and Lomelí 1989: 2).

These resolutions rather than reclaiming a mythic heritage, represent strategies to win political and economic control of Mexican American communities and lands across the south-west. It was in this vein that the importance of the struggle for community control of schools received special emphasis. Using nationalism as a base upon which to build, the resolutions advocated bilingual education and the need for Chicano Studies programmes which would teach Chicanos their history and culture. Many Chicano groups were inspired by this kind of politics, and many of the plan's ideals were put into practice at the community level during the movement's most formative years. According to 'Corky' Gonzales (1972) one community-based educational organisation, La Escuela y Colegio Tlatelolco in Denver, Colorado, established by the Crusade for Justice in 1970, strove to achieve 'adequate educational opportunities for the Chicano' (Esquibel 2001: 173). In his Arizona State University Speech given in 1970 'Corky' Gonzales also stated that the school would disseminate the ideals of *El Plan Espiritual de Aztlán* and thereby inculcate an awareness of the Chicano experience (Esquibel 2001: 39). 'When we start to teach in the *barrio* how we are a colonised people', he claimed, 'then we're able to understand how we live in this country' (Esquibel 2001: 39).

Economic practices based on capitalist goals and values were also rejected in favour of communal values thought to be at the core of Mexican and Mexican American culture. According to the plan, Mexican cultural values, particularly those embedded in the family and home, were to be the most 'powerful weapon to defeat the gringo dollar value system and encourage the process of love and brotherhood' (Anaya and Lomelí 1989: 3). Likewise, capitalist economic institutions were to be replaced by cooperatives that would create, 'economic control, distribution of resources and production to sustain an economic base for healthy growth and development' (Anaya and Lomelí 1989: 2).

In balancing these geo-political and socio-economic concerns on the one hand with cultural politics on the other, the plan served a dual purpose. Reflecting upon this duality Pérez-Torres (1995) states that its 'ambiguous' aims revealed 'its role as a split between a strategic critique of socio-political reality and an iconographic instrument of cultural unity' (Pérez-Torres 1995: 58). Recent studies have indicated that there is more generally a duality to be found within nationalist politics (Hutchinson and Smith 1994: 122–31). Ideologically, it was the two competing strains of cultural nationalism and political nationalism that came to dominate the movement during its most potent years. Whereas cultural nationalists wanted to preserve Aztlán as the birthplace of a distinct civilisation, unique history and culture, political nationalists had differing objectives and saw in the concept of Aztlán the possibility of achieving a representative national state that would guarantee to its members uniform citizenship rights. Political nationalists such as José Angel Gutiérrez considered Chicano culture to be important for purposes of mobilisation because it defined the group, and an understanding of the political history affecting the Chicano experience was thought to be important for purposes of collective action. But rather than drawing on a pre-Columbian hagiography as a source for political motive, political nationalists attacked existing political institutions that blocked the realisation of their goals. The efforts of MALDEF to use the legal system to protect the civil rights of Chicanos, and the urban project of MAYO in Crystal City, Texas are clear examples of this kind of activism during the movement's most formative years. While cultural nationalism made a positive contribution to the task of nation building – in other words, to the identification, organisation and unification of the community, it is clear from these examples that political nationalists worked within specific areas in order to secure a state that would embody their political aspirations.

Though different in their ideology, both forms of nationalism initially coalesced around the idea of a separate nation based on a politicised Chicano community and the concept of a 'natural homeland'. In practice, however, the goal of recovering land proved idealistic and the divergent goals of political and cultural nationalists problematic. Ideologically, the politics of cultural nationalism differed greatly from that of the political nationalist and arguably this difference was responsible for the most significant split in the movement as a whole. This occurred when ideological differences formed a rift between Chicano pragmatists led by José Angel Gutiérrez and Chicano cultural nationalists led by 'Corky' Gonzales. Furthermore, several critics agree that when considering Aztlán as a concrete territorial region, it is difficult to separate fact from myth, and to clearly establish many geographic and socio-political details (Pérez-Torres 1995, Padilla 1989, Neate 1998). Pérez-Torres (1997) defines Aztlán as an 'empty signifier', in other words Aztlán reflects 'that which is ever absent: nation, unity, liberation' (Pérez-Torres 1997: 37). Other critics focus on what they see as the 'inventions' of certain early critics and writers. Some attribute this to 'shrill sloganeering that abused myth' (Padilla 1989: 124). Others focus on the plan's 'incomplete analysis' and its ideological and political vagueness' (Pérez-Torres 1995: 67).

To understand how the idealism of Aztlán was most limited, however, we need only recall how the male *carnalismo* philosophy excluded women. First and foremost the plan overtly reconnects to the forefathers as a basis for land reclamation. According to Chávez (1984), in the minds of Chicanos the territory of the south-west 'remains their patrimony' (Chávez 1984: 1). In other words the south-west and Aztlán are constitutive elements of their *patria*, and are as such an overwhelmingly paternal inheritance. Research has indicated that at the grass-roots level this found its corollary in the reinscription of the heterosexual hierarchisation of male–female relationships. As stated previously, in many organisations associated with the liberation of Aztlán, male domination was the rule and women were often excluded from the decision-making process. In Texas, Los Cinco's dominance in MAYO underwrote the gendered inequalities inherent both to Mexican culture as well as cultural nationalism, and presented an obstacle to women who wanted to play a major role in the organisation (Navarro 1995: 403). Likewise the educational philosophy at La Escuela y Colegio Tlatelolco in Denver placed an emphasis on the importance of brotherhood in the construction of the community and nation. As 'Corky' Gonzales stated in 1973, 'Tlatelolco is based on la familia concept. Carnalismo is the common, living practice at Tlatelolco' (Esquibel 2001: 174). According to the logic of *carnalismo* it would be the sons from the barrios who most profited from Tlatelolco's educational philosophy, giving them an opportunity to merge into high schools and universities, where they become part of a wider sibling community of metaphoric brothers.

Perceiving Aztlán as an ideal site for *carnalismo* to flourish, *El Plan Espiritual de Aztlán* specifically names 'brotherhood' as a necessary and unifying force for group deliverance: 'brotherhood unites us, and love for our brothers makes us a people whose time has come' (Anaya and Lomelí 1989: 1). It is *carnalismo* (brotherhood) that most directly contributes to the formation of *la familia de la raza*, effectively uniting all Chicanos in one family. But for Chicanas, entrenchment within such masculinist family structures automatically impeded their participation in the Chicano nation and prevented them from achieving certain 'rights'.

A tension thus exists between the politics of *El Plan Espiritual de Aztlán* that wanted to achieve equal rights for the nation's community, and its politics of patriarchal nationalism that excluded women from its borders. Following Lowe's (1990) comments on national identity in another context, we might say that the Chicano nationalist narrative 'incorporate[d] the subject according to a relationship that is not dissimilar to the family's oedipalisation, or socialisation, of the son . . . he becomes a citizen when he identifies with the paternal state' (Lowe 1990: 56). Women on the other hand were incorporated into the Chicano nation only indirectly through men, as dependent members of the family. Moreover, according to the logic of *El Plan Espiritual de Aztlán* civil liberties were to be granted only to those people who qualify as subjects of the Chicano nation, in other words, Chicano men. Chicanas as such were denied similar rights.

The complexity of this internal contest for power suggests the embedded nature of gender oppression within Chicano society at that time. Women were implicated in the rise of the Chicano movement and its proposed solutions to oppression, but at the same time they were considered to be potentially or actually against the plan and its programme. Statements made at the Denver Youth Conference reinforced this position by reminding the women attending that their role in the Chicano movement was subordinate to their male counterparts. As López (1977) stated, to threaten this hierarchy was considered to be counterproductive to their national liberation (A. Garcia 1997: 103).

The overwhelming paternalism of the plan and of statements such as these ensured that they would be subsequently challenged and negotiated. Due to pressure from the Chicana feminist movement, three years after writing *El Plan Espiritual de Aztlán*, Alurista addressed the issue of gender and revised the wording for the introduction to his volume of poetry, *Nationchild Plumaroja*. What had been in the plan 'Brotherhood unites us, and love for our brothers' becomes in the revised edition 'brotherhood and sisterhood unites us, and love for our brothers and sisters' and 'the northern land of Aztlán' becomes 'our motherland Aztlán' (Arteaga 1997: 18). During the movement the patriarchal bias of its politics increasingly came to dominate issues of identity, location and meaning. In order to explore male representations of the Chicano nation in further detail the remainder of this chapter will discuss these issues in relation to Rudolfo Anaya's *Heart of Aztlán* (1988), a novel first published seven years after the Denver Youth Conference in 1969 and the first reading of *El Plan Espiritual de Aztlán*. As I go on to state, despite this lapse in time Anaya continues to represent the Chicano nation as a male space in ways that overtly parallel the politics of the movement.

Set in New Mexico in the 1940s, Anaya's protagonist is forced through economic necessity to move his family from the rural *llano* into the barrio of Barelas in Albuquerque, New Mexico. On first arrival there the Mexican American barrio community provides a welcome for the family, 'As they talked about the people they knew they found many neighbours and *compadres* in common and Clemente realised that many of the families he had known in the small towns and *ranchos* were now here in the city' (Anaya 1988: 11). The friendly atmosphere of the close-knit community initially makes the barrio seem like a viable alternative to their home on the New Mexican *llano*. But once in Barelas the wife, Adelita, refers to Clemente Chavez as 'a man lost in a foreign land' as without his farm and his land he soon becomes alienated and without a clear sense of identity. As he astutely observed before leaving for Barelas: 'when I sell my land I will be cast adrift, there will be no place left to return to, no home to come back to' (Anaya 1988: 3).

Chavez's loss of a home and sense of identity is further compounded by his reduction to the status of a dependent wage labourer at the Santa Fe railroad. This in turn results in a dramatic change in the Chavez familial structure, as, without a sense of roots, the family begin to experience the loss of tradition and culture. Accurately reflecting the process of Chicano urbanisation in the twentieth century, Anaya depicts several of the Chavez children's identification with the local *pachuco* brotherhood, the *carnalismo* of the barrio and their subsequent loss of respect for *familia* rules and traditions (de León 2001, Sanchez 1993). Rather than acting as a tool for resistance against the dominant group, the Chavez family undergoes a rapid transformation in its structure and customs during which the *pachuco* gangs provide an alternative sense of identity and social support for the children.

External factors contribute overwhelmingly towards the dysfunctional nature of the Chavez family. Once in the barrio they experience racial restrictions and class barriers, poor and congested housing and unhealthy living conditions, police repression and an underworld economy comprised of *movidas* (crooked deals) drugs and prostitution. Poverty and lack of occupational mobility, in addition to race and cultural prejudice, keep the Mexican American community segregated inside the boundaries of the barrio. The opportunity that city life holds for these newcomers is thus soon tempered by the realities of Mexican American life there. Although initially attracted by the opportunities for employment that the barrio offers, since his arrival Chavez has been a virtual prisoner of the Santa Fe railroad, and is thus unable to leave the barrio or to realise his wife's ambition for greater economic wealth that motivated the family's initial migration. Many other Mexicans similarly suffer exploitation at the railroad yard, an empire carefully constructed and developed using hundreds of men from the Barelas barrio:

> The black tower of steel loomed over everything. Around it trains thrashed like giant serpents, and when they coupled the monstrous act gave unnatural birth to chains of steel. Jason cautiously approached the labyrinth of grimy buildings, steel tracks and boxcars. The houses near the yards were dark with soot and the elm trees withered and bare. A chain link fence surrounded the yard.
>
> (Anaya 1988: 22)

The descriptions of the yard emphasise its capacity for dehumanisation. Its structure integrates work and housing in a way that is designed to maximise the dependence of the workers on the railroad company. The railroad owners are thus not only in control of the social and economic forces which determine Chicano working conditions, but also in control of the neighbourhood and its use value for American industrial and commercial interests. Serrano (2000), in his discussion of Anaya's text as an 'Example of Chicano Proletarianisation within an Internal Colonial Framework', states that Anaya also images the confinement of Chicano workers within these systems as a captive labour force (Lomelí and Ikas 2000: 191–9).[1] Certainly at several points in the text the men of Barelas are portrayed as 'long lines of men bound in chains of steel' (Anaya 1988: 130). At other times they are depicted as 'slaves to the steel' (Anaya 1988: 203). Within this system, jobs are hard to come by and are confined to semi-skilled or unskilled labour. Unemployment is a serious problem, creating a disproportionate number of economic outcasts and a disaffected underclass:

> if you have no job and your kids are going hungry then it doesn't matter if you sell your soul to the devil or to the railroad! Either way, we're in the same pinch all the time, just holding our noses above debts so we won't drown, hoping things at the shops don't get worse.
>
> (Anaya 1988: 16)

Juxtaposed with these scenes are those Chavez experiences with the old Indian, Crispin, a blind poet and musician of the barrio whose 'melody and the magic of his words carried them out their present time and misery to a time of legends and myths' (Anaya 1988: 83). In this sense Anaya follows the logic of other movement narratives such as Rivera's *Y no se lo trago la tierra/ And the Earth Did Not Devour Him* (1987) in which debilitating scenes such as these are counterpoised by other scenes which suggest a collective unity. Aiming to inspire a sense of community by educating the men of the barrio about their common cultural heritage and distinct national civilisation, Crispin tells of the myth of Aztlán and the founding of the Aztec empire:

> It is a simple story . . . a burning god fell from the sky and told the people to travel southward. The sign for which they were to watch was a giant bird in whose claws would be ensnared the poisonous snakes which threatened the people. In that place, under the protection of that plumed bird, the wanderers from Aztlán were to build their new civilisation. There they would meet the second part of their destiny.
>
> (Anaya 1988: 83–4)

Projecting a dynamic vision of Aztlán as a high civilisation with a unique place in the development of Chicano history, Crispin's stories represent a source of collective memory, a memory from which the workers have been estranged because of their experiences in the barrio and at the hands of the Santa Fe railroad. An indication of this occurs when the rest of the men from the barrio after hearing Crispin's story turn their backs on him and return to the relentless realities of barrio life. After listening to the heroic legends of the past, the 'grime and poverty of the *barrio* enveloped them again' the *cuentos* and myths only 'helped to pass the time and ease the despair of going jobless that winter, but that was all' (Anaya 1988: 83–4); '[And] stories of the past didn't put beans and meat on the table for the family' (Anaya 1988: 85).

Passages such as this recall Fanon's discussion of the process through which subjected peoples reject 'the colonial structures that distort, devalue and seek to destroy their history' (Fanon 1990: 168). While he is 'ready to concede that on the plane of factual being the past existence of an Aztec civilisation does not change anything very much in the diet of the Mexican peasant of today', he also acknowledges the power of myth and cultural identity as an effective strategy employed by certain groups in order to avoid 'that Western culture in which they all risk being swamped' (Fanon 1990: 168).

It is in this kind of oppositional vein that Crispin encourages Clemente Chavez to heed the *cuentos* and become leader of the railroad workers who need guidance and representation as they are doubly exploited, both by the corrupt unions as much as the railroad company itself. During the course of the text the workers of Barelas organise a significant pattern of labour activism in a way which has resonance with the issues addressed by the Chicano movement. Recognising that their relegation to the bottom of the occupational and wage hierarchy follows from their exploited position as a despised racial minority, most of the organisational and strike directed efforts among Mexican workers begin as protests over traditional issues like wages and hours. After the death of a fellow employee, however, they expand their initial demands for higher wages to a larger discussion of better working conditions and basic human rights. Working together to press their demands for social justice, a wildcat strike is called to protest conditions at the shops and corruption within the union itself. However, the protests of the Chicano workers are futile and as a result of their efforts the railroad announces a large lay-off. Those Chicano workers who defy the administration of the shops by organising picket lines are also laid off and later put on black lists, which prevent them from finding another job; 'work is scarce all right' comments one character, 'I swear there's not one *pinche jale* in this town!' (Anaya 1988: 160).

Clemente Chavez is one of the workers who rebels against the oppressive conditions of the railroad company and is as a consequence fired. In despair he follows Crispin's advice and looks to myth and tradition as an antidote. Under the tutelage of an old *curandera*, and the guidance of Crispin, Chavez embarks upon a mystical journey in search of Aztlán. Consequently, at this point in the novel it is not certain when 'real' events end and those of an hallucinatory nature begin. Transcending existent temporal and spatial barriers during Chavez's journey 'dreams and visions became reality, and reality was but the thin substance of myth and legends' (Anaya 1988: 129). By transcending the confines of space and time in a dreamlike re-enactment of the myth, Chavez 'metaphorically' leaves New Mexico and the barrio of Barelas and first of all journeys 'towards the south'. Once there 'in the land of the south they walked among the ruins where ancient gods once lived and died, and on the facades of crumbling temples they read the sacred signs' (Anaya 1988: 129).

Following the signs, Chavez and Crispin eventually discover a land patterned after the primordial homeland from which the Aztecs originated. Rooted in a sacred landscape that is charged with the power of an indigenous spirituality, Aztlán is figured in a similar manner to much movement writing as the centre, and as the land encircled by water where 'the seven springs form the sacred lake' by 'the desert of white herons' (Anaya 1988: 129). At the same time, it is not entirely idyllic, as of all the various transformations Chavez experiences on the road in search of Aztlán possibly the most profound is his encounter with the suffering masses who cry for help and freedom from oppression:

> *People tumbled like driftwood in a spring-flooded river. Each ghost clutched at him and cried for help. Deliver us, Clemente Chavez! they cried . . . Strike down the snakes of steel that bind our soul, the people cried. Deliver us from this oppression! Strike down injustice!*
>
> (Anaya 1988: 129)

When Chavez falls into the river, or 'the manswarm', it signals another level in his initiation since it allows him to see the heart of Aztlán: 'time stood still, and in that enduring moment he felt the rhythm of the heart of Aztlán beat to the measure of his own heart' (Anaya 1988: 131). Leal concludes his essay 'In Search of Aztlán' (1989) with the admonition, 'whosoever wants to find Aztlán let him look for it, not on the maps, but in the most intimate part of his being' (Anaya and Lomelí 1989: 13). In much the same way, in Anaya's text at the climactic moment of the conversion scene, Clemente totally surrenders to the myth and experiences 'A joyful power' which 'coursed from the dark womb-heart of the earth into his soul and he cried out I AM AZTLÁN!' (Anaya 1988: 131).

Anaya reconstructs Chavez's difficult and painful journey to Aztlán as a passage through the sedimentary levels of consciousness. By the end of his journey the experiences of displacement and lack of orientation that occur at the beginning of the novel have been replaced by a firm sense of direction and a commitment to social politics and action. Aztlán fills the spiritual, cultural and political void experienced by Chavez in the barrio having been ruptured from his land and home. It enables his rise from abjection into full control, and a man capable of leading the community. Anaya thus foregrounds the potential of the myth to act as a power capable of restoring self-identity and self-determination. Instead of evaporating into an idealised past, Aztlán is figured as socially powerful and capable of providing a viable politics for the future. In this sense the text indicates a level of convergence between cultural nationalism and the rights of Mexican American labour in the US in a parallel manner to *El Plan Espiritual de Aztlán* and the politics of the movement.

In mirroring movement ideology in this way, Anaya's representation of Aztlán remains dominated by cultural nationalist discourse that restricts its concerns to race and class struggles. Chicana subjects are either displaced from group characterisations or mediated by systems of differentiation that privilege male forms of identity and subjectivity. The Chicana activist and scholar Elizabeth Martinez points out that Aztlán has always been 'set forth in super-macho imagery', stating that 'the concept of Aztlán encourages the association of *machismo* with domination' (Martinez 1998a: 127). It is in this vein that during Crispin's retelling of the myth, Anaya foregrounds the formative place of Huitzilopochtli in the development of the Aztec and Mexicano history:

> He came in the form of a fiery serpent and the light he cast was so bright it lit up all of Aztlán . . . and he answered their prayers by walking among them and renewing the life of their fields, and ministering to those who were sick . . . and he spoke to the people of Aztlán and made a covenant with them . . . the people obeyed, and it said he lighted up the skies as they marched south. And it is said that all these things the god promised were delivered, and the people flourished and built a civilisation without equal.
>
> (Anaya 1988: 124)

This crucial aspect of the idealised Aztec society recuperated and valorised in nationalist narratives of Chicana/o identity, implicitly encodes the domination of women. Crispin's stories have the status of authority, resembling a quasi-religious discourse that perpetuates the myth of Huitzilopochtli as a 'cultural hero' who Pina (1989) states intervened 'into the collective experience of his people' (Anaya and Lomelí 1989: 26). In reconnecting to the Aztec warrior past, Anaya endorses this cultural legacy, a legacy that implicitly embraces machismo and paternalism as an integral facet of Chicano identity. Moraga (1993) states that the identification of Huitzilopochtli with Chicano identity endorses the 'machista myth', which implicitly subjugates women (Moraga 1993: 74). Representations of women as a consequence by and large fall into the good woman/bad women stereotypes promoted and upheld throughout the movement decades.

One of the typical 'bad woman' archetypes to appear in the text is the witch whose mystical powers initially set Chavez on his journey towards Aztlán. Her dwelling on the outskirts of the barrio marks her marginalisation from the rest of the community, as she is also portrayed as transgressing the boundaries of female normality and acceptability. Figured as the dark woman, alien and unruly, the witch is capable of disempowering men and so embodies the archetype of the *bruja* as progenitor of evil. These kind of stereotypical characteristics are not however confined solely to the witch as 'Las Golondrinas', the prostitutes who work in the barrio of Barelas, are also positioned in a similarly delimiting way. The young men of the barrio seem unable to acknowledge the prostitutes without being both attracted and repulsed by their sexuality. Anaya thus constructs only one dynamic between the male subjects and the prostitutes, which is that of contract and consumption. As Irigaray (1985a) writes in another context, in terms of sexual exchange Anaya's male characters 'make commerce of [women], but do not enter into any exchanges with them' (Irigaray 1985a: 172).

In a parallel manner Anaya associates the good women archetypes with traditional feminine values such as love, intuition, beauty, virtue, and idealising those women who embody the cardinal virtues of piety, purity, submissiveness and domesticity the most. As the mother of the Chavez family possesses these attributes, Anaya's portraits of her do not validate her heroic, labouring feats so much as her capacity for feminine self-abnegation. By extension, Anaya constructs masculine enterprise as work, and simultaneously omits women from the world of labour. Although the aptly named mother, Adelita (loyalist), performs a significant economic task within the family home, the father's place is primary, as he states, 'you know that the *familia* without a strong father soon falls apart' (Anaya 1988: 83).

Anaya's representation of the Chavez family, in fact, is striking in its recapitulation of *familia* ideology, and in its Oedipalisation as a unit. A gendered division of labour organises the Chavez family home, men being the chief wage earners and women doing the household work. Adelita does not work outside the family home – as a wife and mother she is primarily responsible for caring for Clemente, the Mexican male worker, and the family. Under the division of labour, she has to maintain the male work force as well as reproduce it. At the same time as being oppressed under a sexual division of labour, she helps to sustain the family's male workers and indirectly the American economy that prospers from male Mexican labour. Although Clemente's dream is of a progressive community organisation, women are not considered as prospective members of a social formation in which they are considered labouring subjects. Anaya's social 'message' thus functions to elevate the social and political position of men and to constrain women within accepted roles and spheres.

Some positive portrayals of women come readily to mind as instances that would seem to belie this construction of women as being outside of labour. Two women in the text, Juanita and Ana Chavez, talk about the impossibility of getting either a decent job or the means of living with the small salaries they earn in their present employment. Although they are forced to work from a young age, Juanita tries to encourage her sister to stay on at school, but as her sister points out, 'she didn't need a high school diploma to be a waitress' and seems resigned to remain working 'at the Coney Island downtown' (Anaya 1988: 69). Even with her diploma, Juanita has ended up being 'a clerk selling cosmetics at Payless' (Anaya 1988: 69). So far from being outside of labour these women in fact remain firmly ascribed to the unskilled workforce, members of what Alarcón (1990a) terms the 'surplus sources of cheap labour' (Trujillo 1998a: 375).

Significantly, on Chavez's journey women do not appear as subjects but only as symbols, either for the generative spirit in man or as an erotic object. At one point woman is 'keeper of the rock', a sign to be read on the journey, but as his journey progresses woman is literally constructed as an indicator for the nation:

> They moved north . . . there Aztlán was a woman fringed with snow and ice; they moved west, and there she was a mermaid singing by the sea . . . they walked to the land where the sun rises, and . . . they found new signs, and the signs pointed them back to the centre, back to Aztlán.
>
> (Anaya 1988: 126–30)

Even though these female figures are peripheral, they remain crucial to the text's general representation of women. By constructing a series of related values that cohere around visual appearance these figures become implicated in an already well-established discourse that concerns masculine dominance and feminine subordination. During the journey to Aztlán, passivity and inactivity become the dominant tropes associated with womanhood, and at certain points female muse figures are what the male subjects of the text search for. Even more problematically, the discovery of Aztlán involves a kind of violent baptism with the female body, 'the dark womb-heart of the earth' into which Clemete Chavez plunges his fists (Anaya 1988: 131). The production of Aztlán and the search for racial and collective origins that it entails thus sustains central oppressive discourses associated with Chicano nationalism including machismo politics and an essentialised concept of female identity. In this sense, like *El Plan Espiritual de Aztlán* before it, *Heart of Aztlán* perpetuates a gender-based exclusion in its imagining of a national community.

The concluding chapter explores the response by Mexican American women to the exclusions of the Chicano nation by movement politics. While myths of descent and the reacquisition of land form the basis for rebuilding Aztlán, the nation they imagine is formed through coalitions that move across borders and beyond the confines of the separatism promoted by the movement. The study concludes with the suggestion that it is the rewriting of the Chicano nation that conclusively displaces the nationalist agenda of the protest decades and in so doing supersedes previous manifestations of Chicana/o identity politics.

8 Mestiza Aztlán

A nation without borders

The following and concluding chapter considers some of the implications of the dominant constructions of Aztlán in more detail. The literary and political response from Chicanas and the ways in which they contest Aztlán's gendered contours provides much of the discussion. As previously stated, with the writing of *El Plan Espiritual de Aztlán* (1969) Chicanos claimed a nation through their cultural and ancestral primacy in the south-west. Anaya and Lomelí (1989) state that Aztlán enabled the Chicano group to 'find its tap root of identity in its history so that it could more confidently create the future' (Anaya and Lomelí 1989: ii). But this 'tap root of identity' was problematic. Aztlán as a unifying factor in the construction of Chicano identity was severely limited in the sense that women were unrepresented and were therefore excluded from its discourse. Nationalism and nation building were promoted as the all-encompassing answer to oppression, but at the same time its generically masculinist ideology meant that sexuality and gender were placed second to other issues, 'Once we have concretely placed nationalism as the guiding force within the Chicano/Mexicano movement, we will then begin to develop the means to challenge sexism and all other forms of exploitation as we march to free Aztlán' (Pérez 1999a: 73).

This quotation clearly indicates the hierarchies entrenched within nationalist ideology as gender, sexuality, and other differences appear to be subordinate to the more pressing issues of race and class as Chicanos 'march to free Aztlán'. Such a grading of oppressions featured in much movement literature and programmes including *El Plan Espiritual de Aztlán* (1969), the so-called 'blueprint for emancipation' that dictated the trajectory of the movement. But as previously stated, gender and sexuality are absent as terms of analysis in the plan's original manifesto: 'Nationalism as the key to organisation transcends all religious, political, class and economic factions or boundaries. Nationalism is the common denominator upon which all members of la raza can agree' (Anaya and Lomelí 1989: 1).

In basing these claims on an essentialised and biologically determined masculinity, a collective national identity finally proved to be untenable. Such founding ideas of *carnalismo* and blood brotherhood played a significant part in complicating women's participation in the Chicano nation. The resolutions from the Chicana workshop held during the conference at the same time as the plan was presented addressed these issues, and were some of the first attempts to rectify the situation. First, in response to accusations expressed by some Chicano nationalists that women's politics divided the movement, the female participants stated that, 'Chicanas resolve not to separate but to strengthen Aztlán' (A. Garcia 1997: 147). Second, in opposition to the separatism both cultural and gendered which orientated the plan's perspective they stated that they wanted to free, not only 'our nation of Aztlán' but also 'women and children' (A. Garcia 1997: 147).

This more inclusive agenda not only relocated Chicanas within the Chicano movement but also situated them within the nation's borders. Since then Chicana feminists have continued to reshape Chicana/o discourse, including Aztlán, which they attempt to reformulate as a more collective and inclusive nation of resistance. Ignacio M. Garcia (1997) has recently acknowledged this fact. Chicanas, he states, 'Played a significant role in [the] politics of Aztlán. In Colorado, as in Crystal City and throughout the south-west, women proved hard to intimidate in the political process (I. M. García 1997: 98).

In literary terms many Chicana lesbian texts produced in the 1970s also became an integral part of women's re-definitions of Aztlán. Pérez (1999c) cites Sylvia Alicia Gonzales's *Woman to Woman* (1974), Blanca Sandoval's *Eres mujer Chicana* (1977) and Leona Ruth Chacon's *Nací mujer* as examples of early Chicana lesbian texts which problematised Aztlán in order to reconfigure it as a more inclusive source for Chicanas and Chicana lesbian identity (Kaplan et al. 1999: 26–8). More recently these concerns have been echoed in the writings of Moraga and Anzaldúa in the 1980s, and subsequently in critical productions such as Alarcón's 'Anzaldúa's *Frontera*: Inscribing Gynetics' (1996) and Alicia Arrizon's essay 'Mythical Performativity: Relocating Aztlán in Chicana Feminist Cultural Productions' (2000) as well as Moraga's more recent dramatic production: *The Hungry Woman: A Mexican Medea* (2001).

These texts all follow the pattern established during the Chicana workshop in the sense that they question the gendered construction and representation of Aztlán as an exclusively male nation. In previous chapters I discussed the ways in which theatrical canons promoted this masculinist bias. Luis Valdez in particular considered that Chicano theatre should be intimately related to the 'evolving nationalism in Aztlán', and Hurtado's (1997) analyses of his dramatic production during the movement years substantiate this claim (Trujillo 1998a: 383–428). During this time the combined effects of male domination and nationalism that shaped the company's productions not only replicated the nation's gendered borders, but also effectively limited dramatic representations of women given their relationship to this confining structure.

In her most recent play, *The Hungry Woman: A Mexican Medea* (2001), Moraga presents a radically different perspective on the implications of this ideology. The play is set in a future when a series of ethnic wars have Balkanised the USA into several smaller nations in order to prevent further 'relentless political and economic expansion as well as Euro-American cultural domination' (Moraga 2001: 6). According to the playwright's note and setting, the counter-revolutionary 'Mechicano Nation of Aztlán' has achieved certain of *El Plan Espiritual de Aztlán's* original objectives and has 'established economic and political sovereignty' over 'parts of the south-west and the border states of what was once Northern Mexico' (Moraga 2001: 6). Several years after this 'liberation' was achieved, internal stratification along gender lines created an exclusionary operational structure whereby 'hierarchies were established between male and female, and queer folk were unilaterally sent into exile' (Moraga 2001: 6). *The Hungry Woman* thus emphasises not only the power relations built into the nation's hierarchies, but also critiques the ways in which its ideology implements oppressive systems of gender and sexuality within its borders.

Moraga's representation of Aztlán thus mirrors the basic dichotomy of the earlier nation in terms of the polarisation of gendered spaces. Figured as a separate state ruled over by a patriarchal ideology, possession of citizenship is of major importance since it brings with it many rights and privileges, including ownership of land. Relationships within the nation reflect this political economy and are characterised by systems of property exchange based on the classification of blood. In this sense Moraga's dramatisation accurately reflects earlier conceptions of Aztlán, particularly that presented in the plan which also considered biological factors to be of pre-eminent importance in the construction of the nation. Pérez-Torres states that Aztlán initially presented 'a confusion between geographic claims within a system of property exchange and cultural claims within a system of symbolic exchange' (Pérez-Torres 1995: 73). In much the same way, in the Aztlán of the future, purity of blood also legitimates citizenship and claims to land within its borders.

Medea is a *curandera* and midwife who has fought hard in the play's fictional revolution to help establish Aztlán. As the play opens she is incarcerated in the psychiatric ward of a prison as she has killed her son Chac-Mool for political reasons. Medea was once the wife of Jasón, a poet and high-ranking official in Aztlán, but since the discovery of his wife's relationship with Luna, a Chicana sculptor and stonemason, their marriage has ended (Mayorga 2001: 155–66). Because of the rigidly delineated and juridically bound contracts between citizens and nation, all of the characters experience problematic relationships with its ideology. Despite his masculinity Jasón's position in and with regard to Aztlán is no less problematic than that of his estranged wife Medea. He lacks the necessary Indian blood to grant him citizenship and ownership of land and has come to claim his son Chac-Mool in order to safeguard these privileges. The debates between Medea and Jasón over parental rights dramatise these conflicts and are central to the action. As Medea wryly comments at one point: 'He is your native claim. You can't hold onto a handful of dirt in Aztlán without him. You don't have the blood quantum' (Moraga 2001: 72).

Within Aztlán marriage is commonly seen in these terms. Relationships formed by men with women are a means of securing alliances, male heirs and the transmission of property. Medea and Jasón's relationship takes the form of a contract based on these kinds of exchange. The equivalence of this exchange is, however, fractured by betrayal and issues of gender and sexuality. For women relationships within Aztlán are based on unequal status, whereas relationships between men take the form of an exchange between equals. 'Heterosexuality', as Irigaray observes in another context, is 'the only acceptable sexual relationship' there (Irigaray 1985a: 172). An indication of this phallic economy occurs during the interactions between Medea and Jasón concerning their mutual betrayals. Medea cites the fact that despite her native blood enabling his claim to land, Jasón sexually betrayed her. Jasón in turn evokes the same argument when he accuses her of sexual betrayal with Luna. In this scheme of things Medea's is clearly the most significant betrayal as lesbian sexuality subverted nationalist ideology on a number of differing levels. Despite the fact that she has the necessary native blood she has been displaced outside of the nations boundaries because of her 'deviant' sexuality. In Aztlán, again as Irigaray writes: 'the only sex, the only sexes, are those needed to keep relationships among men running smoothly' (Irigaray 1985: 172).

The scenes between Medea and Jasón accentuate this polarisation and more sharply differentiate the conflict between genders. A significant moment in this polarity occurs with the confrontation between Medea and Jasón, particularly when they state their cases against each other in judicial terms. During these exchanges initially Medea competes on equal terms with Jasón, and deploys a range of rhetorical techniques in order to secure her objectives:

MEDEA: I was wondering about my status . . . Technically I still hold the right
    to return. My land—
JASÓN: I'm glad to see you face-to-face. The letters . . . your words are
    persuasive.

(Moraga 2001: 50)

At this point, instead of a relationship based on a difference of status, theirs is an interaction based on an exchange between equals. In scenes such as these Medea represents women as practitioners of exchange, rather than the objects of exchange normally associated with the nation's phallic economy. Arguably, what is most obvious about these interactions, however, is Jasón's complete lack of macho qualities. The most important male values normally associated with Chicano nationalism and inclusion in the nation were assertive qualities, such as personal honour, bravery and political power. These 'male' attributes are, however, progressively transferred to Medea. Her assertiveness and argumentative skill, also typical of male values, are brought to the fore, as is her role as counter-revolutionary and original founder of the nation. In this sense Medea embodies and deploys the skills of both sexes; she is skilled at argument, debate, bravery and takes over Jasón's male responsibility, particularly in her denial of his paternal role.

Medea's arguments are, however, not solely based on conventional rationality and logic. In other interactions she redefines the discourse used and presents a counter-argument in terms that explicitly oppose those of Jasón:

MEDEA: Betrayal occurs when a boy grows into a man and sees his mother as a woman for the first time. A woman. A thing. A creature to be controlled.
JASÓN: If it is so inevitable, give me the boy. Spare yourself the humiliation.
MEDEA: My son is still innocent, his eye will never see me 'as woman.' I promise you that.

(Moraga 2001: 70–1)

In scenes such as these Medea represents women as active participants rather than the passive roles prescribed by nationalist ideology. The very basis of her speech is the exposure of male power as something that oppresses women. Later and subsequent interactions graphically demonstrate the inequality of these power structures. Jasón's judicial arguments, for instance, are based on what Medea considers to be an unequal and highly differentiated concept of justice:

MEDEA: I sent the papers back because they were unacceptable. You ignored my conditions.
JASÓN: You aren't in a position to negotiate, Medea.
[JASÓN opens his briefcase, takes out a document, puts it on the table.]
JASÓN: The courts have already made their decision, Medea.
MEDEA: Which courts? Those patriarchs who stole my country? I return to the motherland in the embrace of a woman and the mother is taken from me.

(Moraga 2001: 68–71)

In scenes such as these Jasón seeks to polarise himself and Medea in psychological terms. He thinks logically, whereas Medea's speech contrasts with that of Jasón in emotional tone. Arguably, the most significant difficulty in the communication between Medea and Jasón in these major exchanges, though, lies in their differing conceptions of Aztlán. For Jasón, Aztlán signifies citizenship, with all the advantages that entails for the male citizen. For Medea on the other hand Aztlán signifies loss, sacrifice of family and bitter regret:

Men think women have no love of country, that desire for nation is a male prerogative. So like gods, they pick and choose who is to be born and live and die in a land I bled for more than any man. Aztlán how you betrayed me!

(Moraga 2001: 15)

This allusion to the nation reveals how its institutional and social organisation has betrayed Medea. As a lesbian she is not protected or represented by its patriarchal structures, and she indicates the civic wrongs done to her based on these gender inequalities. In terms of the structure of the nation presented in the play, she also belongs nowhere. Once banished and having no home to return to she is precipitated into a kind of no man's land in 'what now remains of Phoenix, Arizona' (Moraga 2001: 6). Phoenix embodies all the characteristics of the post-industrial ghetto as 'the dumping site of every kind of poison and person unwanted by its neighbours' and is located in 'a kind of metaphysical border region between *gringolandia* (USA) and Aztlán (Mechicano country)' (Moraga 2001: 6). An important corollary of Medea's transition to this borderland is the corresponding sense of dislocation. Her profound sense of loss is reflected in her renaming of Phoenix as 'Tamoanchán' (which in translation means, 'We seek our home') and in the way gay subjectivity is likened to the migration of the Aztec tribes in earlier generations, '*Y los homos* became *peregrinos . . . como nomads*, just like our Aztec ancestors a thousand years ago' (Moraga 2001: 24). Excluded from Aztlán's borders she describes herself as 'some huerfana abandoned' (abandoned orphan) and openly searches vainly for 'a motherland' (Moraga 2001: 15). This seemingly elusive space is located outside of the action, which mainly takes place in a psychiatric ward of a prison, as Medea has murdered Chac-Mool rather than have him indoctrinated into Aztlán's paternalistic structures. Moving between Aztlán and Medea's present-day location, the two spaces concur with movement ideology in the sense that they relate the primary association of lesbian women with displacement and liminality, in contrast to the corresponding linkages between maleness and the nation.

This gendered polarisation is invoked from a different perspective in *The Last Generation* (1993) where Moraga provides a critique of Aztlán's economic structures. As previously discussed, much of the rhetoric during the movement was concerned with the advocacy of equal opportunities for Chicano men, while Chicanas were excluded from advancement in many spheres. In *The Last Generation* (1993) Moraga outlines the implications of this ideology more explicitly, particularly in the section titled 'A Divided Nation: A Chicana Lésbica Critique' where she states, 'When "el plan espiritual de Aztlán" was conceived a generation ago, we were not recognised as the sister planting the seeds, the brother gathering the crops. We were not counted as members of the bronze continent' (Moraga 1993: 159).

Here Moraga demands a restructuring of the nation in order that it will represent and recognise women and queers in much the same way as the earlier nationalist paradigms did for students and farm workers. Given that the movement based its national liberation struggle on class, as well as race, and given that the plan was designed to reclaim the nation for its workers, Moraga's pointed critique of the economic exclusion of Chicanas appears to be particularly incisive. As discussed in previous chapters, women were positioned outside of the nation because they were also positioned outside of the world of labour. It follows then that Chicanas were also supplementary to the nationalist narrative of participation and national rights. Yet Chicanas were and are as often 'the surplus sources of cheap labour' as their male counterparts. The findings of Chicana historian Vicki Ruiz (1986) substantiate this claim. Chicanas, she states, 'have been overwhelmingly segregated into semi-skilled assembly line positions. Garment and food-processing firms historically hired Mexicans for seasonal line tasks' (de la Torre and Pesquera 1993: 264).

These labour related issues are naturally also reflected in the more literary writing by and about Chicanas. In the poem 'Metaphor and Reality' (1976) Bernice Zamora writes that 'Working in canneries or / picking beets is the / metaphor of being, of being as it has been / in the scheme of things' (Zamora 1976: 71). 'Cannery Town in August' (1981) by Lorna Dee Cervantes also provides an example of this kind of female labour pattern (Sánchez 1985, Pérez-Torres 1995, Libretti 1998, Villa 2000). In contrast to Chicano writers of the 1960s and 1970s whose work was dominated by references to the relationship between male Mexican labour and an American economy, Cervantes presents the physical and psychological effects experienced by the female workforce in a Californian canning factory where, 'All night it humps the air. / Speechless, the steam rises / from the cannery columns. / I hear / the night bird rave about work / or lunch, or sing the swing shift / home' (Cervantes 1981: 6). Contrary to reader expectations, 'Cannery Town in August' also depicts a night scene. Its explicit setting on a night shift is an effective strategy in the representation of female labour as it heightens the sense of isolation and desolation of the factory women's work. Implicit in the poem then is the recognition that women's work is somehow unseen or covert, and sharply differentiated from the far more usual visibility of male labour patterns.

What distinguishes Cervantes's poetry from that of Chicano nationalists most obviously though are the immediate references to a controlling economy as gendered in the opening line of the poem. Dominating the narrative, the cannery is figured explicitly in gendered terms as male. As Homero Villa (2000) states, 'the monstrous phalluses of the cannery columns call attention to the gendered status and labour conditions affecting Chicana workers' (Villa 2000: 216). As the poem progresses, this gendered status is further emphasised through the linkage established between the women's labour and an increasing sense of alienation and silencing brought about by the dominating phallic economy. The speaker of the poem imagines the women 'not speaking' and 'dumbed by the cans clamour and drop'. These references to muting echo the 'speechlessness' of the steam in line 2, as if both women and steam are equivalent waste products of the machine. Conversely, the poem itself is spare, both in terms of line length and in language, and therefore unlike the cannery nothing is wasted. Despite the leanness of Cervantes's expression, however, very much is said. The sense of alienation established in the preceding lines of the poem is further emphasised through the descriptions of the women's exhaustion and their physical appearance. This occurs in particular when the workers are described in terms that suggest the complete emptying out of the subject, as in the following lines:

> I listen, while bodyless
> uniforms and spinach specked shoes
> drift in monochrome down the dark
> moon-possessed streets . . .
> to the trucks that wait, grunting
> in their headlights below.
> they spotlight those who walk
> like a dream, with no-one
> waiting in the shadows
> to palm them back to living.
>   (Cervantes 1981: 6)

Despite the dystopic representation of women's work, right from the beginning of the poem Cervantes transforms what has been previously designated as male territory where women lead a secondary life confined to the shadows, into a space where women participate, albeit in gendered and exploitative terms, in the economy. By bringing together the dimensions of the women workers' material and political subjection in this way, Cervantes effectively illuminates the intersecting axes of exploitation they inhabit on and within the nation's borders.

During the movement women's exclusion from labour and the nation's economic structures was largely based on one of the most fundamental aspects of movement ideology. This is what Francisco Flores (1971) considered to be the 'erroneous cultural and historical understanding of what is meant by "our cultural heritage"' (A. Garcia 1997: 158). More recently Cherríe Moraga has elaborated this critique when she observed that:

> Nationalist leaders used a kind of 'selective memory' drawing exclusively from those aspects of Mexican and native cultures that served the interests of male heterosexuals. At the same time, they took the worst of Mexican machismo and Aztec warrior bravado, combined it with some of the most oppressive male-conceived idealisations of 'traditional' Mexican womanhood and called that cultural integrity.
>   (Moraga 1993: 156)

This perception of Chicana subjectivity was not confined to movement ideology of the protest decades alone of course, but also continues to influence more contemporary interpretations of Chicana identity. It is a subject Moraga returns to repeatedly in her work and has a strong influence on her rewriting of Aztlán. In order to 'create a broader and wiser revolution', she states, 'we seek a nation strong enough to embrace a full range of racial diversities, human sexualities, and expressions of gender' (Moraga 1993: 150–64).

This critique of Aztlán is not confined to writing by Moraga of course, but nonetheless it is representative of a more widespread reconsideration of the nation's boundaries and structures. Alarcón (1990a) states that for many Chicana writers Aztlán no longer signifies a lost 'utopia' or a source for the '"true" essence of our being' (Trujillo 1998a: 375). Instead, Alarcón (1990a) argues it is now figured in more contemporary terms as an empowering space 'whose resistant political implications must . . . be . . . refocused for feminist change' (Trujillo 1998a: 375). Lorna Dee Cervantes's 'Poem for the Young White Man who Asked Me How I, an Intelligent, Well-Read Person Could Believe in the War between Races', again from the collection *Emplumada* (1981), clearly illustrates this point. This poem opens with a vision of a homeland that has a complex relationship both with America and with the Chicano nation, 'in my land there are no distinctions / The barbed wire politics of oppression / have been torn down long ago. / The only reminder / of past battles, lost or won, is a slight / rutting in fertile fields' (Cervantes 1981: 35). The image of a homeland Cervantes presents here is clearly uto-pian. There are no wars, no 'distinctions' between peoples or 'politics of oppression'. The peacefulness of the present day is only disturbed by evidence of more violent events from the distant past which appear as 'a slight rutting in fertile fields'. These idyllic qualities are emphasised again in lines 10–12, when the speaker states that 'There are no boundaries', 'hunger' or 'compli-cated famine or greed' (Cervantes 1981: 35). Yet as the poem progresses this utopian vision of a homeland is displaced with images of an opposing nature. Pérez-Torres states that Cervantes's poem 'serves to mark the dis-continuity of "Aztlán" in its portrayal of divergent lands' (Pérez-Torres 1995: 85). He continues by discussing how she 'maps a terrain that is both an internal landscape scarred by racism and an external battleground that sounds with blasting and muffled outrage' (Pérez-Torres 1995: 87). Following this interpretation, the 'continent of harmony and home' that began the poem gives way to a nightmare terrain where 'the crosses are burning' where there are 'sharp shooting goose-steppers round every corner' and 'snipers in schools', and where the speaker is 'marked by the color of my skin' (Cervantes 1981: 35–7).

Part of the power of these visions of neo-Nazi racially motivated attacks lies in their realism and uncanny resemblance to more recent events in US and European history. Read in the context of movement ideology they sup-port the view that race was the primary source of Chicano oppression. Yet while I would agree with this interpretation in the sense that race is certainly of major importance in the poem, I would also suggest that the speaker's gender complicates conventional understandings of oppression, and this by implication affects the poetic representation of a homeland.

The title of the poem suggests that the speaker is different not only in race but also in gender from the addressee, and later references to children clearly state this position more explicitly (Sánchez 1985: 91). Race and gender most overtly coalesce, however, in the final lines of the poem when the speaker states that 'every day I am deluged with reminders / that this is not / my land / and this is my land' (Cervantes 1981: 36–7). Initially this presents a view of events that reflect nationalist ideology as the loss of Chicano land to the white oppressor was the pre-eminent issue in movement politics. But on closer reading Cervantes's gender necessarily forces a reconsideration of the implicitly masculinist underpinnings of this closing statement. As a woman she is excluded from the Chicano homeland in political, cultural and gendered terms. The closing lines thus necessarily take on an ambiguity that reflects this position. Instead of upholding the nationalist line, gender and sexuality intersect in the closing lines in ways that suggest the continuing complexity of women's relationship to the land, home and nation.

In effect, Cervantes's poem redraws the boundaries of the Chicano nation, demarcating additional borders because of the previously repressed issue of gender. The work of Moraga and Anzaldúa likewise marks a broadening and a transgression of the political and cultural space of the Chicano nation, again largely through the emphasis they place on gender and body politics. In *The Last Generation* (1993) Moraga reiterates this point, presenting Aztlán in a similarly dualistic manner to that of Cervantes as both a 'physical' and as a 'metaphysical' territory (Moraga 1993: 153). In a similar manner in *Borderlands/La Frontera* (1987) Anzaldúa refers to Aztlán as 'land of herons, land of whiteness, the Edenic place of origin of the Azteca' in much the same way as movement rhetoric (Anzaldúa 1987: 4). Yet her conception of a homeland also differs radically in many ways. Throughout her text, rather than asserting a place of origins, Aztlán is figured as a new politicised mestiza space that she maps onto multiple literal, geo-political and psychic borders.

This radical perspective on the Chicano homeland opens *Borderlands/La Frontera* (1987). The first chapter, titled 'The Homeland, Aztlán', contains three subdivisions which are titled 'El otro México/The Other Mexico', 'El destierro/The Lost Land', and 'El cruzar del mojado/Illegal Crossing' respectively (Anzaldúa 1987: 1–13). These three locations establish an ambiguity that at once suggests a spatial and historical antecedence that is parallel to movement ideology, but at the same time simultaneously transforms the idea of the homeland as a fixed space into a shifting or borderland location. By constituting the US–Mexico border as Aztlán, the homeland, she suggests a radically different interpretation of the Chicano nation to prior interpretations. Using a combination of narrative techniques including poetry and personal autobiography with an analysis of Chicano history, she effectively deconstructs the gendered contours of the nation and its role in the normative production of Chicana subjectivity.

Her assertion of the historical primacy of the Chicano group in the southwest during these opening chapters emphasises the rightfulness of the return of the mestizo race and in this respect on first reading she appears to conform to movement rhetoric. In 'El otro México' she states that, 'For the Indians, this constitute[s] a return to the place of origin, Aztlán, thus making Chicanos originally and secondarily indigenous to the south-west' (Anzaldúa 1987: 5).

Again in 'El cruzar del mojado/Illegal Crossing' she reiterates this point, 'Today we are witnessing *la migración de los pueblos mexicanos*, the return odyssey to the historical/mythological Aztlán' (Anzaldúa 1987: 11). Yet, while these migrations appear to be a moving into familiar territory, this is not necessarily a search for, or a perpetuation of origins along the lines of earlier thought. Taking on board the migratory nature of contemporary Chicano populations means that 'home' likewise becomes a mobile space, and as such cannot be considered a juridically bounded and nationalised geo-political territory. Pérez-Torres (1995) further argues this point and suggests that contemporary manifestations of Aztlán disclose a narrative that is 'not so much ... a ... return to home [the original narrative of Aztlán] as about nomadic passage' (Pérez-Torres 1995: 84). He goes on to state that:

> It marks a significant transformation away from the dream of origin toward an engagement with the construction of cultural identity, the move represents at this point a liberating one that allows for the assumption of various subject positions. The refusal to be delimited, while simultaneously claiming numerous heritages and influences, allows for a rearticulation of the relationship between self and society, self and history, self and land.
>
> (Pérez-Torres 1995: 96)

Anzaldúa addresses these issues from a slightly different perspective in 'El otro México/The Other Mexico'. Here the history of the border between the USA and Mexico, or 'home', is figured as a violent and continuing legacy of US imperialism, '1,950 mile-long open wound / dividing a *pueblo*, a culture, / running down the length of my body, / staking fence rods in my flesh, / splits me splits me / *me raja me raja*' (Anzaldúa 1987: 2). This radically split and violent landscape, which is figured in material terms as a wounded female body and body politic, is the contemporary manifestation of the Chicano nation. Progressively detailing the loss of Mexican and Indian land to American incursion, the chapter proceeds to radicalise previous readings of its history in the sense that local issues to Texas and the borderland as well as of gender and sexuality are central to the analysis (Saldívar-Hull 2000: 70–1).

As a material geographic region, the US–Mexican borderlands can be defined roughly as the territory centred on the international boundary line that stretches from Brownsville in Texas to San Diego in California. The Mexican and US governments settled the location of the border with the signing of the treaty of Guadalupe Hidalgo in 1848 and the Gadsden Purchase in 1853. But long before this Indian communities had settlements in the area. In the seventeenth century, Spanish settlers took possession of these lands in grants made by the Spanish crown and thus established the area as the northern frontier of New Spain and then of Mexico after its war of independence which began in 1810. In the decades following the US–Mexican war (1846–8) ideas of 'Manifest Destiny' dominated land-acquiring practices by the Americans who settled there. US cattle barons and agricultural opportunists from the east and mid-west soon controlled US–Mexican trade across the newly formed border and began to establish economic and social domination in the region. This was despite the fact that mestizas/os, who combined Indian and Hispanic heritages, were already inhabitants of the area. Derogatory perceptions by Americans cast them as a combination of what they perceived to be the worst qualities of their Amerindian and Iberian ancestors. Historian David Weber concurs with this view when he states that:

> Anglo Americans had inherited the view that Spaniards were unusually cruel, avaricious, treacherous, fanatical, superstitious, cowardly, corrupt, decadent, indolent, and authoritarian – a unique complex of pejoratives that historians from Spain came to call the Black Legend, *la leyenda negra* . . .
>
> (Weber 1992: 335–9)

This racially charged ideology ensured the continuing subaltern status of Mexican Americans, as did the treaty of Guadalupe Hidalgo (1848), which likewise 'sanctioned the inferior political status of the Mexican' (Montejano 1987: 311). Many of Anzaldúa's narratives and poems tell of these inequities and the events involved in the forging of an Anglicised Texas out of the Texas–Coahuila territory of New Spain, as well as the eventual production of the geo-political border between Mexico and the USA. Her discomfort at being a border woman stems from the political legacy of the territory and her gendered status. It is not surprising then that she refers to the border as an 'open-wound', when her conception of the borderlands grows out of her own experiences of these injustices. In much the same way as the movement she conceives of the border as 'an unnatural boundary' that has been created by fears about the sovereignty of the American nation-state and the safety of its borders (Anzaldúa 1987: 3). This land she states 'has survived possession and ill use by five powers: Spain, Mexico, The Republic of Texas, The United States, The Confederacy, and the US again. It has survived Anglo-Mexican blood feuds, lynchings, burnings, rapes, pillage' (Anzaldúa 1987: 90). The various claims to ownership of the land 'form a third country, a border culture' (Anzaldúa 1987: 3). In Chicana writing this 'country' is reclaimed and renamed as a feminist state and is strongly associated with ideas of liberation and transition. Some writers call it 'Queer Aztlán' (Moraga); others see it as 'Nepantla, the land in the middle or between' (Pat Mora) whereas for Anzaldúa it represents 'El destierro/The Lost Land' (Anzaldúa 1987: 6).

Displacing the dominant narratives of the nations history, the loss of land in *Borderlands/La Frontera* instead takes the far more personal form of a *recuerdo*, or a remembering. The mixture of genres used, the oral with the written, and family history with autobiography, form discourses which problematise established notions of the Chicano nation. Instead, historical document, legends, anecdotes and discussion of land-grant laws, are combined with her grandmother's and mothers narratives as recourse to historical authority: 'My grandmother lost all her cattle, they stole her land . . . My father's mother, mama locha also lost her terrano' (Anzaldúa 1987: 8). Later on in the text, Anzaldúa responds to this loss in the poem 'Don't Give in Chicanita' where she states in a more oppositional and strongly defiant mode, that 'yes, they've taken our lands. / But they will never take that pride / of being mexicana-Chicana-tejana / nor our Indian woman's spirit' (Anzaldúa 1987: 202–3). Collectively, these reminders of a land irrevocably lost not only construct new histories of the nation but are also set against the limited and marginal perceptions of Aztlán by movement ideology.

Ultimately, this configuration of a borderland or a 'third space' by Anzaldúa can be strongly associated with a strategy that Emma Pérez calls 'third space feminism' (Pérez 1999a: 32). According to Pérez, historically when Mexican women's politics have been subordinated under a nationalist paradigm, they construct their own spaces within nationalism. This she states is the site for 'a third space feminism' a space that is positioned 'within and between dominant male discourses' (Pérez 1999a: 32–3). This radically different and politicised location for Chicanas reverses the nationalist parameters of exclusion and substitutes these with a politics of inclusion. Aztlán is thus loosened from its ideologically inscribed 'place', to become a new space, which in Anzaldúa's reconfiguration is composed of a community of those previously excluded.

This reformulation of the nation's community is formed in opposition to the movement's 'imagined community' of Aztlán, which was based on what Benedict Anderson terms 'a deep horizontal comradeship' (Anderson 1983: 7). This 'fraternity' blended individual identity with community identity by reconstructing *familia* and *carnalismo* (brotherhood) in ways that ensured that Aztlán was the origin of an essentialised masculine identity. When constructing their imagined community, however, both Anzaldúa and Moraga prefer to use the concept of the 'tribe' since it captures identities that are more fluid than the fixed identifications of movement discourse.

Moraga states that there is 'a kind of collective longing to return to our cultures traditional indigenous beliefs and ways of constructing community . . . tribe based on the traditional models of Native Americans is a form of community building that can accommodate socialism, feminism, and environmental protection' (Moraga 1993: 166). Later she expands upon this statement by stating that, 'tribe based on the traditional models of Native Americans is an alternative socio-economic structure to the isolated patriarchal capitalist family structure' (Moraga 1993: 166). Her version of *familia*, and by extension, nation, is not dependent upon male dominance or normative heterosexuality. Concurring with these beliefs, Anzaldúa likewise conceives of the Chicana/o people as a tribe when she states that, 'The *Aztecas del norte*. . . compose the largest single tribe or nation of Anishinabeg [Indians] found in the United States today . . . some call themselves Chicanos and see themselves as people whose true homeland is Aztlán [the US south-west]' (Anzaldúa 1987: 1). For both authors, then, returning to a model based on Native American social practices appears to be an integral part of reclaiming a new Chicana nation. Significantly, as Ramirez (1995) argues, this neo-indigenist turn also figures strongly in the work of other Chicana feminist writers of the 1980s such as Sandra Cisneros, Ana Castillo, Alma Villanueva, Lucha Corpi and Lorna Dee Cervantes (Ramirez 1995: 71–8).

Arguably the most important characteristic of these neo-tribal formations when considering them in relationship to movement dogma is their elective or chosen nature. As they are not limited to an ascribed or given cultural and ancestral code, their modes of sociation reflect the essence of contemporary Chicana and Chicano identities better than that of earlier identity paradigms. Instead of the Chicano nation with its fixed racial boundaries, 'tribe' appears to be better understood as a series of identifications that are characterised by fluidity. These more mobile identifications coexist with the rejection of the attempt to locate identity in an essentialised myth of origins. Rather than encountering the unproblematic, mimetic identities furnished by movement narratives, Anzaldúa's construction of the borderland subject is contested at every turn, in terms of national identity, gender identity, racial and sexual identity and in relation to the politics of the movement.

Moreover, in movement discourse, as Alarcón (1996) points out, the land 'is repossessed in imaginary terms', 'through origins' which produce in 'material and imaginary terms "authentic" and "inauthentic", "legal" and "illegal" subjects' (Lavie and Swedenbourg 1996: 45–6). Anzaldúa's radical revisioning of Aztlán on the other hand incorporates a more egalitarian philosophy than this and not only implies a recognition of those excluded by the politics of the movement, but also grants them similar rights to those of Chicano men. The imagery Anzaldúa associates with this new conception of Aztlán, which she refers to as 'a new mythos' engages with a number of these issues (Anzaldúa 1987: 80). In her revisioning of the nation she calls attention to a history of female disenfranchisement under successive waves of imperialist and patriarchal rule. Among the myths that contributed to this and to the formation of a Chicano national consciousness arguably the most significant was that of Malinche. During the movement either Malinche or Guadalupe were recalled as being present at the 'origins' of the Mexican nation. But whereas Guadalupe symbolised transformative powers and sublime transcendence, Malinche represented the implicit underlying connection between the raped woman and the nation. Malinche, according to Paz (1967) and movement rhetoric, is 'the nation's nightmare, the sole reason for the loss of the nation as it was' (Paz 1967). Many Chicanos emphasised this interpretation of Malintzin as such. For Chicanas on the other hand Malinche was more than a metaphor or a foundation myth, she represented a specific female experience that was being misrepresented and trivialised. According to Anzaldúa, 'the Aztec nation fell not because *Malinali (la Chingada)* interpreted for and slept with Cortés, but because the ruling elite had subverted the solidarity between men and women and between noble and commoner' (Anzaldúa 1987: 34). This view reflects recent trends in Chicano Studies scholarship and emphasises the multiple and complex factors which brought about the fall of the indigenous nation. Rather than blaming a single woman for the loss of an entire civilisation, emphasis is now placed on the study of developing socio-economic factors, stratification and the heterogeneity and diversity of the indigenous population (Menchaca 2001, Gonzales 2000, Griswold del Castillo and de Léon 1996, Hine and Faragher 2000).

Moving on from her analysis of Malinche, Anzaldúa also 'brings to light the centrality of female deities rendered passive' by movement ideology (Saldívar-Hull 2000: 60–1). In the main they are Mexican, specifically Mexic Amerindian, and in particular Coatlicue, multiple deity and mother of the gods of the Mexica pantheon. Arguably, this approach appears at first to be problematic in the sense that it recreates the difficulties and limitations prevalent in Chicano nationalism by simply reversing categories. Many critics substantiate this claim and consider that Anzaldúa seems to attempt to 'recover Aztlán in an essentialised female subjectivity' (Quintana 1996: 158–9). But this is far more complex than at first seems. Retracing the series of colonisations that mark the Chicano past, Anzaldúa focuses on the importance of gender in relation to various important historical moments. In this way patriarchal power structures are highlighted and female deities are granted their legitimate place. In Chapter 3 of *Borderlands/La Frontera*, titled 'Entering into the Serpent', Anzaldúa outlines some of the major areas of disagreement between her formulation of the Chicana/o nation, and that proposed by leaders of movement ideology:

> Before the Aztecs became a militaristic, bureaucratic state where male predatory warfare and conquest were based on patrilineal nobility, the principle of balanced opposition between the sexes existed. The people worshipped the lord and lady of duality, *Ometeuhtli* and *Omecihuatl*. Before the change to male dominance, *Coatlicue*, Lady of the Serpent Skirt, contained and balanced the dualities of male and female, light and dark, life and death.
>
> (Anzaldúa 1987: 31–2)

According to Anzaldúa, Coatlicue is most representative of this duality, being 'life in death' and 'death in life', 'life and death together as parts of one process' (Anzaldúa 1987: 47). In 'The Loss of the Balanced Oppositions and the Change to Male Dominance' she goes onto explain how Coatlicue's pre-eminence began to wane when the Azteca, one of the twenty Toltec tribes, made the pilgrimage from Aztlán. Huitzilpochtli, the god of war, assigned the Azteca-Mexica the task of regulating all earthly matters she states through 'controlled or regulated war to gain and exercise power' (Anzaldúa 1987: 32). The Aztec ruler thus wrote a mythology that validated wars of conquest that inaugurated a 'predatory state'.

In *The Last Generation* (1993) Moraga's strategies of revision include a rewriting of this myth. In her writing she reconnects to the daughter of Coatlicue, *la diosa de la luna* (the goddess of the moon) Coyolxauhqui, rather than to her son, Huitzilpochtli (Moraga 1993: 74). Moraga's reading of the role played by Huitzilpochtli here foregrounds an oppositional stance to that endorsed by leaders of the movement. Rather than embodying heroic attributes, Huitzilpochtli is viewed as a murderer who decapitated and dismembered Coyolxauhqui in order to secure his mother's affections and gain complete power. By reconnecting to Coyolxauhqui rather than Huitzilpochtli in her writing, Moraga rewrites the 'machista myth' that implicitly subjugates women and is enacted every time 'the sun/son (Huitzilpochtli) rises up from the horizon and the moon (Coyolxauhqui) is obliterated by his light' (Moraga 1993: 74).

In *Massacre of the Dreamers* (1994b) Ana Castillo further corroborates this view when she states, 'as man shaped his phallic sun-father god world, he [also] defined the other' (Castillo 1994b: 169). At the time of the conquest the Azteca-Tenochtitlan state was firmly entrenched in a phallocracy and bound by a myth that considered that the first four humans on earth were male (Castillo 1994b: 108). Matrilineal descent nonetheless characterised the Toltec and perhaps early Aztec society and there is evidence to suggest that women played a central role before the Aztec nation became centralised. Later there are indications of Toltec women having power, at least as queens and warriors, in the tenth century and there were matrilineal societies such as the Zapotec people of the Oaxaca region (Castillo 1994b: 64). The great Tenochtitlan, however, did not hold women in high regard (Castillo 1994b: 64). Women's status at the height of the Aztec empire had evolved to the point where their primary role was considered to be subservient to men and to serve male-dominated society. In this society, despite the unified dual principle of Quiche Mayan philosophy, women were given secondary roles (Castillo 1994b: 108).

During this time the militant Mexica transformed Coatlicue (another version of the mother) into a monstrous and hostile deity, and the negative aspect of the dual power of mother/fertility and death became prevalent. Originally an earth goddess, and a goddess of fertility, her icon depicts her dressed in serpents, with serpents meeting to form her head (Castillo 1994b: 106). She later emerges in Chicana/o mythology as *cihuacoatl*, the wailing woman and sixth omen that told of the conquest. Coatlicue then enters Mexica society as Tonantsin sometimes perceived as the decapitated earth goddess:

> when her adversaries had mutilated Coatlicue . . . her hair turned to grass, to trees, to flowers. Her skin was transformed into fertile soil, her eyes to holes filled with water, wells and springs. Her mouth changed into great caves, which offered shelter to men. Out of her nose were formed hills and valleys. She it was who secured life with her sacrifices.
>
> (Anzaldúa 1987: 58–9)

Tonantsin in Nahuatl is the name given to several mountains where the earth mother was worshipped. As Teteoinan she was lifted to the highest level of divinity and played a gynarchic role. It is at this point that Anzaldúa reconnects with Coatlicue, thus illustrating the production and reproduction of patriarchy while simultaneously restoring a maternal genealogy and female relationship to the land. This is a crucial aspect of Chicana/o mythology, and one that is taken up by many other Chicana writers. Women's connection to and relationships with the land is an integral part of Chicana feminist praxis and plays a significant role in reclaiming a place within the nation's borders. Cherríe Moraga further concurs with this point when she states that land remains:

> the common ground for all radical action. But land is more than the rocks and trees, the animals and plant life that make up the territory Aztlán or Navajo nation or Maya Mesoamerica. For immigrant and native alike, land is also the factories where we work, the water our children drink, and the housing project where we live. For women, lesbians, and gay men, land is that physical mass called our bodies. Throughout las Americas, all these 'lands' remain under occupation by an Anglocentric, patriarchal, imperialist United States.
>
> (Moraga 1993: 173)

Moraga's rhetoric here recalls that of the movement, not only in its opposition to what she considers to be an 'imperialist United States', but also in her gendering of the land. The metaphorising of the land, *la tierra*, as the female body was a well-known rhetorical convention used in nationalist discourse (Villa 2000: 207). Villa (2000) argues that characteristics such as fertility, nurturance, desire and penetration were commonly identified with the feminised homeland (Villa 2000: 207). He goes on to outline the ways in which this discourse appears in Anaya's *Heart of Aztlán*, particularly as the metaphorised body of land-as-woman. This, he states, is generally figured as a passive receiving entity that is acted upon by men (Villa 2000: 210). Certainly, during the journey to Aztlán, passivity and inactivity become the dominant tropes associated with womanhood, and at certain points female muse figures are what the male subjects of the text search for. Similarly, Aztlán itself is figured as a point of origin, or 'womb':

> There at the core lay the dark, pounding heart. He had come to the source of life and time and history. He reached out and grasped with bleeding hands the living heart of the earth. A joyful power coursed from the dark womb-heart of the earth into his soul and he cried out I AM AZTLÁN!
>
> (Anaya 1988: 130)

Aztlán is figured in the narrative as a symbolic original place. Clemente's search for the homeland therefore becomes the 'return to the mother' or the womb. The manner in which Clemente plunges his bleeding fist into the 'womb heart', however, is an act of macho violence designed to establish his (male) dominance over this feminised space. 'The earth is female', states Moraga; '*Madre Tierra*. Like woman, Madre Tierra has been raped, exploited for her resources, rendered inert, passive, and speechless' (Moraga 1993: 172). For Chicanas the need to re-establish a profound connection to the 'lost land' includes their need to reclaim this space as the female Chicana body. In 'Queer Aztlán' Moraga proposes a 'new nationalism' that would achieve these ends. By displacing the male-centred nationalistic Chicano homeland with the land of the Chicana mestiza, her radical perspective envisions Aztlán as a 'decolonised space':

> the nationalism I seek is one that decolonises the brown and female body as it decolonises the brown and female earth. It is a new nationalism in which la Chicana indigena stands at the centre, and heterosexism and homophobia are no longer the cultural order of the day.
>
> (Moraga 1993: 150)

For Moraga this new nation began to 'take concrete shape' in the early 1990s. In formulating this space she states that it should not form a replica of 'Queer Nation' whose 'anglocentricity' and white radicalism were an 'alien-nation' to people of colour (Moraga 1993: 147). Neither should it concur with the homophobic nationalism of the movement but instead it should promote a politics that embraces 'all its people, including its joteria' (Moraga 1993: 147).

To conclude, whereas previous conceptions of the nation implied the construction of a patriarchally dominated and bounded space, for Chicana writers Aztlán affirms the power of transgression and the necessity of living without borders. Both Moraga and Anzaldúa repeatedly refer to Aztlán as a land 'sin fronteras' (without borders) as they move away from the separatist politics of the movement, while retaining much of the former militants' agenda. A Chicana feminist Aztlán thus works against the tendency to define nation and instead moves towards 'an interstitial space' that simultaneously displaces a masculine coded nationalism while forming a politics that cuts across racial, ethnic and other borders. In this sense, when Chicanas reconstruct Aztlán they also do so in terms that both reinforce and radically modify the existing parameters of the politics of Chicana/o identity.

Conclusion

The Chicano movement was centrally a non-violent and anti-racist resistance movement which had at its core the concern with improving working conditions, legislation, protection and justice for the Mexican American population in the USA. The twin ideologies of militant civil rights and the radical politics of Chicano cultural nationalism formed the foundations of this resistance. By implication these ideological factors identified the primary source of Chicano oppression in the annexation of northern Mexico by the USA after the US–Mexican war of 1846–8. According to this interpretation, annexation set the context for the formation of races in the south-west, and effectively sanctioned the political and economic subordination of the newly formed Mexican American community there (Montejano 1987: 309). The legacy of dispossession and the resulting patterns of exclusion and disparity accordingly fuelled the revolutionary impetus underlying the movement. Yet in concentrating on class and race as determinants of Mexican American social oppression, rather than achieving a genuine social equality, the movement often marginalised many who would count themselves among its liberation struggle.

Within the movement, efforts to construct a sense of identity were typically undertaken in an environment that was saturated with unresolved gender conflict. The central and unifying concepts of *familia* and *carnalismo* were rife with sexism and internal oppression while simultaneously serving as the movement's mandate for collective action. During this time the family was meant to serve as an organisational model of community cohesion that would both spiritually and materially oppose the subordination of Chicanos in the USA. A strategic familialism was clearly evoked by numerous organisations as well as in *El Plan Espiritual de Aztlán* (1969) that unequivocally stated that, 'our culture unites and educates the family of *la raza* toward liberation with one heart and one mind' (Anaya and Lomelí 1989: 1). Yet the ideological construct of the family of *la raza* in cultural nationalist rhetoric simultaneously oppressed women and gay Chicanos and Chicanas. Chicano literary production reflected this ideology and was often openly didactic in reinforcing separate racial, ethnic and gendered divisions. The search for identity, a major motif in Chicano literature of the period simultaneously exposed a nationalist reliance upon the objectification of women, as the prevailing patriarchal and familial models had at their core a vision of group unanimity that replicated an overlap in cultural and male identity. The *chicanismo* or racial and cultural pride that formed the basis of a collective Chicano identity reinforced this ideology. Myths of descent valorised preconquest Aztec culture and in so doing also asserted an aggressive masculinity as a source of Chicano identity. In one way, women were structurally important to the formation and mobilisation of these collective identities in the sense that they became the markers of loss and absence necessary for the construction of Chicano masculinity and culture. At the same time these negative characterisations excluded them from any political participation and subordinated them to inferior positions within the movement's hierarchy.

Convinced of the masculinist and heterosexist ideologies and practices of the movement, Chicanas began to assert their own identity politics, and to enlarge the political agenda from one concerned with race and class to one that included gender. In order to force male activists to change their rhetoric and accept women's issues they adopted two approaches (A. García 1997, Ruiz 1998, I. M. García 1997). A significant number of Chicanas chose to work outside of the movement by creating alliances with the mainstream women's-rights movement. Others favoured a close role within the movement itself, forcing Chicano men to recognise women's issues including educational, political, social and economic advancement for Chicanas. Within the movement Chicanas fought against traditional stereotypes, initially by taking positions of leadership within movement organisations such as Dolores Huerta in the UFW, Vilma Martinez in MALDEF and eventually Maria Elena Martinez in LRUP. Or they became important spokeswomen in their own right such as Luz Gutiérrez, Rosie Castro, Lupe Castillo, Marta Cotera and Enriqueta Longeaux y Vásquez, who deconstructed the gender roles prescribed by *familia* ideology (Ruiz 1998: 111–14). At the same time, they challenged the American subject of white mainstream feminism by viewing their oppression as a threefold intersection of race and class as well as gender. These experiences within the Chicano movement as well as those with white feminists proved to be decisive factors in the development of a specific Chicana identity. Looking back at the Chicano and women's movement, in 1992 Gloria Molina described the experience of many Chicanas in the 1960s and 1970s thus:

> In the days of the Chicano movement I was finding that the more I got involved, the more I realised there was a tremendous need for women to be involved and to be heard. My strong feeling at the time was . . . and many women who agreed with me ran into opposition . . . that we needed the Chicano movement and the women's movement both to be listening to the Chicana.
>
> (Molina 1992: 4)

By the mid-1970s Chicano nationalism as a political strategy was expressing itself more in the cultural arena than in direct militant confrontation with the Government, and subsequently Chicanas began to depend in large part on their literary production to both defend and define their identity. By the 1980s women's writing began to displace the stasis of the movement and Chicanas were becoming highly visible as political writers in their own right (Arrizón 1999: 7). In *The Last Generation* (1993) Cherríe Moraga states her position unequivocally in this regard: 'I mourn the dissolution of an active Chicano movement . . . its ghost haunts me . . . for me *el movimiento* has never been a thing of the past, it has retreated into subterranean uncontaminated soils awaiting resurrection in a queerer, more feminist generation' (Moraga 1993: 148)

Maintaining the movement's oppositional politics while simultaneously refocusing its gendered divisions, Chicana writing presented a new wave in the development of movement discourse. Just as the publishing house Quinto Sol played a major role in the distribution of Chicano literature during the movement decades, small presses and publications such as Scorpion Press, La Palabra: Revista de Literatura Chicana, Relámpago Books Press and Arte Público Press came to play a significant role in the dissemination of Chicana literature. In the works of the 1980s feminist themes and Chicanas' liberation combine with motifs they shared with their male counterparts such as cultural conflict, racial oppression, alienation and the search for identity. Writers such as Lucha Corpi, Ana Castillo, Sandra Cisneros, Denise Chavez, Helena Maria Viramontes, Cherríe Moraga, and Gloria Anzaldúa emphasised the differences between Chicanas and Chicanos and disputed the fiction of an exclusively male subject and the limited conceptualisation of Chicana identity promoted by cultural nationalist rhetoric. Their works expand upon the essentialised Aztec identity of nationalist discourse in ways that not only recall and reform a collective Chicana/o consciousness, but also in ways that deconstruct the legacies of patriarchy, homophobia and xenophobic nationalism that previously dictated the trajectory of Chicano identity. Rather than replicating the essentialised and dichotomised female subject of movement discourse, in Chicana feminist works identity is viewed as plural, and sexuality and gender become dynamic factors in its construction. In an attempt to subvert the heteronormative sexuality of the Chicano movement gay writers initially were the most responsible for new and more inclusive representations of Chicana/o identity. John Rechy's novel *City of Night* (1964) and Estella Portillo-Trambley's play *Day of the Swallows* ignited much controversy as their gay and lesbian characters clearly fell outside of the imposed gender roles of the movement. Forming precursors to the writing of Anzaldúa and Moraga they clearly formed a radical challenge to the traditional construction of gender specifically in relation to *familia* ideology and the Oedipal narrative. The introduction of lesbian sexuality into modes of representation reserved traditionally as the arena for male desire in particular created a destabilising effect on the gender constructs of the movement.

Rejecting the binary oppositions that structured gender relations throughout the protest decades, both Moraga and Anzaldúa refuse to align lesbian
subjectivity with either masculinity or femininity, but strategically employ it
to expose the artifice of the division between the two. Moraga sees gay subjectivity as a disruptive influence that subversively exposes the gaps and
contradictions in heterosexual structures and systems of thought. Recognising the failures of the Chicano movement, partly because it was dominated by
an ideology that endorsed these structures, in *The Last Generation* (1993) she
states that:

> What was right about Chicano nationalism was its commitment to pre-
> serving the integrity of the Chicano people . . . developing Chicano con-
> sciousness, autonomy and self-determination. What was wrong about
> Chicano nationalism was its institutionalised heterosexism, its inbred
> machismo, and its lack of a cohesive national political strategy.
>
> (Moraga 1993: 148–9)

For Moraga, as for many other Chicana writers, the movement was not only
something positive and fundamentally necessary; it also provided a platform
for new forms of collective action. Yet attempts to shape a politics of unification and nationhood among all Chicanos and Chicanas ultimately proved to
be untenable. In a similar way, as Pesquera and Segura (1993) argue, it is
theoretically possible and likely that Chicanas multiple sources of group
identification conflict at times with one another, rendering the development
of a group consciousness untenable (A. García 1997: 294–309). Yet in displacing the binary logic that underwrote male-authored representations of
women, Chicana writers were able to conceive of female subjectivity in terms
of the multiple contexts of identity. The border rather than Aztlán became
the major signifier for issues such as these. Up until this time women's lives
and experiences on the border was 'a subject almost totally overlooked by
scholars of the United States', and generally 'border scholars either
ignore[d] women entirely or rel[ied] on well-worn stereotypes' (Ruiz and
Tiano 1987: 4). The works of Chicana feminists and feminist writers on the
other hand reflect 'difference' and demographic changes in ways that have
developed a self-defined political programme of border feminism that superseded previous manifestations of their politics. Sonia Saldívar-Hull states
that, 'Chicana feminist theories present material geopolitical issues that
redirect feminist discourse, again pointing to a theory of feminism that
addresses a multiplicity of experiences, what I call "feminism on the border" '(Saldívar-Hull 2000: 48). In Chicana writing the border is figured as a
multi-level concept, representing on the one hand the transgression of cultural and political constraints that often impede women's self-realisation. On
the other hand crossing borders and establishing new frontiers is a metaphor
frequently evoked in order to indicate a personal and often radical transformation. As a metaphor it represents the heterogeneity of Chicano/a identity as

well as suggesting a more successful means of coming to terms with non-hegemonic and hierarchical group thinking. As a paradigm for Chicana/o subjectivity it keeps the Chicano movement's goals of self-determination and cultural solidarity alive. While the militant strategies of the movement may have long since disappeared, its legacy in the form of women's writing and new conceptions of identity mean that its unique *resistencia* continues to endure.

Notes

Introduction

1 The Chicano people have been given a number of terms of identification. These have included Americans of Mexican descent, Latin Americans, Spanish Americans, Latinos, Tejanos, Mexican Americans, Mexicanos, Mexicans, Hispanos, Chicanos and Californios. Originally a derisive in-group label given to lower class Mexican immigrants, during the movement the term 'Chicano' became repoliticised as a positive form of identification and symbolised solidarity against what activists argued was a history of racial, cultural and political oppression. The term 'Chicano' refers to people of Mexican descent now resident in the USA who are of a particular politicised consciousness.

1 The Chicano movement

1 The Ford Foundation, established in 1938 by the motor-car company, funded Chicano advocacy groups and supported activists all over the south-west. It provided $2.2 million to MALDEF and financed the formation of the National Chicano Council on Higher Education. It also made grants to MAYO, the south-west council of La Raza, and the Brown Berets, the Chicano equivalent of the African American militant group the Black Berets (Meier and Gutiérrez 2000: 83–4).
2 There were also some organisations that clearly went beyond the militancy of these groups. These included the Chicano Liberation Front, the Zapata Liberation Front and the August Twenty-Third Movement, all of which advocated self-defence or violence and became involved in acts of sabotage (I. M. García 1997: 107).
3 Language is another important component in the literary construction of Chicano and Chicana identity. This is because not only standard Spanish is used but also a non-standard colloquial and communal language, often calo or a 'hybrid slang' of Spanish and English. It is particularly salient in poetry, which uses varieties of code-switching between different languages. Additionally a further level of language complexity includes shifts in male and female usage. Some of these matters are discussed quite fully in several other sources including Sanchez (1994), Pérez-Torres (1995, Anzaldúa (1987).

2 Chicana feminism

1 *Mutualistas* or mutual-aid organisations helped to maintain Mexican culture and provided the working class and poor with a broad range of benefits and services by pooling their limited resources. See Gutiérrez (1995: 395–9).

3 Critical approaches to Chicana/o literature

1 The essay has been consistently expanded and updated as, 'The Space of Chicano Literature Update: 1978' (1978); 'Charting the Space of Chicano Literature' (1980); 'Chicano Literary Production, 1960–1980' (1985); 'The Topological Space of Chicano Literature' (1988); and 'Chicano Literary Space: Cultural Criticism/ Cultural Production' (1990) in Bruce-Novoa (1990).

6 Women, confinement and *familia* ideology

1 The Klail City Death Trip Series by Rolando Hinojosa includes the following texts: *Rites and Witnesses* (1982); *The Valley* (1983); *Dear Rafe* (1985); *Claros Varones De Belken/Fair Gentlemen of Belken County* (1986); *Klail City: A Novel* (1987).

7 The search for Aztlán: the Chicano nation

1 Serrano suggests that there are five constituents to Chicano labour subordination within the internal colony: (1) labour repression and captive labour force; (2) a dual wage system; (3) labour stratification and class ascription; (4) Chicanos as a reserve labour force; and (5) Chicanos as a labour buffer (to the white working class). According to Serrano 'The Dual Wage System' and 'Labour Stratification and Class Ascription' are responsible for the secondary position of Chicanos in 'the economy and the colonial labour market'. See Serrano (2000), Lomelí and Ikas (2000).

Bibliography

PRIMARY SOURCES

Special collections

The Chicano Research Collection Arizona State University.

Books

Acosta, O. Z. (1989b) *The Revolt of the Cockroach People*, New York: Vintage.
Anaya, R. (1991) *Bless Me, Ultima.* Berkeley, Calif.: T. Q. S. Publications.
——— (1988) *Heart of Aztlán*, Albuquerque, N. Mex.: University of New Mexico Press.
Anaya, R. and Lomelí, F. (ed.) (1989) *Aztlán: Essays on the Chicano Homeland*, Albuquerque, N. Mex.: University of New Mexico Press.
Anzaldúa, G. (1987) *Borderlands/La Frontera: The New Mestiza*, San Francisco, Calif.: Aunt Lute Books.
Cabeza de Baca, F. (1994) *We Fed Them Cactus*, Albuquerque, N. Mex.: University of New Mexico Press.
Castillo, A. (1994a) *So Far from God*, London: The Women's Press.
——— (1994b) *Massacre of the Dreamers*, New York: Plume/Penguin.
Cervantes, L. D. (1981) *Emplumada*, Pittsburgh, Pa.: University of Pittsburgh Press.
Cisneros, S. (1991) *The House on Mango Street*, New York: Vintage Contemporaries.
——— (1993) *Woman Hollering Creek*, London: Bloomsbury.
Corpi, L. (1989) *Delia's Song*, Houston, Tex.: Arte Público Press.
Cota-Cardenas, M. (1989) *Marchitas de mayo: sones pa'l pueblo*, Texas: Relámpago Press.
Esquibel, A. (2001) *Message to Aztlán: Selected Writings of Rodolfo 'Corky' Gonzales*, Houston, Tex.: Arte Público.
Hernández-Gutiérrez, M. de Jesús and Foster, D. W. (eds) (1997) *Literatura Chicana 1965–1995: An Anthology in Spanish, English and Caló*, New York: Garland.
Moraga, C. (1983) *Loving in the War Years/Lo nunca pasó por sus labios*, Boston, Mass.: South End Press.
——— (1986) *Giving up the Ghost*, Los Angeles, Calif.: West End Press.
——— (1993) *The Last Generation: Prose and Poetry*, Boston, Mass.: South End Press.
——— (2001) *The Hungry Woman*, Los Angeles, Calif.: West End Press.
Moraga, C, and Anzaldúa, G. (eds) (1983) *This Bridge Called My Back: Writings by Radical Women of Colour*, New York: Kitchen Table Press.

Paredes, A. (1958) *With a Pistol in his Hand: A Border Ballad and its Hero*, Austin, Tex.: University of Texas Press.

Paz, O. (1967) *The Labyrinth of Solitude*, trans. Lysander Kemp, London: Penguin.

Rebolledo, T. D. and Reviro, E. (eds) (1993) *Infinite Divisions: An Anthology of Chicana Literature*, Tucson, Ariz.: University of Arizona Press.

Rivera, T. (1987) *Y no se lo Trago la Tierra . . . And the Earth Did Not Devour Him*, trans. Evangelina Vigil-Pinon, Houston, Tex.: Arte Público Press.

Rivera, T. (1975) 'Chicano Literature: Fiesta of the Living', Books Abroad, 49 (Summer): 439–52.

Rodriguez, L. J. (1995) *Always Running: Gang Days in L.A.,* London: Marion Boyars.

Tijerina, R. L. (2000) *They Called Me 'King Tiger': My Struggle for the Land and Our Rights*, Houston, Tex.: Arte Público Press.

Valdez, L. (1992) *Zoot Suit and Other Plays*, Houston, Tex.: Arte Público Press.

Vigil, E. (1985) *Thirty an' Seen A Lot*, Houston, Tex.: Arte Público Press.

Viramontes, H. M. (1995a) *The Moths and Other Stories*, Houston, Tex.: Arte Público Press.

SECONDARY SOURCES

Books

Acosta, O. Z. (1989a) *The Autobiography of A Brown Buffalo*, New York: Vintage.

Acuña, R. (1988) *Occupied America: A History of Chicanos*, 3rd edn, New York: Harper & Row.

—— (1996) *Anything but Mexican, Chicanos in Contemporary Los Angeles*, London: Verso.

—— (1984) *A Community under Siege: A Chronicle of Chicanos East of the Los Angeles River 1945–1975*, Chicano Studies Research Center Publications, UCLA, Monograph no. 11.

Ainley, R. (1998) *New Frontiers of Space, Bodies and Gender*, London and New York: Routledge.

Alarcon, F. (1992) *Snake Poems: An Aztec Invocation*, San Francisco, Calif.: Chronicle Books.

Alarcon, N., Castro R., Perez E., Pesquera, B., Adaljisa, S. R. and Zavella, P. (eds) (1993) *Chicana Critical Issues*, Berkeley, Calif.: Third Woman Press.

Alarcon, N., Castillo, A. and Moraga, C. (eds) (1993) *The Sexuality of Latinas*, Berkeley, Calif.: Third Woman Press.

Aldama, A. J. and Quinones, N. H. (eds) (2002) *Decolonial Voices: Chicana and Chicano Cultural Studies in the 21st Century*, Bloomington, Ind.: Indiana University Press.

Almaguer, T. (1994) *Racial Faultlines: The Historical Origins of White Supremacy in California*, Berkeley, Calif.: University of California Press.

Alvarez, S. E., Daguina, E. and Escobar, A. (eds) (1998) *Cultures of Politics/Politics of Cultures: Revisioning Latin American Social Movements*, Boulder, Col.: Westview Press.

Anaya, R. (1989) *Tierra: Contemporary Short Fiction of New Mexico*, El Paso Texas: Cinco Puntos Press.

Anaya, R. and Marquez, A. (eds) (1984) *Cuentos Chicanos: A Short Story Anthology*, Albuquerque, N. Mex.: University of New Mexico Press.

Anderson, B. (1983) *Imagined Communities: Reflections on the Origin and Spread of Nationalism*, London: Verso.

Anzaldúa, G. (1990) *Making Face, Making Soul: Haciendo Caras: Creative and Critical Perspectives by Feminists of Color*, San Francisco, Calif.: Aunt Lute Books.

Arrizón, A. (1999) *Latina Performance: Traversing the Stage*, Bloomington, Ind.: Indiana University Press.

Arteaga, A. (1997) *Chicano Poetics: Heterotexts and Hybridities*, New York: Cambridge University Press.

—— (1994) *Another Tongue: Nation and Ethnicity in the Linguistic Borderlands*, Durham, NC: Duke University Press.

Baca, J. S. (1987) *Martin and Meditations on the South Valley*, New York: New Directions.

—— (1992) *Working in the Dark: Reflections of a Poet of the Barrio*, Santa Fe, N. Mex.: Red Crane Books.

Barkham, E. and Shelton, M. D. (eds) (1998) *Borders, Exiles, Diasporas*, Stanford, Calif.: Stanford University Press.

Behar, R. and Gordon, D. G. (eds) (1995) *Women Writing Culture*, Berkeley, Calif.: University of California Press.

Bhabha, H. K. (1994) *The Location of Culture*, New York and London: Routledge.

—— (1990) *Nation and Narration*, New York and London: Routledge.

Blea, I. (1992) *La Chicana and the Intersection of Race, Class and Gender*, Westport, Conn.: Praeger.

Brady, M. P. (2002) *Extinct Lands, Temporal Geographies: Chicana Literature and the Urgency of Space*, Durham, NC: Duke University Press.

Brown, R. L. A. and Ward, J. (eds) (1990) *Redefining American Literary History*, New York: The Modern Language Association of America.

Bronfen, E. (1999) *Dorothy Richardson's Art of Memory: Space, Identity, Text*, Manchester: Manchester University Press.

Bruce-Novoa, J. (1980a) *Chicano Authors: Inquiry by Interview*, Austin, Tex.: University of Texas Press.

—— (1982) *Chicano Poetry: A Response to Chaos*, Austin, Tex.: University of Texas Press.

—— (1990a) *RetroSpace: Collected Essays on Chicano Literature*, Houston, Tex.: Arte Público Press.

Butler, J. (1997) *Excitable Speech: A Politics of the Performative*, New York: Routledge.

Calderon, H. and Saldívar, J. D. (eds) (1991) *Criticism in the Borderlands: Studies in Chicano Literature, Culture and Ideology*, Durham, NC: Duke University Press.

Camarillo, A. (1979) *Chicanos in a Changing Society: From Mexican Pueblos to American Barrios in Santa Barbara and Southern California 1848–1930*, Cambridge, Mass.: Harvard University Press.

Cambell, F. (1995) *Tijuana: Stories on the Border*, trans. E. Hicks, Berkeley, Calif.: University of California Press.

Candelaria, C. (1986) *Chicano Poetry: A Critical Introduction*, Westport, Conn.: Greenwood Press.

Castillo, A. (1990) *Sapogonia*, New York: Anchor Books.

—— (1992) *The Mixquiahuala Letters*, New York: Anchor Books.

—— (1995) *My Father Was a Toltec and Selected Poems*, New York and London: W. W. Norton & Co.

Castillo, D. (1998) *Easy Women: Sex and Gender in Modern Mexican Fiction*, Minneapolis, Minn.: University of Minnesota Press.

—— (1992) *Talking Back: Toward a Latin American Feminist Literary Criticism*, Ithaca, NY and London: Cornell University Press.

Cervantes, L. D. (1991) *From the Cables of Genocide: Poems on Love and Hunger*, Houston, Tex.: Arte Público.

Chavez, D. (1986) *The Last of the Menu Girls*, Houston, Tex.: Arte Público Press.

—— (1995) *Face of an Angel*, New York: Warner Books.

—— (2001) *Loving Pedro Infante*, New York: Washington Square Press.

Chávez, E. (2002) *'¡Mi Raza Primero!' Nationalism, Identity, and Insurgency in the Chicano Movement in Los Angeles, 1966–1978*, Berkeley, Calif.: University of California Press.

Chávez, J. R. (1984) *The Lost Land: The Chicano Image of the South-West*, Albuquerque, N. Mex.: University of New Mexico Press.

Chodorow, N. (1978) *The Reproduction of Mothering: Psychoanalysis and the Sociology of Gender*, Berkeley, Calif.: University of California Press.

Christie, J. S. (1998) *Latino Fiction and the Modernist Imagination: Literature of the Borderlands*, New York: Garland.

Cisneros, S. (1987) *My Wicked Wicked Ways*, Berkeley, Calif.: Third Woman Press.

—— (1994) *Loose Woman*, New York: Random House.

—— (2002) *Caramelo*, London: Bloomsbury.

Clifford, J. (1997) *Routes, Travel and Translation in the Late 20th Century*, Cambridge, Mass.: Harvard University Press.

Cota-Cardenas, M. (1977) *Noches Despertando in Conciencias*, Tucson, Ariz.: Scorpion Press.

—— (1978) *Siete Poetas*, Tucson, Ariz.: Scorpion Press.

—— (2000) *Puppet: A Chicano Novella*, Albuquerque, N. Mex.: University of New Mexico Press.

Cull, N. J. and Carrasco, D. (eds) (2004) *Alambrista*, Albuquerque, N. Mex.: University of New Mexico Press.

De La Cruz, Sor Juana Inés (1997) *Poems, Protest, and a Dream*, trans. Margaret Sayers Peden, London: Penguin Books.

de la Torre, A. and Pesquera, B. M. (eds) (1993) *Building with Our Hands: New Directions in Chicana Studies*, Berkeley, Calif.: University of California Press.

De Lauretis, T. (1994) *The Practice of Love: Lesbian Sexuality and Perverse Desire*, Bloomington, Ind.: Indiana University Press.

de León, A. (2001) *Ethnicity in the Sunbelt: Mexican Americans in Houston*, Houston, Tex.: Texas A. & M. University Press.

del Castillo, R., McKenna, T. and Yarbro-Bejarano, Y. (eds) (1991) *Chicano Art: Resistance and Affirmation, 1965–1985*, Los Angeles, Calif.: Wight Art Gallery, University of California.

Fanon, F. (1990) *The Wretched of The Earth*, Harmondsworth: Penguin.

—— (1986) *Black Skin/White Masks*, London: Pluto.

Fregoso, L. (1993) *The Bronze Screen: Chicana and Chicano Film Culture*, Minneapolis, Minn.: University of Minnesota Press.

Galván, R. A. (1996) *The Dictionary of Chicano Spanish/El Diccionaro del Español Chicano*, Lincolnwood, Ill.: NTC Publishing Group.

Garcia, A. (ed.) (1997) *Chicana Feminist Thought: The Basic Historical Writings*, New York: Routledge.

García, I. M. (1997) *Chicanismo: The Forging of a Militant Ethos among Mexican Americans*, Tucson, Ariz.: University of Arizona Press.

Garcia, M. T. (1989) *Mexican Americans: Leadership, Ideology and Identity*, London and New Haven, Conn.: Yale University Press.

—— (ed.) (1995) *Ruben Salazar Border Correspondent: Selected Writings, 1955–1970*, Berkeley, Calif. and London: University of California Press.

Gaspar de Alba, A. (1998) *Chicano Art: Inside/Outside the Master's House: Cultural Politics and the Cara Exhibition*, Austin, Tex.: University of Texas Press.

Gaspar de Alba, A., Herrera-Sobek, M. and Martínez, D. (eds) (1989) *Three Times a Woman: Chicana Poetry*, Tempe, Ariz.: Bilingual Press.

George, R. M. (1996) *The Politics of Home: Postcolonial Relocations, and 20th Century Fiction*, New York and Cambridge: Cambridge University Press.

Gilmore, L. (1994) *Autobiographics: A Feminist Theory of Women's Self-Representation*, Ithaca, NY and London: Cornell University Press.

Gómez-Peña, G. (1996) *The New World Border*, San Francisco, Calif.: City Lights.

Gomez-Quiñones, J. (1994) *Roots of Chicano Politics, 1600–1940*, Albuquerque, N. Mex.: University of New Mexico Press.

Gonzales, M. G. (2000) *Mexicanos: A History of Mexicans in the United States*, Bloomington, Ind.: Indiana University Press.

Griswold del Castillo, R. and de León, A. (eds) (1996) *North to Aztlán: A History of Mexican Americans in the United States*, New York: Twayne Publishers.

Grossberg, L. and Nelson, G. (eds) (1992) *Cultural Studies*, London: Routledge.

Gutiérrez, D. (1995) *Walls and Mirrors, Mexican Americans, Mexican Immigrants and the Politics of Ethnicity*, Berkeley, Calif.: University of California Press.

Gutiérrez, R. (ed.) (1997) *Home Altars of Mexico*, London: Thames & Hudson.

Gutiérrez, R. and Padilla, G. (eds) (1993) *Recovering the US Hispanic Literary Heritage*, Houston, Tex.: Arte Público Press.

Gutiérrez-Jones, C. (1995) *Rethinking the Borderlands: Between Chicano Culture and Legal Discourse*, Berkeley, Calif.: University of California Press.

Hedges, E. and Fisher Fishkin, S. (eds) (1994) *Listening to Silences: New Essays in Feminist Criticism*, New York and Oxford: Oxford University Press.

Herrera-Sobek, M. (1993) *Northward Bound: The Mexican Immigrant Experience in Ballad and Song*, Bloomington, Ind.: Indiana University Press.

—— (ed.) (1994) *Reconstructing a Chicano/a Literary Heritage: Hispanic Colonial Literature of the South-West*, Tucson, Ariz.: University of Arizona Press.

—— (1995) *Chicana (W)riters on Word and Film*, Berkeley, Calif.: Third Woman Press.

Herrera-Sobek, M. and Viramontes, H. M. (eds) (1988) *Chicana Creativity and Criticism: Charting New Frontiers in American Literature*, Houston, Tex.: Arte Público Press.

Hine, R. V. and Faragher, J. M. (eds) (2000) *The American West: A New Interpretive History*, New Haven, Conn.: Yale University Press.

Hinojosa, R. (1982) *Rites and Witnesses*, Houston, Tex.: Arte Público.

—— (1983) *The Valley*, Tempe, Ariz.: Bilingual Press.

—— (1985) *Dear Rafe*, Houston, Tex.: Arte Público Press.

—— (1986) *Claros Varones De Belken/Fair Gentlemen of Belken County*, Tempe, Ariz.: Bilingual Press.

—— (1987) *Klail City: A Novel*, Houston, Tex.: Arte Público Press.

—— (1990) *Becky and her Friends*, Houston, Tex.: Arte Público Press.

Hogue, W. L. (1996) *Race, Modernity, Postmodernity*, New York: State University of New York Press.

Hollinger, D. (1995) *Postethnic America: Beyond Multiculturalism*, New York: Basic Books.

Huerta, J. (2000) *Chicano Drama: Performance, Society and Myth*, New York and Cambridge: Cambridge University Press.

Hutcheon, L. (1988) *A Poetics of Postmodernism: History, Theory, Fiction*, New York and London: Routledge.

Hutchinson, J. and Smith, A. D. (eds) (1994) *Nationalism*, Oxford: Oxford University Press.

Irigaray, L. (1985a) *This Sex Which Is Not One*, Ithaca, NY: Cornell University Press.

—— (1985b) *Speculum of the Other Woman*, trans. Gillian C. Gill, Ithaca, NY: Cornell University Press.

Islas, A. (1984) *The Rain God*, New York: Avon Books.

Jameson, F. (1991) *Postmodernism or the Cultural Logic of Late Capitalism*, London: Verso.

Janmohamed, A. and Lloyd, D. (eds) (1990) *The Nature and Context of Minority Discourse*, New York: Oxford University Press.

Jensen, R. J. and Hammerback, J. C. (eds) (2002) *The Words of César Chávez*, Houston, Tex.: A. & M. University Press.

Jonas, S. and Thomas, S. D. (eds) (1999) *Immigration: A Civil Rights Issue for the Americas*, Wilmington, Del.: SR Books.

Kaplan, C., Alarcón, N. and Moallem, M. (eds) (1999) *Between Woman and Nation*, Durham, NC and London: Duke University Press.

Kaup, M. and Rosenthal, D. J. (2002) *Mixing Race, Mixing Culture: Inter-American Literary Dialogues*, Austin, Tex.: University of Texas Press.

Kowalewski, M. (1996) (ed.) *Reading the West: New Essays on the Literature of the American West*, Cambridge: Cambridge University Press.

Krupat, A. (1992) *Ethnocriticism: Ethnography, History, Literature*, Los Angeles, Calif.: University of California Press.

—— (1996) *The Turn to the Native: Studies in Criticism and Culture*, Lincoln, Nebr. and London: University of Nebraska Press.

Lavie, S. and Swedenbourg, T. (eds) (1996) *Displacement, Diaspora, and Geographies of Identity*, Durham, NC: Duke University Press.

Lee, R. (1999) *The Americas of Asian American Literature: Gendered Fictions of Nation and Transnation*, Princeton, NJ: Princeton University Press.

Limón, J. E. (1992) *Mexican Ballads, Chicano Poems: History and Influence in Mexican American Social Poetry*, Berkeley, Calif.: University of California Press.

—— (1998) *American Encounters: Greater Mexico, the United States, and the Erotics of Culture*, Boston, Mass.: Beacon Press.

Lomelí, F. A. (ed.) (1993) *Handbook of Hispanic Cultures in the United States: Literature and Art*, Houston, Tex.: Arte Público Press.

Lomelí, F. A. and Ikas, K. (eds) (2000) *US Latino Literatures and Cultures: Transnational Perspectives*, Heidelberg: C. Winter.

López, T. A. (1993) *Growing Up Chicana/o*, New York: Avon Books.

Lowe, L. (1990) *Immigrant Acts: On Asian American Cultural Politics*, Durham, NC: Duke University Press.

Lyotard, J.-F. (1988) *The Differend: Phrases in Dispute*, trans. Georges Van den Abbeele, Minneapolis, Minn.: University of Minnesota Press.

MacLachlan, C. and Beezeley, W. H. (1994) *El Gran Pueblo: A History of Greater Mexico*, Englewood Cliffs, NJ: Prentice Hall.

McClintock, A., Mufti, A. and Shohat, E. (eds) (1997) *Dangerous Liasons: Gender, Nation and Postcolonial Perspectives*, Minneapolis, Minn.: University of Minnesota Press.

McClintock, A. (ed.) (1995) *Imperial Leather: Race, Gender and Sexuality in the Colonial Context*, New York: Routledge.

McKenna, T. (1997) *Migrant Song: Politics and Protest in Contemporary Chicano Literature*, Austin, Tex.: University of Texas Press.

Marin, M. V. (1991) *Social Protest in an Urban Barrio: A Study of the Chicano Movement 1966–74*, Lanham, Md. and London: University Press of America.

Mariscal, G. (ed.) (1999) *Aztlán and Vietnam: Chicano and Chicana Experiences of the War*, Berkeley, Calif.: University of California Press.

Martinez, E. (1998a) *De Colores Means All of Us*, Cambridge, Mass.: South End Press.

Martinez, R. (1992) *The Other Side: Fault Lines, Guerilla Saints and The True Heart of Rock 'n' Roll*, New York: Verso.

Mazón, M. (1984) *The Zoot Suit Riots: The Psychology of Symbolic Annihilation*, Austin, Tex.: University of Texas Press.

Meier, M. S. and Gutiérrez, M. (eds) (2000) *Encyclopaedia of the Mexican American Civil Rights Movement*, London and Westport, Conn.: Greenwood Press.

Menchaca, M. (2001) *Recovering History Constructing Race: The Indian, Black, and White Roots of Mexican Americans*, Austin, Tex.: University of Texas Press.

Montejano, D. (1987) *Anglos and Mexicans in The Making of Texas 1836–1986*, Austin, Tex.: University of Texas Press.

—— (1999a) *Chicano Politics and Society in the Late 20th Century*, Austin, Tex.: University of Texas Press.

Mora, P. (1993) *Nepantla: Essays from The Land in The Middle*, Albuquerque, N. Mex.: University of New Mexico Press.

—— (1985) *Chants*, Houston, Tex.: Arte Público Press.

—— (1997) *House of Houses*, Boston, Mass.: Beacon Press.

—— (1984) *Borders*, Houston, Tex.: Arte Público Press.

Morales, A. (1988) *The Brick People*, Houston, Tex.: Arte Público Press.

—— (1992) *The Rag Doll Plagues*, Houston, Tex.: Arte Público Press.

Muller, T. and Espenshade, T. J. (eds) (1985) *The Fourth Wave: California's Newest Immigrants*, Washington, DC: Urban Institute Press.

Mulvey, L. (1989) *Visual and Other Pleasures*, London: Macmillan.

Muñoz, C. (1989) *Youth Identity Power: The Chicano Generation*, London: Verso.

Murphet, J. (2001) *Literature and Race in Los Angeles*, Cambridge: Cambridge University Press.

Neate, W. (1998) *Tolerating Ambiguity: Ethnicity and Community in Chicano/a Writing*, New York: Peter Lang Publishing.

Noriega, C., Avila, E. R., Davalos, K. M., Sandoval, C. and Pérez-Torres, R. (eds) (2001) *The Chicano Studies Reader: An Anthology of Aztlán, 1970–2000*, Los Angeles, Calif.: UCLA Chicano Studies Research Center.

Olivares, J. (ed.) (1986) *International Studies in Honor of Tomás Rivera*, Houston, Tex.: Arte Público Press.

Omi M. and Winant, H. (1986) *Racial Formation in the United States: From the 1960s to the 1980s*, New York and London: Routledge & Kegan Paul.

Padilla, G. M. (1993) *My History, Not Yours: The Formation of Mexican American Autobiography*, Madison, Wisc.: University of Wisconsin Press.

Palmer, P. (1993) *Contemporary Lesbian Writing: Dreams, Desire, Difference*, Philadelphia, Pa.: Oxford University Press.
Paredes, A. (1991) *Between Two Worlds*, Houston, Tex.: Arte Público Press.
Pérez, E. (1999a) *The Decolonial Imaginary: Writing Chicanas into History*, Bloomington, Ind.: University of Indiana Press.
Pérez-Torres, R. (1995) *Movements in Chicano Poetry: Against Myths Against Margins*, New York: Cambridge University Press.
Quintana, A. E. (1996) *Home Girls: Chicana Literary Voices*, Philadelphia, Pa.: Temple University Press.
Rebolledo, T. D. (ed.) (1995) *Women Singing in the Snow: A Cultural Analysis of Chicana Literature*, Tucson, Ariz.: University of Arizona Press.
Rechy, J. (1964) *City of Night*, London: MacGibbon & Kee.
—— (1991) *The Miraculous Day of Amalia Gómez*, New York: Grove Press.
Rendon, A. (1972) *Chicano Manifesto*, New York: Macmillan.
Rodriguez, L. J. (1991) *The Concrete River*, Willimatic, Conn.: Curbstone Press.
Rodriguez, R. (1983) *Hunger of Memory: An Autobiography/The Education of Richard Rodriguez*, London: Bantam Books.
Romo, R. and Paredes, R. (eds) (1977) *New Scholar*, Monographs in Chicano Studies, Santa Barbara, Calif.: University of California Press; Center for Chicano Studies.
Rosaldo, R. (1993a) *Culture and Truth: The Remaking of Social Analysis*, London: Routledge.
Ruiz, V. (1998) *From Out of the Shadows: Mexican Women in 20th Century America*, New York: Oxford University Press.
Ruiz, V. and Tiano, S. (eds) (1987) *Women on the US–Mexico Border: Responses to Change*, Boston, Mass.: Allen & Unwin.
Ruiz, V. and Dubois, E. C. (eds) (1990) *Unequal Sisters: A Multi-Cultural Reader in US Women's History*, London and New York: Routledge.
Rutherford, J. (ed.) (1990) *Identity, Community, Cultural Difference*, London: Lawrence & Wishart.
Said, E. (1994) *Culture and Imperialism*, London: Vintage.
Saldívar, J. D. (ed.) (1985) *The Rolando Hinojosa Reader: Essays, Historical and Critical*, Houston, Tex.: Arte Público Press.
—— (1991a) *The Dialectics of Our America: Genealogy, Cultural Critique, and Literary History*, Durham, NC: Duke University Press.
—— (1997) *Border Matters: Remapping American Cultural Studies*, Berkeley, Calif.: University of California Press.
Saldívar, R. (1990a) *Chicano Narrative: The Dialectics of Difference*, Madison, Wisc.: University of Wisconsin Press.
Saldívar-Hull, S. (2000) *Feminism on the Border: Chicana Gender Politics and Literature*, Berkeley, Calif.: University of California Press.
Salinas, R. (1980) *Un Trip through the Mind Jail y Otras Excursions*, San Francisco, Calif.: Editorial Pocho-Che.
Sanchez, G. (1993) *Becoming Mexican American: Ethnicity Culture and Identity in Chicano Los Angeles, 1900–1945*, New York: Oxford University Press.
Sánchez, M. (1985) *Contemporary Chicana Poetry: A Critical Approach to an Emerging Literature*, Berkeley, Calif.: University of California Press.
Sánchez, R. (1990) *Eagle-Visioned/Feathered Adobes*, El Paso, Tex.: Cinco Punto Press.
—— (1994) *Chicano Discourse: Socio-Historic Perspectives*, Houston, Tex.: Arte Público Press.

—— (1995) *Telling Identities: The Californio Testimonies*, Minneapolis, Minn.: University of Minnesota Press.

Sedgwick, E. K. (1990) *Epistemology of the Closet*, Berkeley, Calif.: University of California Press.

Serros, M. (1993) *Chicana Falsa and Other Stories of Death, Identity and Oxnard*, New York: Riverhead Books.

Siemerling, W. and Schwenk, K. (eds) (1996) *Cultural Difference and the Literary Text: Pluralism and the Limits of Authenticity in North American Literatures*, Iowa City, Iowa: University of Iowa Press.

Singh, A., Skerrett, J. K. and Hogan, R. E. (eds) (1996) *Memory and Cultural Politics: New Approaches to American Ethnic Literatures*, Boston, Mass.: Northeastern University Press.

Stanley, S. K. (1998) *Other Sisterhoods: Literary Theory and US Women of Colour*, Urbana, Ill.: University of Illinois Press.

Takaki, R. (1993) *A Different Mirror: A History of Multicultural America*, New York: Little, Brown & Co.

Tallack, D. (1993) *The 19th Century Short Story: Language, Form and Ideology*, New York and London: Routledge.

Trujillo, C. (ed.) (1998a) *Living Chicana Theory*, Berkeley, Calif.: Third Woman Press.

Urrea, L. A. (1993) *Across the Wire: Life and Hard Times on the Mexican Border*, New York: Anchor Books.

Vargas, Z. (ed.) (1999) *Major Problems in Mexican American History: Documents and Essays*, New York: Houghton Mifflin.

Vasconcelos, J. (1979) *La raza cósmica*, trans. Didier T. Jaén, Pensamiento Mexicano 1, Los Angeles, Calif.: Centro de Publicaciones.

Vigil, E. B. (1999) *The Crusade for Justice: Chicano Militancy and the Government's War on Dissent*, Madison, Wisc.: University of Wisconsin Press.

Villa, R. H. (2000) *Barrio-Logos: Space and Place in Urban Chicano Literature and Culture*, Austin, Tex.: University of Texas Press.

Villanueva, A. (1982) *Bloodroot*, Austin, Tex.: Place of Herons Press.

Viramontes, H. M. (1995b) *Under the Feet of Jesus*, New York: Dutton.

Weber, D. (1992) *The Spanish Frontier in North America*, New Haven, Conn.: Yale University Press.

Williams, R. (1977) *Marxism and Literature*, Oxford: Oxford University Press.

Yarbro-Bejarano, Y. (2001) *The Wounded Heart: Writing on Cherríe Moraga*, Austin, Tex.: University of Texas Press.

Zamora, B. (1976) *Restless Serpents*, Menlo Park, Calif.: Disenos Literarios.

Theses

Brady, M. P. (1996) 'Extinct Lands, Scarred Bodies: Chicana Literature and the Reinvention of Space', University of California Los Angeles.

Duncan, K. (1998) 'Contemporary Chicano Literature: From Roots to Rhizomes', University of Birmingham.

Eagar, G. D. (1996) 'The Chicana Female Hero and the Search for Paradise: Estella Portillo Trambley's Archetypal Discourse on Liberation', Arizona State University.

Hepworth, R. (1997) 'Autobiography as Cultural Process: Chicano Writing from the 1970s and 1990s', University of Birmingham.

168 *Bibliography*

Articles and chapters

Alarcón, N. (1983) 'Chicana Feminist Literature: A Revision Through Malintzin/or Malinche: Putting Flesh Back on the Object', in G. Anzaldúa and C. Moraga (eds) *This Bridge Called My Back: Writings by Radical Women of Colour*, New York: Kitchen Table Press, pp. 182–90.

—— (1987) 'Making "Familia" from Scratch: Split Subjectivities in the Work of Helena Maria Viramontes and Cherríe Moraga', in M. Herrera-Sobek and H. M. Viramontes (eds) (1988) *Chicana Creativity and Criticism: Charting New Frontiers in American Literature*, Houston, Tex.: Arte Público Press, pp. 220–32.

—— (1989) 'Traddutora, Traditora: A Paradigmatic Figure of Chicana Feminism', in A. McClintock, A. Mufti and E. Shohat (eds) (1997) *Dangerous Liasons: Gender, Nation and Postcolonial Perspectives*, Minneapolis, Minn.: University of Minnesota Press, pp. 278–97.

—— (1990a) 'Chicana Feminism: in the Tracks of "The" Native Woman', in C. Trujillo (ed.) (1998a) *Living Chicana Theory*, Berkeley, Calif.: Third Woman Press, pp. 371–82.

—— (1990b) 'The Theoretical Subject[s] of This Bridge Called My Back and Anglo-American Feminism', in G. Anzaldua (ed.) (1990) *Making Face, Making Soul: Haciendo Caras: Creative and Critical Perspectives by Feminists of Color*, San Francisco, Calif.: Aunt Lute Books, pp. 356–69.

—— (1994a) 'Conjugating Subjects: The Heteroglossia of Essence and Resistance', in A. Arteaga (ed.) (1994) *Another Tongue: Nation and Ethnicity in the Linguistic Borderlands*, Durham, NC: Duke University Press, pp. 125–38.

—— (1994b) 'Cognitive Desires: An Allegory of/for Chicana Critics', in E. Hedges and S. Fisher Fishkin (eds) *Listening To Silences: New Essays in Feminist Criticism*, Oxford: Oxford University Press, pp. 260–73.

—— (1996) 'Anzaldua's *Frontera*: Inscribing Gynetics', in S. Lavie and T. Swedenbourg (eds) *Displacement, Diaspora, and Geographies of Identity*, Durham, NC: Duke University Press, pp. 41–54.

Arrizón, A. (2000) 'Mythical Performativity: Relocating Aztlán in Chicana Feminist Cultural Productions', *Theatre Journal*, 52: 23–49.

Baca Zinn, M. (1975) 'Political Familism: Toward Sex-Role Equality in Chicano Families', in C. Noriega, E. R. Avila, K. M. Davalos, C. Sandoval, and R. Pérez-Torres (eds) (2001) *The Chicano Studies Reader: An Anthology of Aztlán, 1970–2000*, Los Angeles, Calif.: UCLA Chicano Studies Research Center, pp. 455–72.

Benjamin-Labarthe, E. (2000) 'American Cinema: *The Mask of Zorro* and the Chicano Canon', in F. Lomelí and K. Ikas (eds) *US Latino Literatures and Cultures: Transnational Perspectives*, Heidelberg: C. Winter, pp. 81–98.

Browdy de Hernandez, J. (1998) 'Mothering the Self: Writing through the Lesbian Sublime in Audre Lorde's *Zami* and Gloria Anzaldúa's *Borderlands/La Frontera*', in S. K. Stanley (ed.) (1998) *Other Sisterhoods: Literary Theory and US Women of Colour*, Urbana, Ill.: University of Illinois Press, pp. 244–62.

Bruce-Novoa, J. (1978) 'The Space of Chicano Literature Update: 1978', in J. Bruce-Novoa (1990a) *RetroSpace: Collected Essays on Chicano Literature*, Houston, Tex.: Arte Público Press, pp. 93–113.

—— (1980b) 'Charting the Space of Chicano Literature', in J. Bruce-Novoa (1990a) *RetroSpace: Collected Essays on Chicano Literature*, Houston, Tex.: Arte Público Press, pp. 114–24.

—— (1985) 'Chicano Literary Production, 1960–1980', in J. Bruce-Novoa (1990a) *RetroSpace: Collected Essays on Chicano Literature*, Houston, Tex.: Arte Público Press, pp. 75–90.

—— (1988) 'The Topological Space of Chicano Literature', in J. Bruce-Novoa (1990a) *RetroSpace: Collected Essays on Chicano Literature*, Houston, Tex.: Arte Público Press, pp. 147–56.

—— (1990b) 'Chicano Literary Space: Cultural Criticism/Cultural Production', in J. Bruce-Novoa (1990a) *RetroSpace: Collected Essays on Chicano Literature*, Houston, Tex.: Arte Público Press, pp. 157–75.

Bus, H. (2000) ' "Keep This Chicano/a Running": Geography and the Dynamics of Spatial Movement and Stasis in Chicano Literature', in F. A. Lomelí and K. Ikas (eds) *US Latino Literatures and Cultures: Transnational Perspectives*, Heidelberg: C. Winter, pp. 115–30.

Calderon, H. (1991) 'Rereading Tomás Rivera's y no se lo trago la tierra', in H. Calderon and J. D. Saldívar (eds) *Criticism in the Borderlands: Studies in Chicano Literature, Culture and Ideology*, Durham, NC: Duke University Press, pp. 97–113.

Castañeda, A. I. (1990) 'Gender, Race, and Culture: Spanish-Mexican Women in the Historiography of Frontier California', *Frontiers: A Journal of Women Studies*, 9 (1): 8–20.

—— (1992) 'Women of Color and the Rewriting of Western History: The Discourse, Politics, and Decolonisation of History', *Pacific Historical Review*, 51 (4): 501–33.

Chabram-Dernersesian, A. (1991) 'Conceptualising Chicano Critical Discourse', in H. Calderon and J. D. Saldívar (eds) *Criticism in the Borderlands: Studies in Chicano Literature, Culture and Ideology*, Durham, NC: Duke University Press, pp. 127–48.

—— (1990) 'Chicana/o Studies as Oppositional Ethnography', *Cultural Studies*, 4 (3): 228–47.

—— (1992) 'I Throw Punches for My Race, but I Don't Want to Be a Man: Writing Us Chica-nos [Girl /Us]/Chicanas into the Movement Script', in L. Grossberg and G. Nelson (eds) *Cultural Studies*, London: Routledge, pp. 81–95.

—— (1993) 'And, Yes . . . The Earth Did Part: On the Splitting of Chicana/o Subjectivity', in A. de la Torre and B. M. Pesquera (eds) *Building with Our Hands: New Directions in Chicana Studies*, Berkeley, Calif.: University of California Press, pp. 34–56.

Chávez, J. R., (1989) 'Aztlán, Cíbola, and Frontier New Spain', in R. Anaya and F. A. Lomelí (eds) *Aztlán: Essays On The Chicano Homeland*, Albuquerque, N. Mex.: University of New Mexico Press, pp. 49–71.

Cixous, H. (1980) 'Sorties', in E. Marks and I. de Courtivron, *New French Feminisms*, Amherst, Mass.: University of Massachusetts Press, pp. 366–71.

Cotera, M. (1977) 'Our Feminist Heritage', in A. Garcia (ed.) (1997) *Chicana Feminist Thought: The Basic Historical Writings*, London: Routledge, pp. 41–4.

de la Fuente, P. (1986) 'Invisible Women in the Narrative of Tomás Rivera', in J. Olivares (ed.) *International Studies in Honor of Tomás Rivera*, Houston, Tex.: Arte Público Press, pp. 81–9.

del Castillo, A. R. (1974) 'Malintzín Tenepal: A Preliminary Look into a New Perspective', in A. Garcia (ed.) (1997) *Chicana Feminist Thought: The Basic Historical Writings*, London: Routledge, pp. 122–6.

Escobar, E. J. (1993) 'The Dialectics of Repression: The Los Angeles Police Department and the Chicano Movement, 1968–1971', *Journal of American History*, 79 (4, March): 1483–514.

Flores, F. (1971) 'Conference of Mexican Women in Houston: Un Remolino
[A Whirlwind]', in A. Garcia (ed.) (1997) *Chicana Feminist Thought: The Basic
Historical Writings*, London: Routledge, pp. 157–61.

Fregoso, R. L. (1999) 'Re-Imagining Chicana Urban Identities in the Public Sphere,
Cool Chuca Style', in C. Kaplan, N. Alarcon and M. Moallem (eds) *Between Woman
and Nation*, Durham, NC and London: Duke University Press, pp. 72–91.

Garcia, A. (1989) 'The Development of Chicana Feminist Discourse, 1970–1980', in
E. C. Dubois and V. Ruiz (eds) (1990) *Unequal Sisters: A Multi-Cultural Reader in
US Women's History*, New York and London: Routledge, pp. 418–29.

García, Ignacio M. (1989) *United We Win: The Rise and Fall of La Raza Unida Party*,
Tucson, Ariz.: University of Arizona Press.

Garcia, M. T. (1999) 'Mexican Immigrant Women in El Paso, Texas', in Z. Vargas
(ed.) (1999) *Major Problems in Mexican American History: Documents and Essays*,
New York: Houghton Mifflin, pp. 216–22.

Garcia, R. (2002) 'New Iconographies: Film Culture in Chicano Cultural Produc-
tion', in A. J. Aldama and N. H. Quiñones (eds) *Decolonial Voices: Chicana and
Chicano Cultural Studies in the 21st Century*, Bloomington, Ind.: Indiana University
Press, pp. 64–77.

Gaspar de Alba, A. (1995) 'The Alter-native Grain: Theorising Chicana/o Popular
Culture', in A. Darder (ed.) (1995) *Culture and Difference: Critical Perspectives on
the Bi-Cultural Experience in the United States*, Westport, Conn: Bergin & Garvey,
pp. 105–15.

—— (1989) 'Malinchista, A Myth Revisited', in A. Gaspar de Alba, D. Martinez,
M. Herrera-Sobek (eds) *Three Times a Woman*, Tempe, Ariz.: Bilingual Press, pp.
16–17.

Gomez, A. N. (1974) 'La Feminista', in A. Garcia (ed.) (1997) *Chicana Feminist
Thought: The Basic Historical Writings*, London: Routledge, pp. 86–92.

—— (1976) 'Chicana Feminism', in A. Garcia (ed.) (1997) *Chicana Feminist Thought:
The Basic Historical Writings*, London: Routledge, pp. 52–7.

González, D. (1997) 'Chicana Identity Matters', in C. Noriega, E. R. Avila, K. M.
Davalos, C. Sandoval, R. Pérez-Torres (eds) (2001) *The Chicano Studies Reader: An
Anthology of Aztlán, 1970–2000*, Los Angeles, Calif.: UCLA Chicano Studies
Research Center, pp. 411–26.

Gonzales, R. C. (1967) *I Am Joaquín: An Epic Poem*, Denver, Col.: The Crusade for
Justice.

—— (1967) 'Yo Soy Joaquín' in M. de Jesús Hernández-Gutiérrez and D. Foster
(eds) (1997) *Literatura Chicana 1965–1995: An Anthology in Spanish, English and
Caló*, New York: Garland, pp. 207–22.

—— (1968) 'El Plan del Barrio', in A. Esquibel (ed.) (2001) *Message to Aztlán: Selected
Writings of Rodolfo 'Corky' Gonzales*, Houston, Tex.: Arte Público Press, pp. 32–4.

—— (1970) 'Arizona State University Speech', in A. Esquibel (ed.) (2001) *Message to
Aztlán: Selected Writings of Rodolfo 'Corky' Gonzales*, Houston, Tex.: Arte Público
Press, pp. 35–55.

—— (1972) 'Message to El Congreso on Land and Cultural Reform', in A. Esquibel
(ed.) (2001) *Message to Aztlán: Selected Writings of Rodolfo 'Corky' Gonzales*, Houston,
Tex.: Arte Público Press, pp. 238–42.

—— (1972) 'Maintaining a Positive Direction for the Chicano Movement', in
A. Esquibel (ed.) (2001) *Message to Aztlán: Selected Writings of Rodolfo 'Corky'
Gonzales*, Houston, Tex.: Arte Público Press, pp. 62–6.

Gutiérrez, D. (1989) 'The Third Generation; Reflections on Recent Chicano Historiography', in *Mexican Studies/Estudios Mexicanos*, 15 (2): 281–96.

—— (1993) 'Significant to Whom? Mexican Americans and the History of the American West', *Western Historical Quarterly*, 24 (4): 519–39.

Gutiérrez, R. (1971) 'Community, Patriarchy and Individualism: The Politics of Chicano History and the Dream of Equality', in A. de la Torre and B. M. Pesquera (eds) (1993) *Building with Our Hands: New Directions in Chicana Studies*, Berkeley, Calif.: University of California Press, pp. 587–606.

—— (1986) 'Unravelling America's Hispanic Past: Internal Stratification and Class Boundaries', in *Aztlán*, 17 (1, spring): 79–101.

—— (1989) 'Aztlán, Montezuma, and New Mexico: The Political Uses of American Indian Mythology', in R. Anaya and F. A. Lomelí (eds) *Aztlán: Essays on the Chicano Homeland*, Albuquerque, N. Mex.: University of New Mexico Press, pp. 172–90.

Hall, S. (1990) 'Cultural Identity and Diaspora', in J. Rutherford (ed.) (1990) *Identity, Community, Cultural Difference*, London: Lawrence & Wishart, pp. 222–37.

Herrera-Sobek, M. (1988) 'The Politics of Rape: Sexual Transgression in Chicana Fiction', in M. Herrera-Sobek and H. M. Viramontes (eds) *Chicana Creativity and Criticism: Charting New Frontiers in American Literature*, Houston, Tex.: Arte Público Press, pp. 245–56.

—— (1993) 'Canon Formation and Chicano Literature', in R. Gutiérrez and G. Padilla (eds) *Recovering the US Hispanic Literary Heritage*, Houston, Tex.: Arte Público Press, pp. 209–19.

Hurtado, A. (1997) 'The Politics of Sexuality in the Gender Subordination of Chicanas', in C. Trujillo (ed.) (1998a) *Living Chicana Theory*, Berkeley, Calif.: Third Woman Press, pp. 383–428.

Juárez, N. (1972) 'José Vasconcelos and La Raza Cósmica', *Aztlán*, 3 (1): 51–76.

Lamadrid, E. R. (1994) '*Entre Cíbolos Criado:* Images of Native Americans in the Popular Culture of Colonial New Mexico', in M. Herrera-Sobek (ed.) (1994) *Reconstructing a Chicano/a Literary Heritage: Hispanic Colonial Literature of the South-West*, Tucson, Ariz.: University of Arizona Press, pp. 158–200.

Leal, L. (1994) 'Poetic Discourse in Perez de Villagra's Historia de la Nueva Mexico', in M. Herrera-Sobek (ed.) (1994) *Reconstructing a Chicano/a Literary Heritage: Hispanic Colonial Literature of the South-West*, Tucson, Ariz.: University of Arizona Press, pp. 95–117.

—— (1989) 'In Search of Aztlán', in R. Anaya and F. A. Lomelí (eds) *Aztlán: Essays on the Chicano Homeland*, Albuquerque, N. Mex.: University of New Mexico Press, pp. 6–13.

Libretti, T. (1998) 'Rethinking Class from a Chicana Perspective', in S. K. Stanley (ed.) (1998) *Other Sisterhoods: Literary Theory and US Women of Colour*, Urbana, Ill.: University of Illinois Press, pp. 200–27.

Lizárraga, S. (1986) 'The Patriarchal Ideology in "La noche que se apagaron las luces" ', in Julián Olivares (ed.) (1986) *International Studies in Honor of Tomás Rivera*, Houston, Tex.: Arte Público Press, pp. 90–5.

López, S. A. (1977) 'The Role of the Chicana within the Student Movement', in A. Garcia (ed.) (1997) *Chicana Feminist Thought: The Basic Historical Writings*, London: Routledge, pp. 100–6.

McKenna, T. (1997) 'On Chicano Poetry and the Political Age: *Corridos* as Social Drama', in T. McKenna (1997) *Migrant Song: Politics and Protest in Contemporary Chicano Literature*, Austin, Tex.: University of Texas Press, pp. 27–48.

Martinez, E. (1998b) 'Chingon Politics Die Hard', in E. Martinez (ed.) *De Colores Means All of Us*, Cambridge, Mass.: South End Press, pp. 172–81.

Mayorga, I. (2001) 'Homecoming: The Politics of Myth and Location in Cherríe L. Moraga's *The Hungry Woman: A Mexican Medea* and *Heart of the Earth: A Popol Vuh Story*', in C. Moraga, *The Hungry Woman*, Los Angeles, Calif.: West End Press, pp. 155–66.

Miller Matthei, L. (1999) 'Gender and International Labor Migration: A Networks Approach', in S. Jonas and S. D. Thomas (eds) *Immigration: A Civil Rights Issue for the Americas*, Wilmington, Del.: SR Books, pp. 69–84.

Molina, G. (1992) 'Chicano!' TV Series Newsletter 1 (1): 4. Chicano Research Collection, Arizona State University.

Montejano, D. (1999b) 'On the Future of Anglo-Mexican Relations in the United States', in D. Montejano (ed.) (1999a) *Chicano Politics and Society in the Late 20th Century*, Austin, Tex.: University of Texas Press, pp. 234–57.

Navarro, A. (1995) 'The Mexican American Youth Organisation', in Z. Vargas (ed.) (1999) *Major Problems in Mexican American History: Documents and Essays*, New York: Houghton Mifflin, pp. 392–404.

Nieto Gomez, A. (1995) 'La Chicana: Legacy of Suffering and Self-Denial', in A. Garcia (ed.) (1997) *Chicana Feminist Thought: The Basic Historical Writings*, New York and London: Routledge, pp. 48–50.

—— (1974) 'La Feminista', in A. Garcia (ed.) (1997) *Chicana Feminist Thought: The Basic Historical Writings*, New York and London: Routledge, pp. 86–92.

Orozco, C. (1986) 'Sexism in Chicano Studies and the Community', in A. Garcia (ed.) (1997) *Chicana Feminist Thought: The Basic Historical Writings*, London: Routledge, pp. 265–70.

Padilla, G. (1994) 'Discontinuous Continuities: Remapping the Terrain of Spanish Colonial Narrative', in M. Herrera-Sobek (ed.) (1994) *Reconstructing a Chicano/a Literary Heritage: Hispanic Colonial Literature of the South-West*, Tucson, Ariz.: University of Arizona Press, pp. 24–36.

—— (1989) 'Myth and Comparative Cultural Nationalism: The Ideological Uses of Aztlán', in R. Anaya and F. A. Lomelí (eds) *Aztlán: Essays on the Chicano Homeland*, Albuquerque, N. Mex.: University of New Mexico Press, pp. 111–34.

—— (1991) 'Imprisoned Narrative? Or Lies, Secrets, and Silence in New Mexico Women's Autobiography', in H. Calderon and J. D. Saldívar (eds) *Criticism in the Borderlands: Studies in Chicano Literature, Culture and Ideology*, Durham, NC: Duke University Press, pp. 43–60.

Pardo, M. (1990) 'Mexican American Women Grassroots Community Activists: "Mothers of East Los Angeles" ', *Frontiers: A Journal of Women Studies*, 11 (1): 1–7.

Pérez, E. (1993) 'Speaking from the Margin: Uninvited Discourse on Sexuality and Power', in A. de la Torre and B. Pesquera (eds) *Building with Our Hands: New Directions in Chicana Studies*, Berkeley, Calif.: University of California Press, pp. 57–71.

—— (1999b) 'Feminism-in-Nationalism: The Gendered Subaltern at the Yucatán Feminist Congresses of 1916', in C. Kaplan, N. Alarcón and M. Moallem (eds) *Between Woman and Nation*, Durham, NC: Duke University Press, pp. 219–39.

Pérez, L. Elisa. (1999c) '*El desorden*, Nationalism, and Chicana/o Aesthetics', in C. Kaplan, N. Alarcón and M. Moallem (eds) *Between Woman and Nation*, Durham, NC and London: Duke University Press, pp. 19–46.

Pérez-Torres, R. (1997) 'Refiguring Aztlán', *Aztlán: A Journal of Chicano Studies*, 22 (2): 37.

Pesquera B. M. and Segura, D. A. (1993) 'There Is No Going Back: Chicanas and Feminism', in A. Garcia (ed.) (1997) *Chicana Feminist Thought: The Basic Historical Writings*, London: Routledge, pp. 294–309.

Pina, M. (1989) 'The Archaic, Historical and Mythicised Dimensions of Aztlán', in R. Anaya and F. A. Lomelí (eds) *Aztlán: Essays on the Chicano Homeland*, Albuquerque, N. Mex.: University of New Mexico Press, pp. 14–45.

Pratt, M. L. (1993) 'Yo Soy La Malinche: Chicana Writers and the Poetics of Ethnonationalism', *Callaloo* 16 (4): 859–73.

Quintana, A. E. (1991) 'Ana Castillo's *The Mixquiahuala Letters*: The Novelist as Ethnographer', in H. Calderon and J. D. Saldivar (eds) *Criticism in the Borderlands: Studies in Chicano Literature, Culture and Ideology*, Durham, NC: Duke University Press, pp. 72–83.

Ramirez, A. (1995) 'Feminist Neo-Indigenism in Chicana Aztlán', *SAIL*, 7 (4, winter): 71–8.

Rebolledo, T. D. (1988) 'The Politics of Poetics: Or, What am I, A Critic, Doing in This Text Anyhow?' in M. Herrera-Sobek and H. M. Viramontes (eds) (1988) *Chicana Creativity and Criticism: Charting New Frontiers in American Literature*, Houston, Tex.: Arte Público Press, pp. 203–12.

Riddell, A. S. (1974) 'Chicanas and El Movimiento', in C. Noriega, E. R. Avila, K. M. Davalos, C. Sandoval, R. Pérez-Torres (eds) (2001) *The Chicano Studies Reader: An Anthology of Aztlán, 1970–2000*, Los Angeles, Calif.: UCLA Chicano Studies Research Center, pp. 359–70.

Romano-V, O. I., (1969) 'The Historical and Intellectual Presence of Mexican Americans', in M. de Jesús Hernández-Gutiérrez and D. W. Foster (eds) (1997) *Literatura Chicana 1965–1995: An Anthology in Spanish, English and Caló*, New York: Garland, pp. 47–61.

Rosaldo, R. (1993b) 'Imperialist Nostalgia', in *Culture and Truth: The Remaking of Social Analysis*, New York and London: Routledge, pp. 68–87.

—— (1993c) 'Border Crossings', in *Culture and Truth: The Remaking of Social Analysis*, New York and London: Routledge, pp. 196–217.

—— (1991) 'Fables of the Fallen Guy', in H. Calderon and J. D. Saldívar (eds) *Criticism in the Borderlands: Studies in Chicano Literature, Culture and Ideology*, Durham, NC: Duke University Press, pp. 84–93.

Rose, M. (1990a) 'The Significant Role of Chicanas in the United Farm Worker's Boycott', in Z. Vargas (ed.) (1999) *Major Problems in Mexican American History: Documents and Essays*, New York: Houghton Mifflin, pp. 404–10.

—— (1990b) 'Traditional and Nontraditional Patterns of Female Activism in the United Farm Workers of America, 1962 to 1980', *Frontiers: A Journal of Women Studies*, 11 (1): 24–32.

Ruiz, V. (1986) 'A Promise Fulfilled: Mexican Cannery Workers in Southern California', in A. de la Torre and B. M. Pesquera (eds) (1993) *Building with Our Hands: New Directions in Chicana Studies*, Berkeley, Calif.: University of California Press, pp. 264–75.

Saldívar, J. D. (1991b) 'Chicano Border Narratives as Cultural Critique', in H. Calderon and J. D. Saldívar (eds) *Criticism in the Borderlands: Studies in Chicano Literature, Culture and Ideology*, Durham, NC: Duke University Press, pp. 167–80.

Saldívar, R. (1990b) 'Beyond Good and Evil: Utopian Dialectics in Tomás Rivera and

Oscar Zeta Acosta', in R. Saldívar, *Chicano Narrative: The Dialectics of Difference*, Madison, Wisc.: University of Wisconsin Press, pp. 74–98.

Saldívar-Hull, S. (1991) 'Feminism on the Border: From Gender Politics to Geopolitics', in H. Calderon and J. D. Saldívar (eds) *Criticism in the Borderlands: Studies in Chicano Literature, Culture and Ideology*, Durham, NC: Duke University Press, pp. 203–20.

Sanchez-Tranquilino, M. and J. Tagg (1991) 'The Pachuco's Flayed Hide: The Museum, Identity, and Buenas Garras', in R. del Castillo, T. McKenna and Y. Yarbro-Bejarano (eds) *Chicano Art: Resistance and Affirmation, 1965–1985*, Los Angeles, Calif.: Wight Art Gallery, University of California, pp. 97–119.

Segura, D. A. and B. Pesquera (1988–90) 'Beyond Indifference and Antipathy: The Chicana Movement and Chicana Feminist Discourse', in C. Noriega, E. R. Avila, K. M. Davalos, C. Sandoval, R. Pérez-Torres (eds) (2001) *The Chicano Studies Reader: An Anthology of Aztlán, 1970–2000*, Los Angeles, Calif.: UCLA Chicano Studies Research Center, pp. 389–410.

Segura, D. A. and Pierce, J. (1993) 'Chicana/o Family Structure and Gender Personality: Chodorow, Familism, and Psychoanalytic Sociology Revisited', *Signs* (autumn): 62–91.

Serrano, J. C. (2000) 'Rudolfo Anaya's Narrative as an Example of Chicano Proletarianisation within an Internal Colonial Framework', in F. A. Lomelí and K. Ikas (eds) *US Latino Literatures and Cultures: Transnational Perspectives*, Heidelberg: C. Winter, pp. 191–9.

Sommers, J. (1977) 'From the Critical Premise to the Product: Critical Modes and their Application to a Chicano Literary Text', in Romo, R. and Paredes, R. (eds) (1977) *New Scholar*, Monographs in Chicano Studies, Santa Barbara, Calif.: University of California Press, Center for Chicano Studies, pp. 51–80.

Spivak, G. (1993) 'Woman in Difference', *Outside in the Teaching Machine*, New York: Routledge, pp. 77–95.

Tatum, C. (1990) 'Grappling with Difference: Gender, Race, and Ethnicity in Contemporary Chicana/o Literature', *Renato Rosaldo Lecture*, Series 6: Mexican American Studies & Research Center, University of Arizona, 1988–9, pp. 1–23.

—— (1993) 'Some Considerations on Genres and Chronology for Nineteenth-Century Hispanic Literature', in R. Gutiérrez and G. Padilla (eds) *Recovering the US Hispanic Literary Heritage*, Houston, Tex.: Arte Público Press, pp. 199–208.

Tonn, H. (2000) 'Hispanic Film in the United States: The Past Two Decades', in F. Lomelí and K. Ikas (eds) *US Latino Literatures and Cultures: Transnational Perspectives*, Heidelberg: C. Winter, pp. 71–80.

Torres, H. A. (2000) 'Space, Difference, Mestizaje: The Erasure Mark in Contemporary Chicana/o Critical Discourse', in F. A. Lomelí and K. Ikas (eds) *US Latino Literatures and Cultures: Transnational Perspectives*, Heidelberg: C. Winter, pp. 143–57.

Trujillo, C. (1998b) 'La Virgen de Guadalupe and her Reconstruction in Chicana Lesbian Desire', in C. Trujillo (ed.) *Living Chicana Theory*, Berkeley, Calif.: Third Woman Press, pp. 214–31.

Vargas, Z. (2001) 'In the Years of Darkness and Torment: The Early Mexican American Struggle for Civil Rights, 1945–1963', *New Mexico Historical Review*, 76 (4): 383–413.

Virdal, M. (1971) 'New Voice of La Raza: Chicanas Speak Out', in A. Garcia (ed.) (1997) *Chicana Feminist Thought: The Basic Historical Writings*, London: Routledge, pp. 21–4.

Wiley, C. (1998) 'Teatro Chicano and the Seduction of Nostalgia', *MELUS*, 23 (1): 99–115.

Xavier, R. E. (1999) 'Politics and Chicano Culture: Luis Valdez and El Teatro Campesino, 1964–1990', D. Montejano (ed.) *Chicano Politics and Society in the Late 20th Century*, Austin, Tex.: University of Texas Press, pp. 175–200.

Yarbro-Bejarano, Y. (1988) 'Chicano Literature from a Chicana Feminist Perspective', in M. Herrera-Sobek and H. M. Viramontes (eds) *Chicana Creativity and Criticism: Charting New Frontiers in American Literature*, Houston, Tex.: Arte Público Press, pp. 213–19.

Index

Acuña, R. 7, 14, 31, 111, 122
agabachadas 27, 64
Alarcón, N. 29, 50–1, 57–9, 79, 96, 101, 116, 132, 135, 142, 147
Alianza Federal de Mercedes 1, 3, 7–9
Alurista 2, 20, 22, 42, 65, 69, 99–100, 118, 125
Anaya, R. 2, 21–2, 34, 41, 46–7, 60, 65, 70, 72, 80, 99, 118–23, 125–32, 134, 150, 152
Anzaldúa, G. 2, 4, 29, 36–7, 50–3, 55–9, 61, 77–80, 89, 107, 110, 135, 143–51, 154–5
Arizona 2, 3, 8, 20, 30, 123, 139
Arteaga, A. 7, 20, 69, 121, 126
assimilation 8, 17, 20, 24, 58, 68, 112
Aztecs 15, 20, 68–9, 70, 86, 119, 129, 148
Aztlán 2, 4–5, 20–1, 34, 60, 64, 69–70, 77, 80, 118–21, 123–6, 128–39, 141–8, 150–1, 155
Aztlán 2, 65, 118

Bless me Ultima 46–7, 60
border 3, 5, 9, 20, 24, 26, 37, 47, 54–5, 61–3, 66, 79–80, 92, 118, 125, 133–6, 139, 141, 143–7, 150–1, 155
Borderlands/la Frontera 29, 37, 51, 55, 57, 77, 143, 145, 148
Braceros 11, 102, 110
Bruce-Novoa, J. 4, 13, 37, 39, 43–5, 48, 54, 65–6, 71–2, 94, 107

California 1, 3, 6, 8, 11–12, 16, 20, 31, 35, 67, 81, 140, 144
Candelaria, C. 59, 69, 71–2, 74
carnalismo 27, 72–3, 87, 100, 124–6, 134, 146, 152

Castillo, A. 2, 32, 50–1, 60–2, 114, 147, 149, 154
catholicism 13, 35, 57, 67, 92, 95, 107–8, 113
Cervantes, L.D. 2, 50, 75, 140–3, 147
Chávez, C. 3, 6, 8, 11–14, 31, 39, 56, 81, 101
Chávez, E. 7, 23, 82
Chávez, J. 3–4, 7, 12–13, 18, 20, 56, 118, 124
Chicana feminism 26–9, 33, 35–6, 38, 50, 52, 63–4, 89, 110; *see also* feminism
Chicano movement 2–4, 6, 8, 14–15, 17, 21, 23–4, 26, 28–34, 37, 39, 42, 55, 65, 73, 81, 87, 91, 99, 101, 105, 125, 128, 135, 152–4, 155–6; *see also el movimiento*
church 35, 57, 67, 89, 92, 95, 105, 107, 109
Cisneros, S. 2, 50, 53, 55, 62, 98, 110–17, 147, 154
civil rights 1, 3, 6, 8, 10–12, 17–18, 21–3, 27, 30, 124, 152
Cixous, H. 51–2, 74
class 6, 8, 10, 12, 16–17, 27–34, 39, 46–7, 53, 64, 67, 72, 74–5, 78, 83, 89, 99, 104, 110, 126–7, 130, 136, 139, 152–3
Coatlicue 29, 57, 79, 148–50
colonisation 3, 16, 19, 57, 68, 79–80, 148
community 1, 3, 5, 16–17, 20, 22, 28, 32–3, 37, 43, 45, 58, 61, 64, 67, 82, 87–8, 94, 98–100, 104–5, 107–9, 112, 115–16, 120, 122–6, 128, 130–1, 133, 146, 152; organisations 15, 18, 120, 123, 132

conquest 9, 17, 30, 59, 61, 69–71, 73, 77, 79, 96, 121, 148–9, 153
Cotera, M. 26–7, 36, 153
Crusade for Justice 3, 6, 18–19, 23, 99, 120, 123
cultural nationalism 1, 16, 21, 23, 99, 123–4, 130, 152; *see also* nationalism
culturalist criticism 39, 40–2, 45

de León, A. 3, 8, 10, 17, 83, 118, 126
del Castillo, G. 3, 10, 52, 59, 66, 83, 118, 148
Denver Youth Conference 6, 20, 33, 70, 118, 125–6

El Louie 94–5
el movimiento 1, 22, 24, 27, 42, 154
El Plan de Delano 7, 12
El Plan Espiritual de Aztlán 4, 7, 20, 41, 70, 72, 80, 99, 118, 120, 122–3, 125–6, 130, 133–4, 136, 139, 152
El Plan de Santa Bárbara 7, 33

farm workers 1, 3, 6, 11–14, 56, 81, 101–2, 108, 111, 139; *see also* UFW
familia 27, 47, 53, 62, 87–8, 97–101, 105–11, 113–14, 116–17, 125–6, 131, 146, 152–4
family 2, 27, 32–3, 36–7, 41, 47, 53, 57, 68–9, 85, 87–8, 91, 98–101, 104–9, 111–16, 123, 125–8, 131–2, 138, 145–6, 152
feminism 4, 26–9, 33, 35–6, 38, 50–2, 54, 58, 61, 63–4, 89, 99, 110, 146, 153, 155; *see also* Chicana feminism
feminist criticism 38, 49, 51, 53, 57, 95
Flores, F. 35, 141
Fregoso, L. 88, 93

Garcia, A. 4, 24, 26–9, 32–5, 57, 59, 99–101, 105–6, 125, 135, 141
García, I. M. 26, 135
Gaspar de Alba, A. 60, 64, 94
gender 4–5, 26–9, 32–4, 36–7, 41, 43, 47, 49–54, 57, 60, 64–5, 73–6, 78–81, 87–9, 91–2, 95–7, 99, 105–10, 112–13, 115–18, 124, 126, 131, 133–7, 139–45, 147, 150, 152–5
Giving up the Ghost 53, 81, 89–97
Gonzales, M. 3, 10, 18, 35–6, 67, 83, 98, 116, 148
Gonzales, R. C. 2–3, 18–20, 22, 24, 42, 65, 66–77, 80, 99, 120–5

Gutiérrez, D. 4, 8, 11–13, 17, 21–4, 26–7, 56, 66–7, 82, 98, 102, 122
Gutiérrez, J. A. 17–18, 24, 123–4
Gutiérrez, R. 3, 17, 70
Gutiérrez-Jones, C. 45, 72–3, 85, 87

Heart of Aztlán 118, 126, 129, 133, 150
Hernández-Gutiérrez and Foster 19, 41–2, 67–72, 74–5, 94
Herrera-Sobek, M. 50, 53–4, 66, 115
Hinojosa, R. 22, 65, 104
historical dialectical 40, 45
history 1, 6, 12–13, 19, 30, 36, 46–8, 50, 59–60, 63, 66–8, 70, 72–4, 76–8, 80, 82, 91, 101, 104, 109, 113, 118, 120, 123, 128, 130, 134, 142–5, 147, 150
home 2, 31, 82, 88–9, 98–100, 102, 106–7, 111–16, 123, 126, 130–1, 139–40, 143–4
homeland 4, 20, 34, 38, 69–70, 77, 117–19, 121, 124, 129, 142–3, 147, 150–1
House on Mango Street 53, 99, 110, 112–13
Huerta, D. 11, 31, 153
Huerta, J. 40, 84, 87
Hungry Woman: A Mexican Medea 135–6, 139

identity 1–5, 7, 17, 19, 22, 26–8, 35–7, 41, 45, 50–1, 55–7, 63, 67–8, 70, 72, 74–81, 85–7, 93–6, 99–100, 104, 115–16, 120, 126, 130, 133–5, 146–7, 152–6; Chicano/a 3–5, 7, 10, 15, 18–21, 24, 64–5, 68, 70–3, 75–85, 87, 89, 91, 97, 130–1, 133–4, 141, 151, 153, 155; collective 4, 64, 104, 120; cultural 7, 24, 85, 99, 128, 144; female 52, 64, 75, 89, 97–8, 105, 116; national 4, 56, 125–6, 134, 147; native 21, 29, 54, 120, 136, 137, 141, 150
immigration 17, 24, 62, 83, 85

Labyrinth of Solitude 59, 83, 108
land 3, 5–7, 9–10, 12, 14, 20–1, 60, 67, 70, 77–8, 104, 119, 120–4, 126, 129–30, 132–3, 136–9, 142–7, 150–1; *see also* border; homeland
La Raza Unida Party 2; *see also* LRUP
League of United Latin American Citizens 8, 17; *see also* LULAC
Limón, J. 48, 60, 62, 67, 73–4, 93–4

Llorona 55–6, 60–2, 114
Lomelí, F. 21, 34, 41, 45, 49, 70, 72, 80, 99, 110, 119–23, 125, 127, 130–1, 134, 152
Loving in the War Years 37, 51, 55, 92, 96, 106, 109
LRUP 2, 7, 15–16, 18, 23–4, 26, 33, 36, 153
LULAC 8, 17, 23–4

machismo 2, 30, 31–2, 34, 58, 87, 106, 113–16, 130–2, 141, 155
MALDEF 2, 7, 21–2, 124, 153
malinche(s) 27, 55–6, 58–61, 64, 96–7, 99, 106, 108–9, 147–8
Martinez, E. 27, 130, 153
Massacre of the Dreamers 51, 60, 149
MAYO 2, 7, 15, 17–18, 26, 30, 124
MEChA 2, 7, 15–16, 20, 23
Meier and Gutiérrez 9–10, 18, 21
mestiza 37, 55, 58–9, 77, 79–80, 134, 143, 145, 151
mestizaje 71–2, 79–80
mestizo 17, 34, 41, 58–9, 66, 69, 71–2, 77, 120, 143
Mexican American 1–8, 10–15, 18, 20–4, 26–7, 30–3, 35–6, 41–2, 48, 50, 55–6, 66–8, 77, 81–3, 85, 87, 98, 103–4, 106, 108, 110–11, 116, 118, 120, 122–3, 126–7, 130, 133, 145, 152
Mexican revolution 7, 12, 28, 41, 56, 58, 71, 73, 88, 121
Mexico 7, 9, 11, 13, 19–20, 26, 37, 41, 56, 58–60, 86, 102, 119, 121, 136, 143, 144–5, 152
Montejano, D. 8, 22, 24, 102–3, 145
Mora, P. 51, 94, 96, 145
Moraga, C. 2, 4, 36–7, 50–3, 55, 57, 59, 81, 89–97, 106, 109–10, 131–9, 141–3, 145–6, 149–51, 154–5
Muñoz, C. 4, 14–16, 20, 23, 26, 32, 82, 103

nation 4, 5, 12, 17, 20, 34, 58, 96, 117–18, 120, 124–6, 132–6, 138–9, 141–7, 149–51; American 21, 122, 145
nationalism 1, 10, 14, 16–17, 19–21, 23–4, 74, 81, 87, 99, 118, 123–5, 130, 134–5, 137, 146, 148, 151–2, 154–5
Native American 1, 18, 46, 146–7

Navarro, A. 17, 26, 30, 124
Neate, W. 4, 39–40, 43, 46–7, 49, 55, 57–8, 65–6, 68, 71–2, 74, 77–8, 81, 91, 124
New Mexico 1, 3, 6, 8–10, 16–17, 20, 23, 46–7, 55, 120, 126, 129

pachucos 82–6; *pachucas* 90, 94
Paredes, A. 47, 66–7
Paz, O. 42, 58–9, 83, 96, 108, 147
Pérez, E. 4, 7, 26, 58, 71, 73, 96, 134–5, 146
Pérez-Torres, R. 4, 37, 45, 48, 119, 121, 123–4, 136, 140, 142, 144

race 12, 15, 27–9, 31, 33–4, 36–7, 40–1, 46–7, 53, 58–9, 64, 71, 77–80, 89, 92, 102–4, 109, 122, 126, 130, 134, 139, 142–3, 152–3
raza 2, 14, 23, 27, 29, 35, 41, 64–5, 71, 77, 99, 120, 125, 134, 152
Rebolledo, T.D. 37, 49, 54–6, 60–1, 65, 75–6, 110
Rendon, A. 30, 58, 64
revolutionary 7, 23, 30, 41–2, 71, 121, 136–7, 152
Rivera, T. 2, 13, 22, 65, 98, 100–1, 103–11, 113–14, 116, 127
Rose, M. 31–3
Ruiz, V. 4, 23, 26–7, 29, 35–6, 83, 98, 140, 153, 155

Saldívar, J. D. 32, 45–7, 60, 62, 66–7, 104, 112
Saldívar, R. 45–8, 101, 104
Saldívar-Hull, S. 4, 52, 54–5, 61, 63, 98–9, 110, 144, 148, 155
Sanchez, G. 7, 83, 98, 111–12, 126
Sánchez, M. 50
Sanchez, R. 7, 50, 55, 84
sexuality 29, 33, 36–7, 43, 50–3, 57–8, 64, 75, 79–80, 89–93, 109, 115, 131, 134, 136–7, 143–4, 146, 154; queer 36, 136, 139, 145, 151, 154
So Far from God 32, 61, 114
Sommers, J. 39, 40, 43, 45

Teatro Campesino 13, 14, 81; *see also* theatre
Texas 1–3, 6, 8, 11–13, 16–18, 27, 30, 36, 55, 67, 77, 101–4, 108, 121, 124, 144–5
theatre 14, 22, 81–97, 135
This Bridge Called My Back 4, 36, 55

Tijerina, R.L. 3, 6, 8–10, 14, 16, 23
treaty of Guadalupe Hidalgo 9, 20–1,
  77, 121, 144–5

UFW 1, 3, 6–8, 11–14, 23–4, 31–3, 39,
  56, 81, 153
US–Mexican War 9, 17, 66, 70, 73,
  121–2, 144, 152

Valdez, L. 2, 12, 14, 56, 65, 80–6, 88–9,
  97, 118, 135
Vasconcelos, J. 41, 71
vendidas 27, 64, 92, 106, 109
Vigil, E.B. 18, 23–4
Villanueva, A. 2, 50, 59, 75, 76, 77, 147

Viramontes, H. M. 50, 53–5, 62, 63,
  110, 115, 154
Virgin of Guadalupe 13, 19, 55–9, 74,
  79, 97, 101, 105, 107–8

Y no se lo trago la tierra/*And The
  Earth Did Not Devour Him* 13,
  98–109
Yarbro-Bejarano, Y. 50, 53, 55, 80,
  92
'Yo Soy Joaquín' 19, 65–7, 74, 76–8, 82,
  99

Zapata 7, 19, 56
Zoot Suit 80–9

CPSIA information can be obtained at www.ICGtesting.com
Printed in the USA
243472LV00002B/7/P

9 780415 544061